The Politics of Challengin
Term Limits in Africa

Jack R. Mangala
Editor

The Politics of Challenging Presidential Term Limits in Africa

palgrave
macmillan

Editor
Jack R. Mangala
Grand Valley State University
Wyoming, MI, USA

ISBN 978-3-030-40812-1   ISBN 978-3-030-40810-7 (eBook)
https://doi.org/10.1007/978-3-030-40810-7

© The Editor(s) (if applicable) and The Author(s), under exclusive license to Springer Nature Switzerland AG 2020
This work is subject to copyright. All rights are solely and exclusively licensed by the Publisher, whether the whole or part of the material is concerned, specifically the rights of translation, reprinting, reuse of illustrations, recitation, broadcasting, reproduction on microfilms or in any other physical way, and transmission or information storage and retrieval, electronic adaptation, computer software, or by similar or dissimilar methodology now known or hereafter developed.
The use of general descriptive names, registered names, trademarks, service marks, etc. in this publication does not imply, even in the absence of a specific statement, that such names are exempt from the relevant protective laws and regulations and therefore free for general use.
The publisher, the authors and the editors are safe to assume that the advice and information in this book are believed to be true and accurate at the date of publication. Neither the publisher nor the authors or the editors give a warranty, expressed or implied, with respect to the material contained herein or for any errors or omissions that may have been made. The publisher remains neutral with regard to jurisdictional claims in published maps and institutional affiliations.

This Palgrave Macmillan imprint is published by the registered company Springer Nature Switzerland AG
The registered company address is: Gewerbestrasse 11, 6330 Cham, Switzerland

Preface

In the aftermath of the end of the Cold War, the vast majority of African presidential regimes adopted the constitutional rule limiting the number of terms their chief executives could serve in office. Among other political and institutional reforms initiated at that time, this cardinal rule of democratic governance was intended to create constitutionally binding constraints on the presidents in order to move the countries past the era of big men that had defined Cold War politics, and anchor them on the path to democracy. The adoption of term limits is generally credited with having contributed to an emerging political culture in which it is no longer acceptable for leaders to remain in power *ad infinitum* as had been the case decades earlier. The institution of presidential term limits has, however, been challenged by many African leaders since its inception. From Namibia's San Nujoma in 1998 to Rwanda's Paul Kagame in 2017, the institution of term limits has come under repeated onslaughts from African leaders convinced of their indispensability and seeking political immortality by subverting the constitution to suit their personal ambitions.

The trajectory of the institution of presidential term limits in Africa since its adoption in the early 1990s presents a contrasting picture. While the institution has survived alteration attempts in some countries (e.g. Benin, Burkina Faso, Senegal, and Nigeria), it has suffered important setbacks in others (e.g. Congo, Burundi, Rwanda, and Uganda). However, the emerging new international era, marked by global trends toward authoritarianism (the so-called rise of strong men), a realignment of Western countries' priorities (stability and the fight against terrorism taking precedence over democracy), and the ascendance of China and Russia in Africa (both countries invested neither in matters of democracy at home nor democracy promotion abroad), all of which seem to suggest that the fragile institution of presidential term limits is entering a time of great political turbulence.

"Why so many African presidents are ditching term limits?" asks *The Economist*. It is because, increasingly and within the context of the emerging international era succinctly described above, "they calculate that the costs of doing so are low."[1] Current trends seem to indicate that the term limits debate will occupy center stage in African politics in decades to come as various actors bring their best arguments and strategies to the fore to battle for the maintenance or removal of "the institutional demarcation line that separates democratic rulers, however powerful, from tyrants."[2]

Against this backdrop, the present volume seeks to contribute to the unfolding debate by shedding much-needed scholarly light on the core arguments pro and against the institution of presidential term limits, by discussing the key findings from empirical and non-empirical studies on term limits, and by comparatively dissecting six national experiences where attempts at altering constitutional term limits have either failed (Burkina Faso, Nigeria, and Zambia) or succeeded (Uganda, Gabon, and Rwanda). The whole exercise is intended to provide the overarching framework through which the debate over presidential term limits in Africa can be fruitfully pursued.

I am thankful to colleagues who have agreed to be part of this scholarly endeavor by graciously contributing a chapter. It has been a pleasure working with them individually and collectively. They have been very understanding and patient as this volume went through the long publishing process. In the end, we all are proud of the final product and hope the readers would find it insightful, intellectually enriching, and policy-relevant as the debate over presidential term limits unfolds in Africa and elsewhere around the world.

Allendale, MI, USA Jack R. Mangala
October 2019

NOTES

1. "Why So Many African Presidents are Ditching Term Limits," *The Economist*, August 4, 2017.
2. Alexander Baturo, Democracy, *Dictatorship, and Term Limits* (Ann Arbor, The University of Michigan Press, 2014), 11.

Contents

1 Presidential Term Limits, the Never-Ending Debate   1
  Jack R. Mangala

Part I   J'Y Suis, J'Y Reste

2 The Battle for Term Limits in Rwanda   37
  David E. Kiwuwa

3 The Making of a Monarchical Republic: The Undoing of Presidential Term Limits in Gabon Under Omar Bongo   65
  Daniel Mengara

4 Presidential Term Limits in Uganda: Do Elections Provide an Avenue for Alternate Power Succession?   105
  Sabiti Makara

Part II Touche pas à ma Constitution

5 The Undoing of a Semi-authoritarian Regime: The Term Limit Debate and the Fall of Blaise Compaoré in Burkina Faso   141
Daniel Eizenga and Leonardo A. Villalón

6 Failed Elongation of Presidential Term Limits in Nigeria Under Olusegun Obasanjo   171
Hassan A. Saliu and Abdulrasheed A. Muhammad

7 Frederick Chiluba's Third Presidential Term Bid in Zambia   205
Cephas Lumina

8 Constitutionalism and the Future of Presidential Term Limits in Africa   227
Jack R. Mangala

Index   235

NOTES ON CONTRIBUTORS

Dr. Daniel Eizenga is a Research Fellow at the National Defense University's Africa Center for Strategic Studies in Washington, DC. His research primarily focuses on countering violent extremism in the Sahel and the intersecting roles of civil–military relations, traditional institutions, and civil society across various regime trajectories of African states. Prior to joining the Africa Center, Dr. Eizenga was a postdoctoral fellow with the Centre FrancoPaix at the Université du Québec à Montréal and a research associate with the Sahel Research Group based at the University of Florida.

Dr. David E. Kiwuwa is an Associate Professor in the School of International Studies at the University of Nottingham Ningbo China campus. He is also the School Director of Research. Most recently he was a visiting Fellow at the Sydney Democratic Network, University of Sydney, and a Fung Global Fellow, Princeton Institute of International and Regional Studies, Princeton University. His research mainly looks at democratic transition and democratization processes in deeply divided societies, ethnic and nationalism politics, conflict analysis, electoral studies, and China–Africa contemporary political relations.

Professor Cephas Lumina is a lawyer and a human rights expert. He is an Advocate of the High Court of Zambia, a Member of the United Nations Committee on the Rights of the Child, and a Visiting Professor of Law at the University of Lusaka, Zambia. From March 2008 to May

2014, he served as the UN Independent Expert on the effects of foreign debt and other related international financial obligations of States on the full enjoyment of all human rights, particularly economic, social, and cultural rights. He was also, until recently, a full Research Professor of Constitutional and Human Rights Law at the University of Fort Hare, South Africa. He co-edited *Sovereign Debt and Human Rights* (Oxford University Press, 2018).

Dr. Sabiti Makara is a Senior Lecturer in the Department of Political and Public Administration at Makerere University, Uganda. His research interests are in the areas of urban governance, decentralization, civil society, and electoral processes. He has co-edited two volumes, *Elections in a Hybrid Regime* (Fountain Publishers, 2014) and *Electoral Democracy in Uganda* (Fountain Publishers, 2008).

Dr. Jack R. Mangala is a Professor of Global Studies and Political Science at Grand Valley State University, Michigan, where he also serves as Chair of the Area and Global Studies Department. His scholarly interest centers on the nexus between international law and human security with a regional focus on Africa and EU–Africa relations. He is the editor of *Africa and its Global Diaspora: The Policy and Politics of Emigration* (Palgrave Macmillan, 2017), *Africa and the European Union: A Strategic Partnership* (Palgrave Macmillan, 2013), *Africa and the New World Era: From Humanitarianism to a Strategic View* (Palgrave Macmillan, 2010), and *New Security Threats and Crises in Africa: Regional and International Perspectives* (Palgrave Macmillan, 2010).

Dr. Daniel Mengara is a native of Gabon and a Professor of French and Francophone Studies at Montclair State University. His scholarly interest focuses on precolonial and pre-Islamic African political and thought systems. He is the author of *La Représentation des groupes sociaux chez les romanciers noirs sud-africains* (L'harmattan, 1996), *Images of Africa: Stereotypes and Realities* (World Africa Press, 2001), as well as two novels *Mema* (Heineman, 2003), and *Le Chant des chimpanzés* (L'Harmattan, 2008).

Dr. Abdulrasheed A. Muhammad is a Senior Lecturer in Political Science at the University of Ilorin, Nigeria. His primary areas include Federalism, Political Parties and Legislative Studies.

Dr. Hassan A. Saliu teaches in the Department of Political Science, University of Ilorin, Nigeria, where he previously served as Head of Department and Dean of Faculty of Business and Social Sciences. He focuses on International Relations and Governance Issues.

Dr. Leonardo A. Villalón is a Professor of African Politics and Dean of the International Center at the University of Florida, where he also coordinates the Sahel Research Group. He is also the former director of the UF Center for African Studies. He has carried out research on religion and politics, democratization and elections, and the politics of educational reform across the Francophone Sahel for some 30 years. He is author of numerous works on the region, and editor of *Oxford Handbook of the African Sahel*.

LIST OF TABLES

Table 1.1	Institutional matrix for studying the bids to remove term limits in Africa	22
Table 3.1	Presidential elections results and turnout, 1993–2016	82
Table 3.2	Legislative elections results and turnout, 1990–2018	86
Table 6.1	Nigeria's Debt Profile, 1985–2004 in Dollars	182
Table 6.2	Nigeria's External Debt Service Payment, 1985–2004 in Dollars	183

CHAPTER 1

Presidential Term Limits, the Never-Ending Debate

Jack R. Mangala

The aftermath of African independence in the early 1960s was marked by the emergence of imperial presidencies across the continent and the total disregard for any notion of power alternation in the constitutional and political order of most countries. Adept at playing Cold War politics and manipulating the masses, many African leaders succeeded in being crowned de facto or de jure life presidents. They came to symbolize the "Big Man" syndrome, a landmark of African political landscape that spoke to the centrality of personal rule and various systems of patronage orchestrated by the leader to ensure his longevity in office. In such a system, there was no ontological separation between the leader and the state. The leader was the state. Congo's Mobutu Sese Seko, Ivory Coast's Felix Houphouet Boigny, Egypt's Hosni Mubarak or Gabon's Omar Bongo were some of the archetypal Big Men, a breed of life presidents or "dinosaurs" of African politics that would hold a firm grip on power and dominate their societies for decades.

J. R. Mangala (✉)
Grand Valley State University, Wyoming, MI, USA
e-mail: mangalaj@gvsu.edu

© The Author(s) 2020
J. R. Mangala (ed.), *The Politics of Challenging Presidential Term Limits in Africa*, https://doi.org/10.1007/978-3-030-40810-7_1

1

The crisis of the African state in the 1980s, combined with the geopolitics of the post-Cold War era, opened up the political and social space needed to challenge big men's hold on power and advocate for presidential term limits, which would become a key feature of post-Cold War constitutional orders engineered across the continent in the 1990s. It is important to note that the embrace of presidential term limits as a new democratic norm in the early years of the post-Cold War era was not the subject of much discussion on the continent. No major political or social forces openly stood against it. It was easily included in the package of reforms that countries were quick to adopt to assert their democratic credentials and chart a new political path. In some instances, it was even supported by the same big men who had ruled their countries for decades, only to challenge it in years to come.

Since its adoption by the majority of African presidential regimes in the years following the end of the Cold War, the institution of presidential term limits has come under successive waves of assault in many countries whose leaders have contemplated or sought its removal or alteration in order to extend their time in office. The first wave, which began in the early 2000s, was led by incumbents such as Namibia's Sam Nujoma, Zambia's Frederick Chiluba, Guinea's Lansana Conte, Uganda's Yoweri Museveni, Nigeria's Olusegum Obasanjo, Gabon's Omar Bongo and Tunisia's Ben Ali, some of who succeeded whereas others failed to achieve their goal of removing or altering term limits. The most recent wave (2015–2017) has put the institution of term limits at the forefront of political debate and maneuvering in countries such as Rwanda, Burundi, Burkina Faso, the Democratic Republic of the Congo, and the Republic of the Congo. It has resulted in various outcomes that are dissected in the case studies included in this volume.

Overall, a numerical overview of the institution shows that in the early 1990s, 33 out of 48 constitutions had enabled presidential term limits, thus raising the hope of a new constitutional era in Africa and "reflecting a new logic of power alternation, a novelty at the time."[1] However, between 1990 and 2009, 26 incumbents representing 72% of the total number of countries with term limits considered altering them to prolong their tenure. Of this group of leaders, only 15 would actually attempt a constitutional amendment with an alarmingly high rate of success. Bids to remove term limits succeeded in 12 countries and were rejected only in 3, representing a success rate of 80% relative to the number of attempts.[2] This situation raises serious concerns over the long-term viability of the institution of term limits and its impact on Africa's democratic trajectory even though, as of 2017, 32 countries still had the principle of power alternation through presidential term limits enshrined in their constitutions.

It is important to note that assaults on the institution of presidential term limits in Africa over the past two decades have been part of a global and long trend that has seen incumbent presidents from Latin America to post-Soviet Eurasia questioning its legitimacy. It has been reported that, between 1960 and 2010, more than a quarter of 200 term-bounded presidents that had exhausted their term in office succeeded, in various forms and manners, in extending their stay beyond constitutionally mandated terms.[3] This number does not include incumbents whose attempts failed as well as those who contemplated the idea of extending their stay but did not, in the end, table a constitutional amendment to that effect or engage in extra constitutional actions to stay in office. This global context must be kept in mind when discussing the institution of term limits in Africa. Even though there are certain dynamics that are particular to African societies, the latter does not need to be exoticized as is often the case in social sciences debates. The questioning of term limits by incumbents or attempts to remove them are not some kind of African "pathology" that leaders and societies elsewhere would be immune against.

Onslaughts on presidential term limits in Africa and globally over the two past decades, and the ensuing political debates, have generated a great deal of scholarly interest and empirical studies shedding new insights on the classical institution of term limits through the examination of a number of variables influencing incumbents' propensity to seek term alteration as well as those impacting the success or failure of such attempts at term elongation. To place the discussion of the politics of presidential terms limits in Africa in its proper context, the following sections will successively offer some historical and global perspectives on presidential term limits, revisit the core political and philosophical arguments in the debate over presidential term limits, review key theoretical contentions and empirical insights on presidential term limits, and outline the present book's added value and structure.

Historical and Global Perspectives on Term Limits

The democratic institution of presidential term limits, which stipulates a president's maximum length of tenure in office, has deep historical roots that can be traced back to ancient Greece and the Roman republic. It has survived the vicissitudes and convulsions of history and has spread across the globe to become a landmark of modern democratic presidential regimes, often contested by rulers imbued with their own sense of indispensability and seeking political immortality, but reaffirmed through trials and tribulations that speak to its universality and enduring relevance across times and cultures.

History teaches that the institution of term limits was first practiced by ancient Greeks who sought to dilute the dangers of power usurpation on the part of elected officials by mandating they served, with very limited exceptions, only a single or two terms in office. Underlining this mandate was the view that by limiting the number of terms one could serve in a particular office, all citizens are given the opportunity to seek that office if they so desire, thus reinforcing the idea of equality among the citizens. Frequent office rotation was thought to contribute to the good of the city by compelling moderation on the part of elected officials.

Following ancient Greece, the Roman republic (509–27 B.C.) would also enact term limits for the majority of its magistrates.[4] Expanding on the rationale put forward earlier in Greece, republican Rome emphasized the need, through mandated office rotation, to prevent personal rule and moderate political competition, thus ensuring the stability of its aristocratic political system. In broad strokes, it is worth observing that, with a few exceptions pertaining to specific emergency situations and a few successful second consulships, term limits were generally enforced—alongside other checks and balances—during the Roman republic until Julius Caesar decided to deviate from this republican norm by having himself declared Father of the Country and *dictator perpetus* in 44 B.C. It is worth noting that Caesar's assassins would justify his killing on the imperative of returning the republic to its proper course by delivering it from the claws of a de facto, if not the jure, king.[5] The practice of term limits lasted until the demise of the republic in 27 B.C., which led to a long era of perpetual and personal rule. Following the demise of the Roman Republic, the practice of term limits would later resurface, in various forms and contours, in a number of medieval and early modern European cities and republics such as Novgorod, Pskov, Genoa, and Florence. In the latter, for example, members of the executive council, in which power was vested, enjoyed only a two-month term of office.[6] By all historical accounts, there is little evidence to suggest that tenure limitation was practiced, at that time, outside of the European theater.

Fast-forwarding to the emergence of modern democratic constitutions, it is important to note that the notion of term limits was not initially part of the constitutional engineering that took place in the late 1700s. Neither the US Constitution of 1788 nor the French Constitution of 1793 made any reference to term limits. In the case of the USA, even though term limits for officeholders, especially in regard to the office of the president, was discussed during the Constitutional Convention, it would not, *in fine*, figure in the constitution that was adopted by the delegates. Presidential term limits would however quickly become an informal institution of American politics following President George Washington's decision to voluntarily step down after his second term in 1796. As for France, following the silence of the initial constitution of 1793, term limitation would be mandated, two years later, for the five-man executive directory established by the new constitution of 1795.[7]

George Washington's decision would prove to be of great historical and political significance. It revived the debate about term limitation in presidential regimes, and influenced presidential constitutions engineering that took place in subsequent decades in a number of newly independent countries in Latin America (Bolivia, Venezuela, and Argentina).[8] Even though not formally embedded in the US Constitution, the tradition started by George Washington would be scrupulously followed by all his successors with the exception of President Franklin D. Roosevelt who went on to seek and win four terms in office. The precedent set by President Roosevelt generated the necessary impetus to codify, through a 1951 constitutional amendment, the informal rule started by the first American president.

A snapshot of presidential term limits among the independent nations of the world at the time of the US constitutional amendment shows a rather limited global appeal for the institution of term limitation in the office of the president. While it had gained currency in Latin America and had been enshrined in the US Constitution, European presidential regimes (France being the most notable) and a few of the existing independent countries elsewhere in the world (Liberia, for example) did not embrace it. The emergence of new independent nations in Africa and Asia in the aftermath of WWII would mark a new phase for presidential term limits in the contemporary period, and the start of a long process of universalization.

The independence wave that swept across the world in the middle of the twentieth century resulted in a significant increase in the number of states that adopted presidential systems of government in Africa and Asia. The vast majority of these new presidential regimes did not, however, include term limits for the office of the president. Between 1950 and 1970, a total of fifty-two new presidential-system Constitutions were enacted globally of which only seven (13%) included term limitation rules. With particular reference to Africa, only the Democratic Republic of the Congo, Gabon, Rwanda, and Togo initially imposed term limits at the time of independence in the early 1960s, only to abandon them quickly in the ensuing years. Of all new presidential regimes in the Middle East, only Lebanon adopted term limitation. The same dynamic was at play in Asia where, with the exception of the Philippines, presidential system countries either did not initially impose term limits (Indonesia and Taiwan) or quickly eliminated them (South Korea). This trend was reinforced throughout the Cold War, making term limits a rather rare commodity in presidential systems of government worldwide. It was not until the end of the Cold War in the closing decades of the twentieth century—a period that also coincided with the third wave of democratization—that presidential term limits became a central feature of presidential-regime constitutions across the globe and achieved universal status.[9]

The decade between 1990 and 1999 coincided with tremendous expansion in the institutionalization of presidential term limits. Out of a total of sixty-six constitutions that were promulgated during this period, 89% incorporated presidential term limits. This evolution represented an important substantive change compared to the early 1960s.[10] The 1990s witnessed the transformation of presidential term limits from a norm that was embraced only by a handful of presidential regimes across the world a few decades earlier to a major institutional feature of modern democratic life within the context of an increased globalization of culture, commerce, and politics. With the demise of the Soviet Union and the end of the Cold War, newly sovereign countries in Eastern Europe and Central Asia, as well those that had been caught in Cold War politics in Africa and other parts of the world, decided to codify presidential term limits through new multiparty constitutions to guard against a history of dictatorship and autocratic rule. The movement of universalization of term limits warrants further comments, especially in regard to African countries.

It is worth noting that foreign organizations and groups engaged in democracy promotion in Africa did not initially posit presidential term limits as a core demand of their governance agenda. At the inception of the post-Cold War era, the initial focus seems to have been on good governance, not on democratic governance. Even though the question of term limits was not high on the reform priorities put forward by organizations such as the US National Endowment for Democracy or the National Democratic Institute, it appears however that local civil society organizations (CSOs) and new political parties either funded or trained by these foreign groups were determined to fight for term limitation. Having experienced the social, economic, and political costs of personal rule and big men governance since independence, local actors seized on the political space created by the end of the Cold War to chart a new democratic path for African countries by insisting that presidential term limits be included in the new constitutional order. Foreign donor governments would bring to bear pressure on the issue of term limits later in the decade that followed the start of democratization process in Africa.[11] As rightly noted by Alexander Baturo, "…the initiative to restrict tenure was largely homegrown and was regarded as evident by democratic activists."[12]

Besides the repudiation of life presidencies and the determination on the part of African local actors to stop the crisis of the state, other interesting dynamics are also credited to have contributed to the almost universal adoption of the democratic norm of term limits on the continent in the 1990s and early 2000s. First, through a process of "constitutional diffusion" that saw virtually similar provisions constraining the president to two consecutive terms coupled with a number of other constitutional limitations on the office of the president being adopted, country after country, across the vast African continent. Second, many long-serving leaders whose democratic credentials were dubious supported the inclusion of term limits in new constitutions as a cosmetic measure aimed mostly at foreign consumption. Teodoro Obiang Nguema of Equatorial Guinea, Omar Bongo of Gabon, and Gnassingbé Eyadéma of Togo were chiefs among African presidents who engaged in this cosmetic constitutional operation. However, as Alexander Baturo remarks, "Perhaps inadvertently, by imposing tenure restrictions at the onset of democratization, whether genuine or not, many presidents created very powerful focal points for future societal, elite and international coordination against dictatorial takeover."[13]

If the 1990s and the early years of 2000 witnessed the almost universal adoption of term limits in presidential systems of government in Africa and other regions of the world, this trend has seen a reversal in the past two decades. The proportion of global Constitutions that enshrined presidential term limits slowed significantly in the first nine years of the twenty-first century. Of the forty-one Constitutions enacted or amended during this period, just slightly over half (51%) provided for presidential term limits.[14] As more term-limited presidents began to reach the end of their maximum tenures toward the end of the 1990s, several began to initiate processes aimed at either removing term-limit provisions or altering them in order to elongate their stay in office. From Russia, Azerbaijan, Tunisia, to Venezuela, presidential term limits came under worldwide assault that seemed to dampen the democratic enthusiasm that had followed the end of the Cold War.

In Africa, the process of reversal or contestation of term limits began in 1998 when Namibia amended her Constitution to allow the country's founding president, Sam Nujoma, to contest for a third term in the 1999 elections. Other African leaders, both from the older generation that self-imposed restrictions in the 1990s and those that came later, would follow on the same path over the years since then, some succeeding and others failing in their attempts to extend their stay in office. Recent successful, albeit contested, presidential term elongation in Rwanda, Burundi, and the Republic of Congo, failed attempts in Burkina Faso, and elongation maneuvering in the Democratic Republic of the Congo are clearly indicative of the slow erosion suffered by the institution of term limits since the end of the Cold War as captured in Table 1.1.

If the establishment of presidential term limits in the early years of the post-Cold War era did not generate much debate and was regarded as evident by democracy activists, the worldwide reversal movement observed over the past two decades has, however, ignited an intense debate that has revived old philosophical and political arguments for and against presidential term limits, the substance of which will be captured in the following section.

Debating Presidential Term Limits: The Philosophical and Political Arguments

From ancient Greece to Gabon, from Russia to Rwanda, the core philosophical and political arguments pro and against term limits in general, and presidential term limits more specifically, have remained pretty constant. Beyond oratorical sophistications and local eccentricities by opponents and proponents on each side of this debate, the essence of arguments on term limits has not changed much across times and cultures. Even though the idea of term limits is popular among the wider citizenry, it remains a contested institution that often generates passionate arguments from various groups and actors. The following sections will consider key arguments in support of the institution before turning to those against it.

Arguments in Support of Term Limits

Today, as in classical times, arguments in support of term limits have centered on four core contentions. Proponents argue that term limits promote rotation of leadership, reduce the likelihood of tyranny, help to improve participation in politics, and promote efficiency and effectiveness in government policy.

The Leadership Rotation Argument
The first argument posits that term limits serve as an important institution that promotes alternation for elected public office holders by opening up opportunities for other members of the society to hold political office. The Greek political philosopher Aristotle was among the first to articulate this position. He argued that term limits were a necessary institution of democratic politics as they help to ensure that all individuals in society would have the opportunity to serve in leadership roles. Here is how Aristotle in *The Politics* (Book VI, Section II) expressed this equal opportunity argument:

> …the characteristics of democracy are as follows: the election of officers by all out of all; that the appointment to all offices, or to all but those which require experience and skill, should be made by lot…that a man should not hold the same office twice, or not often, or in the case of few except military officers; that the tenure of all offices, or of as many as possible, should be brief.

The essence of Aristotle's argument is grounded on the notion of equality among the citizens, and term limits is posited as a public good, a democratic norm that ensures moderation in office and the commonality between public and private individuals based on the principle of "ruled and being ruled in turn." In his letter to James Madison during the debates on the drafting of the US Constitution, Thomas Jefferson also framed term limits as an important institutional barrier aimed, among other things, at neutralizing the advantages of incumbency. He wrote, "reason and experience tell us the First Magistrate will always be reelected if he may be reelected."[15]

Although rotation of officeholders in democratic politics can be achieved through competitive elections, term limits are thought to play an important role by neutralizing the advantage of incumbency, which significantly reduces the chances for challengers to win elections. Even though the causes of incumbency advantage are contested, there is a large body of literature that has established that the incumbent advantage is not only real but, more importantly, seems to increase over time. For example, Gary King and Andrew Gelman find that incumbency increases a representative's expected vote share by 11%.[16] This finding is corroborated by a number of other studies that stress that both the sources of incumbency advantage and its multifaceted nature that allow incumbents to win sixteen times as often as their challengers, have higher margins of victory, and participate in more unopposed elections than do challengers.[17]

In addition to encouraging turnover in holders of political office, opponents of term limits also contend that the resultant rotation of public office holders, especially at the executive level of government, can have a corresponding effect that increases the prospects of party alternation, which is considered a key feature of democratic politics.[18] This claim is supported by empirical evidence. It has been shown that when an incumbent gives way to other candidates, the chances of electoral victory for the ruling party slide down from a 93% probability of success to a modest 52%.[19] In other words, term limits increase the likelihood of alternation of the party in power.

Furthermore, advocates of term limits argue that rotation of office is not the end in itself. Rotation of office presents opportunities for democratic consolidation, a point backed by strong scholarly evidence that indicates, for example, that both intra-party leadership alternation and partisan turnovers are typically followed by a significant improvement in the quality of political rights and civil liberties.[20] For proponents of term limits, partisan alternation is seen as "the ultimate indicator of (…) democracy and democratic quality"[21] in that it generates shared levels of legitimacy between winners and losers in the general population, thus furthering democratic consolidation.[22]

The Tyranny Argument
The possibility of power usurpation or the danger of tyranny has always been and remains a central argument for proponents of term limits. This point was eloquently articulated by Thomas Jefferson during the founding years of the American republic. A strong supporter of tenure limitation as an institutional insurance against self-perpetuated personal rule, Jefferson did not hide his dislike for "…the abandonment in every instance of the necessity of rotation in office, and most particularly in the case of the President. If some termination to the services of the Chief Magistrate be not fixed by the Constitution or supplied by practice, his office, normally four years, will in fact, become for life; and history shows how easily that degenerates into an inheritance."[23]

In the absence of term limits, the danger of tyrannical rule appears to be particularly acute in presidential regimes where the chief executive is at the pinnacle of the government machinery. The literature has explored a number of dynamics that contribute to this situation. First is the idea that with great powers entrusted in the office of the president, there is a great threat that democratically elected presidents can easily use their positions to become tyrants. The danger of tyranny and the demise of democracy become even more pronounced when the exercise of presidential powers is accompanied by lengthy tenure.[24]

Term limits is thus regarded a constitutional safety mechanism aimed at preventing the hijacking of democracy by very popular leaders who might be inclined to utilize the formal mechanics of democracy to advance personal ambitions, consolidate their own power, and ensure their durability in office, leading to a situation of electoral authoritarianism, a growing phenomenon around the world.[25] This argument carries particular resonance in Africa with its history of long-tenured and life presidents. The imperative of preventing a return to tyrannical presidencies of the past was front and center in the national debates leading up to the almost universal adoption of presidential term limits on the continent in the early 1990s.

The Political Participation Argument
In classical Athens, the argument that rotation of public officials helped to increase participation in politics emanated from the idea of equality among the citizens alluded to earlier. Term limitation was conceived of as a political equalizer that gave everyone, including people of humble origin and modest means, a shot at public service, thus contributing to the greater good of the city through a number of particular processes that

have reverberated in contemporary debates over term limits and have been dissected by term limits scholars.

One process by which office rotation contributes to the greater good of the city is by increasing the stock of citizens that are knowledgeable about public affairs and by endowing the society with politically experienced individuals that can be relied upon to play various political roles, including monitoring the performance of the government and offering advice on the affairs of government. Another process through which term limits is said to contribute to the greater good of the city is by increasing political participation. By shaking up power structures and mitigating the advantages of incumbency, term limits have the potential to rejuvenate the country's political life in a manner that can excite the electorate and contribute to higher voter turnout. Without the people's participation in the political process, it is argued, democracy itself will lose its true essence and cannot ultimately survive. The prospect of power alternation is thought of as one of democracy's safety mechanisms in that it keeps the citizens motivated and engaged in the affairs of the city. This argument was on full display in 2002 in Arkansas during the debate to impose term limits for the state's congressional delegation. Among other things, the proposal in support of term limits stated the following:

> The people of Arkansas find and declare that elected officials who remain in office too long become preoccupied with reelection and ignore their duties as representatives of the people. Entrenched incumbency has reduced voter participation and has led to an electoral system that is less free, less competitive, and less representative than the system established by the Founding Fathers.[26]

Central to this proposal is the idea that the lack of term limits undermines democracy by depressing voter participation and contributing to a political system dominated by a few and in which the vast majority of citizens do not feel like they have a stake.

The Good Governance Argument
By encouraging regular leadership rotation and neutralizing the advantages of incumbency, term limits are thought to promote efficiency and effectiveness in government policy in two fundamental ways. First, and with particular regard to the office of the president, term limits are credited with increasing the likelihood of new leadership that can bring new

and fresh ideas in solving the country's problems. Entrenched incumbency tends to lead to political myopia, a condition in which the leader recycles the same old mantras and becomes resistant to change and fresh ideas, thus impeding the country's ability to confront the complex problems it faces which often require new and creative thinking in government policymaking and implementation.[27] Second, perpetual incumbency in the office of the president tends to lead to a situation in which the leader shirks his/her responsibilities and becomes unresponsive to the wishes and needs of the people. The "shirking-deviation theory" elucidates this phenomenon by demonstrating how incumbency advantage serves as a relaxation of the election constrain. In other words, the theory asserts, as the leader is assured of being reelected *ad vitam aeternam*, he or she can afford to ignore the wishes of the voters.[28]

Against this backdrop, rotation of public officials is seen as a mechanism that contributes to good governance by facilitating a people-centric leadership and enhancing a sense of legitimacy on the part of the leader and the policies being pursued, whereas political careerism generates political ossification by which the leader becomes too concerned with his or her own reelection, often risk-averse, and disconnected from the citizenry.

Arguments Against Term Limits

On the other hand, opponents of term limits usually outline four central points. They argue that term limits are undemocratic, reduce accountability, do not prevent former leaders from influencing policymaking, and promote inefficiency. In the making of modern constitutions, these arguments were first eloquently outlined by Alexander Hamilton in *The Federalist Papers n.71* published in 1788. They have been echoed, since then, by opponents of term limits across the globe. They are worth revisiting, albeit succinctly.

The Democracy Argument

The main argument put forward by opponents of term limits is that they are substantively undemocratic in that they infringe upon the right of citizens to elect a president or leader of their choice for as long as they wish. Te Mann sums up the essence of this first line of reasoning when he contends that term limits "diminish democracy by restricting it unnecessarily, by taking away the power to end the careers of politicians from the electorate."[29] The ultimate power of the people to reward or sanction its leaders, it is argued, is the true measure of democracy, not artificial tenure restrictions that take away the people's power. Several micro arguments are usually outlined in support of this broad contention on the undemocratic nature of term limits.

First is the idea that term limits devalue the role of elections by reducing the field of candidates that can compete for political office. Although the rotation of public officials is acknowledged to be an essential feature of democratic politics, critics of term limits often maintain that leadership alternation should only be achieved through elections in which no individual is barred from contesting. In other words, let the people decide. By restricting the people's power through innate constitutional rules, term limits are portrayed as being, at their core, democratically flawed.[30]

Second, opponents of term limits often argue that incumbency advantage must be regarded, especially in well-functioning democracies, as indicative of voter satisfaction, even if the lack of alternation is considered undesirable. Imposing term limits in order to neutralize incumbency advantage, as claimed by proponents of term limits, would amount to punishing responsive public officials, while taking away the ability of the voters, through the ballot box, to reward performers and punish non-performers. Limiting the freedom of choice of the electorate and that of individuals to stand for public office is thus considered antithetical to the idea of a free and democratic society.

Third, instead of contributing to consolidating democracy, term limits can have the opposite effect of eroding it. Along these lines, Juan Linz and Arturo Valenzuela contend that the winner-takes-all nature of presidential elections, when juxtaposed against term limits on the presidency, means that presidents seeking to extend their tenure might have to resort to non-democratic means to remain in office. The consequences, they point out, can be violent protests and coups as the only way to ensure *continuissimo*, or tenure prolongation.[31] Within this school of thought, the fight over term limits is viewed as a major challenge and threat to political stability, especially in new and emerging democracies where democratic institutions are rather weak and political stability is often assured through the leadership of particular individuals. When such leaders are forced to leave office as a result of term limits, it is argued, the leadership vacuum created can contribute to political instability that might pose a challenge to democratic survival.

This argument against term limits is, to say the least, weak and intellectually deceptive. It plays right into the hands of tyrants quick to portray an apocalyptic landscape after they leave office, and often working toward that outcome so as to prove their point. The aim of democracy is to build political stability on strong and impersonal institutions. Any political instability or uncertainty that arises from leadership alternation would be reflective of the weaknesses of the political system as a whole and cannot simply be blamed on term limits.

The Accountability Argument
By curtailing the right of the people to reelect those who have performed well in office, term limits are said to reduce accountability by diminishing the incentive for elected officeholders to serve those who voted them into power. In so doing, term limits are criticized for severing the bond between electors and the elected.[32] This problem is said to be particularly acute in a country like Mexico where almost all elected officials are not allowed to stand for reelection. In such scenarios, public officials, once elected, become unresponsive to the needs of the people since they cannot be obligated or pressured to perform and respond because the threat of being "fired" during elections has been eliminated.

Term limits are also criticized for reducing accountability by encouraging a type of leadership that shirks its responsibilities when approaching the end of their tenure in office, a situation that often contributes to irresponsible spending by lame-duck leaders who become more concerned about their own professional prospects after leaving office than serving the people who elected them.[33]

The Policymaking Argument
Another rationale for term limits is that it can facilitate turnover and, in so doing, create opportunities for new leadership to emerge and influence public policymaking through the infusion of new ideas and approaches. To that argument, critics of term limits reply that the mere removal of certain individuals from office does not ipso facto prevent them from influencing public policy from outside or from other high-profile public positions. In many instances, there are, for example, no rules barring term-limited leaders from assuming other high-profile public functions. The case of Vladimir Putin who swapped the presidency of Russia for the post of prime minister in 2008 is often cited to illustrate this point.

Critics of term limits also argue that the institution puts too much emphasis on individual leaders, and yet their policies can still be continued after their tenures have ended. Even after the leader leaves office, his or her policy can still be pursued through a handpicked successor and other clients and associates who occupy key public positions. Cristina Fernandez Kirchner succeeding her husband Nestor Kirchner as President of Argentina in 2007 clearly speaks to this dynamic of policy continuation and influence of former leaders barred from seeking office.

Even though term limits can produce leadership alternation, concede critics of the institution, this alone, they argue, is insufficient to achieve the more important objective of infusing new ideas and fresh perspectives into the public policymaking process.

The Inefficiency Argument
The inefficiency argument put forward by critics of term limits has several legs to it. The first leg underscores the fact that leadership rotation promotes inefficiency because it constantly entrusts critical public decision-making in the hands of novices instead of experts. This line of criticism was espoused by opponents of term limits in classical Athens and Rome. Socrates, for example, contended that strict enforcement of leadership rotation ultimately promoted "mediocrity" as it "deprived Athens of the services of professional experts that were equipped with superior governing skills."[34] This point would be reiterated by Alexander Hamilton who asserted that term limits can restrict the voters' choice and deprive the latter of experienced representatives. He asked: "What more desirable and more essential than this quality in the governors of the nations? Can it be wise to put this desirable and essential quality under the ban of the Constitution…?"[35] The experience argument found its way in the debates leading up the adoption of the 22nd Amendment to the US Constitution during which opponents pointed out that term limits were flawed because they contributed to the removal of experienced candidates who were more aware of their public responsibilities than newcomers. Victor Kamber echoes the same view when he writes that term limits "remove seasoned professionals [from office and] depriving them of the experience, institutional memory, wisdom and judgment needed to govern effectively…leaving the affairs of government in the hands of amateurs."[36] This argument has been reverberating in term limits debates in Africa and other parts of the world over the past three decades.

The second leg of the inefficiency argument rests on the contention that term limits carry the potential of increasing inefficiency as a result of their indiscriminate removal of good and bad leaders from political office. Term limits are thought to interfere with the normal electoral process—which allows voters the choice of rewarding good performers and punishing bad ones—by forcing the removal of the candidacy of both good and bad performers. This criticism of term limits seems to be based on the assumption that elections can be a sufficient tool for voters to reward or punish public officeholders. However, in order to do so, voters not only need to be well-informed to make sound electoral choices but, more importantly, the playing field also needs to be leveled so that all candidates have an equal chance of winning. However, as the literature on incumbency advantage has demonstrated, this is rarely possible. The unevenness of the electoral playing field is especially pronounced in new and emerging democracies such as those of Africa where high illiteracy rates, limited access to news as well as very weak and poor-resourced opposition parties often conspire to make it difficult for voters to make informed electoral choices.[37]

The third line of criticism against term limits based on the inefficiency argument highlights the fact that leadership rotation can disrupt, or indeed reverse, policy gains made by previous administrations. This argument was part of Alexander Hamilton's multilayered stance against term limits. He contended that term limits would hinder policy continuity. He wrote: "To reverse and undo what has been done by a predecessor, is very often considered by a successor as the best proof he can give of his own capacity and desert. ..."[38] In regard to situations where continuity is considered essential, such as in post-conflict or economic recovery situations, it has been asserted that breaks in administration enforced by office rotation can slow down the recovery process. Along the same line, it has also been argued that the possibility of remaining in office for long periods might enhance the likelihood that public officials would adopt long-term plans. Conversely term limits are thought to encourage short-termism as public officials know they would not have time to fulfill long-term plans, even if these would ultimately be more beneficial. Short-termism deriving from enforced term rotation is therefore framed as an impediment to good public policy and governance.[39]

Proponents of term limits have addressed the inexperience argument by counter-arguing that the average person is competent to carry out the routine affairs of the government.[40] In other words, this counter-argument seeks to return the institution of term limits to its original *ratio legis*, which rests on the idea of equality among the citizenry and faith in the common sense of all citizens, not in the knowledge of experts and career politicians, to be able to exercise leadership for the greater good of the society. In a democracy, no one is indispensable. All are able.

Since the end of the Cold War and in light of the new Caesarism—a phenomenon which has seen leaders from Africa, Latin America, Asia, to post-Soviet Eurasia, question the *raison d'être* of constitutional term limits and, through the use of various legal and political subterfuges, seek to extend their terms in office—the topic of presidential term limits has benefited from a growing scholarly interest that has opened new theoretical grounds and provided empirical insights into the question of presidential term limits alteration. The next section seeks to capture the substance of scholarly directions and insights emerging from the new body of literature on presidential term limits alteration with a particular reference to Africa.

Theoretical and Empirical Insights on Presidential Term Limits Alteration

An incumbent president who is approaching the end of his tenure within a term-limited polity has two primary choices: abide by the tenure limitations and step down, or get the term limits removed or relaxed in such a manner as to allow for tenure extension. If the decision is to seek a third term, this would trigger a second phase of the game that requires the removal of term limits, and which can take any one of these four options: abolishing the term-limit rule to allow indefinite reelection, increasing the maximum number of allowed terms, classifying a prior term as falling outside the term-limit ambit, and increasing the length of presidential term without removing term limits. The president then has to navigate and meander through a number of institutions, both formal and informal, before he can get over the limitations. The outcomes of these processes ultimately depend on the strength or weakness of the existing institutions in preventing or aiding the removal of term limits, as well as the ability of the incumbent to successfully negotiate around them.

James March and Johan Olsen define institutions as the "relatively enduring collection of rules and organized practices, embedded in structures of meanings and resources, that are collectively invariant in the face of turnover of individuals and relatively resilient to the idiosyncratic preferences and expectations of individuals and changing external circumstances..."[41] In other words, institutions create capabilities for acting, while at the same time constraining and shaping political interactions by prescribing what actions are acceptable or not. Institutions provide structures of meaning, common purposes, and accounts of political actors.

While the role that institutions play in providing opportunities and constraints for political action in the bids to remove presidential term limits has long been at the center of scholarship on the third-term phenomenon, recent scholarly inquiries have underscored a new institutional analysis in the study of term limits by re-examining some of the conclusions reached in the early studies and focusing on the importance of informal institutions, in the developing world in general and in Africa in particular. The new institutional analysis has thus expanded the portfolio of institutions to be accounted for as variables in explaining the outcomes of bids to remove term limits. Before discussing the core approaches and findings of this new line of inquiry, a further elaboration on informal institutions and their centrality in African politics seems warranted.

The above definition of institutions from March and Olsen includes not only "the enduring collection of rules" of a formal kind, but also informal norms that are based on "organized practices." Drawn from socially shared values and usually unwritten, informal institutions are often created, communicated, and enforced outside of formally sanctioned channels. While formal rules are easy to observe, decipher, and study (and therefore the focus of most works on institutions), there is an increasing recognition that informal rules that include organizational structures and cultural practices have much influence, and sometimes more, in shaping political affairs and outcomes as do formal ones.[42]

The competing effects of formal and informal institutions in shaping politics and political outcomes can be fully observed in the African political arena. A number of scholars of African politics have rightly observed that even though the political transitions that started in the early 1990s were expected to increase the influence of formal institutions while reducing the effect of informal ones, the reality remains that the latter continue to shape political action on the continent in profound and significant ways.[43] Beatrice Hibou writes:

The relationships, institutions and people most prominently in public view are not necessarily the most powerful...public administration and institutions in Africa are indeed weak...personal relations, and personal networks, whether economic, political, religious or regional nature, frequently offer far more effective instruments of public management....[44]

One should not, however, conclude that informal rules always trump formal ones. Rather, the two are in constant competition, the outcome of which depends on a number of complex factors that affect various processes within a particular political, social and cultural context. For example, the formal new institutions introduced following the political transitions of the 1990s included, among other changes, competitive elections, constitutional supremacy, and maximum presidential age. These have been in competition and dynamic relationships with other informal institutions, not always easily observable and quantifiable, such as respect for the elderly and authority, father-figure, and patronage, but which are culturally embedded and socially potent in Africa. Because informal institutions can create, strengthen, or negate incentives to comply with formal rules, they may also shape attempts to change existing formal rules in important ways. Even in situations where Constitutions establish super-powerful presidencies, informal institutions may limit the exercise of presidential power to advance a personal agenda as vividly illustrated in the case of President Olusegun Obasanjo's failed attempt at term elongation in 2007.

Despite sweeping powers entrusted to him by the Nigerian Constitution, Obasanjo failed miserably in his attempt to stay in power beyond the allowed two terms. Although the President's People's Democratic Party (PDP) had a comfortable parliamentary majority and his quest for a third term was skillfully orchestrated through a major campaign of patronage to entice supporters, it was ultimately defeated due to the PDP's policy stipulating that its presidential candidates should be rotated between the largely Muslim North and the predominantly Christian South after every two terms. Obasanjo's third-term bid was thus seen as a flagrant deviation from the long-established informal rule of leadership rotation within the PDP. As a result, Obasanjo faced a rebellion among his own party instigated by Vice President Atiku Abubakar who convinced the PDP members in the Senate to vote against the bill that sought to remove term limits when it was tabled in May 2006.[45]

In the wake of the democratic transitions of the 1990s, some scholars of African politics expressed an early optimism by suggesting that the era of informal rule domination in Africa might be coming to an end, and the formal institutions will increasingly assume center stage in post-transition African politics.[46] However, the vast majority of scholars do not seem to share the view that Africa's emerging democracies are transforming politics beyond the informal institutional paradigm. They have expressed skepticism about the potency of formal institutions to reign in Africa's personal rules. While conceding that formal institutions have had only a limited impact, they contend that informal institutions continue to provide the dominant framework within which politics is practiced and can best be understood in Africa.[47] Nicholas Van de Walle best echoes this view when he writes that, despite the adoption of new and ostensibly democratic Constitutions, the reality in Africa's emerging party systems is that "power is [still] intensely personalized around the figure of the President."[48]

Recent scholarly studies on presidential term limits in Africa underscore the need for a holistic approach that focuses on the complex dynamics between both sets of institutions (formal and informal) on the outcomes of bids to remove term limits. This approach accounts for the full range of institutions, formal and informal, that influence the outcomes of bids to remove tenure limits. It stresses a broad definition of institutions that includes organizational structures and cultural practices that all serve as important drivers of politics at different levels of the African political arena. From the body of work published on presidential term limits over the past decade, the broad conceptualization and institutional framework adopted in this volume identify up to sixteen institutional variables that may affect the outcomes of the bids to remove term limits, which are visually captured in Table 1.1.

The below four-layered institutional matrix calls for some succinct explanation. The meta institutional level includes institutions and rules stemming from the overarching legal framework that define the political regime, mostly the national Constitution. The state-level is concerned with the set of rules that govern the activities of political actors at the state level, including both local and extant factors that influence the outcomes of political action at this level. The third level focuses on the political society level, which encompasses groups of actors that form political goals, such as political parties and the person of the president. The fourth and final tier in the matrix deals with institutions that regulate the activities

Table 1.1 Institutional matrix for studying the bids to remove term limits in Africa

Institutional level	Type of institutional arena	
	Formal arena	Informal arena
Meta-level	Constitution: maximum length of tenure, checks and balances	Path dependency, the precedence of alternation
State-level	Extent of democracy, legislative majority of ruling party, effective number of parties	Patronage, influence of extant economic factors
Political society	Political parties, electorate	Alliances, factions, age of the president(gerontocracy), deference for authority and father-figure leadership, military background of president, history of long-tenured presidents
Civil society	NGOs, religious groups, media, trade unions	Ethnic fragmentation, public opinion

of civil society actors, such as non-governmental organizations (NGOs), the media, religious groups, trade unions, and others. At each of these four levels, institutional variables that affect the outcomes of the bids to remove term limits are organized in two sub-groups dealing, respectively, with formal and informal institutions.

What are the predicted effects of institutions on third-term outcomes? Within the framework of this holistic institutional analysis, the literature underscores a number of scenarios and expected relationships between the rules and the actors and how they impact third-term outcomes as illustrated in Fig. 1.1.

Figure 1.1 indicates that an incumbent president's ability to remove tenure limits is affected by both formal and informal institutional channels to secure the removal of term limits. The removal of term limits is a complex process, and the interaction and interpenetration of formal with informal institutions, as shown in the diagram, suggests that the distinction between the two is only an analytical tool, not necessarily an empirical one. The diagram also shows that, overall, the two sets of institutions have a reversal effect on term limits removal. It appears that the majority of formal institutions (five of seven) tend to frustrate the removal of

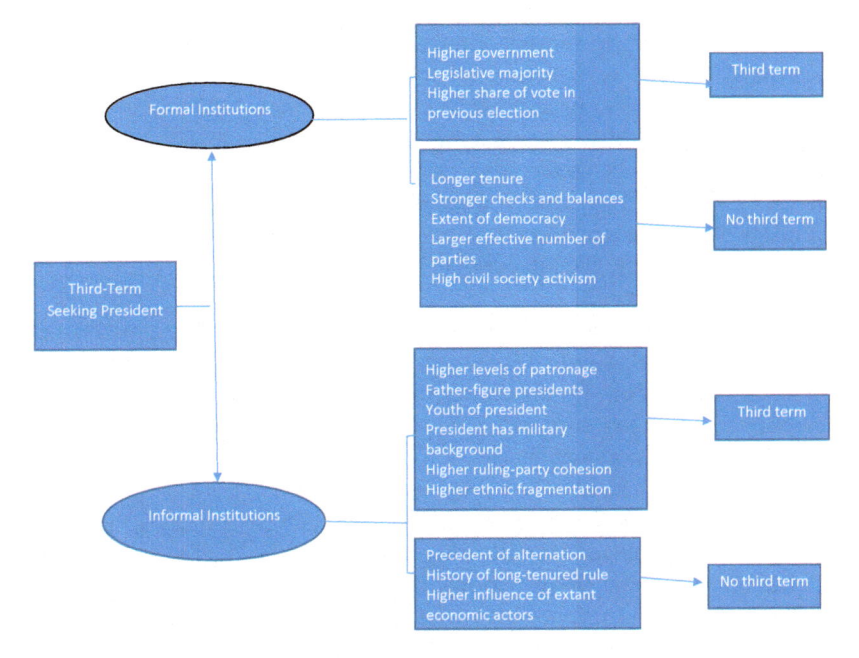

1 PRESIDENTIAL TERM LIMITS, THE NEVER-ENDING DEBATE

Fig. 1.1 Predicted effects of institutions on third term outcomes

term limits whereas the bulk of informal institutions (nine of thirteen) are expected to increase the likelihood of the removal of term limits.

The various variables gathered from the scholarship on term limits and shown in the above diagram are explored at length in the case study chapters. Within the confines of this introductory chapter, I would like, for illustrative purposes only, to further discuss the relationship between two variables (path dependency and share of the presidential vote in previous elections) and term limits removal.

In Fig. 1.1, path dependency (precedent of alternation) is shown to frustrate third-term bid. As James March and Johan Olsen point out, long periods of institutional continuity can facilitate the reproduction of institutions and thus help to establish political equilibrium which, in turn, can help establish a legacy of path dependency where the institution is continuously reproduced.[49] As illustrated by President George Washington, leaders who step down at the end of their terms are thought to instill the "precedent of succession," thereby making it less likely for their successors to tamper with the institutions of term limits. It can thus be expected that countries with leaders that have previously stepped down from either voluntarily (South Africa) or at the end of their tenure in office (e.g. Ghana, Benin, Tanzania, and Botswana, among others) will establish path dependencies of observance of term limits. New incumbents in these countries will be less likely to pursue the removal of term limits. Conversely, in countries where the tradition of honoring term limits is less established, there will be a higher likelihood that leaders will attempt to remove term limits and even succeed.

In regard to the share of presidential vote in previous elections, Daniel Posner and Daniel Young identify it as one of the three predictors of the likelihood of a bid to remove term limits being attempted and passed. More specifically, they contend that presidents who secured high electoral majorities in the most recent elections are likely to use it as a retrospective indicator of the public's willingness to endorse a term elongation.[50] Daniel Vencovsky echoes the same argument when he contends that "the outcome of third-term struggles may hinge…on the degree of popularity that the president enjoys among the population."[51] If the argument advanced by these authors holds true, presidents who had a high share of the vote in previous presidential elections would be expected to pursue the removal of term limits and succeed in doing so than those with a smaller share of the votes in previous elections.

While the holistic institutional framework discussed above offers important insights into the variables impacting the third-term outcomes, and while the strength of institutions can certainly act as constraints on a leader contemplating a change to term limits rules, institutions in themselves do not, however, fully answer the question as to why one leader would step down whereas another would seek to subvert the constitution to extend his term in office. What explains the president's behavior when confronted with term limits? What are the factors that can ensure that political leaders will honor term limits constitutional norms across presidential regimes? Answering these fundamental questions, to which the institutional approach provides only limited answers, requires taking a step back from variables that affect the outcomes of third-term bids after the decision to stay in office longer than required by the constitution has already been made by the dealer, and focus instead on the onset of personalism, that critical juncture when a leader ponders whether to go or stay. Why do certain leaders choose the latter and subvert the constitution?

In his seminal work, *Democracy, Dictatorships, and Term Limits*, Alexander Baturo addresses this central question through a novel approach that attempts to understand the motivation of a national political leader, the value of holding political office and, on the basis of various cross-national data, the likely factors that determine this value—and thus what rulers stand to lose—in the context of term limits. Baturo's study sheds much-needed scholarly light on the phenomenon of new Caesarism which has seen leaders, across Africa and elsewhere in the world, convinced of their own indispensability, seek political immortality through a subversion of constitutional term limits. In so doing, they are following in the historical footstep of Julius Caesar who, after crossing the Rubicon, claimed for himself the consecutive titles of consul, dictator, and dictator for life in 44 B.C. To set the stage for this novel approach that investigates the interplay between presidential power, rent-seeking and political regimes, and personal survival, Baturo writes:

> Presidents contemplating whether to comply with constitutional term limits or extend their stay instead have to be able to implement such extension—hence constraints on the executive capacity matter—but they also have varying monetary and personal incentives to remain in that office—hence individual motives are also crucial. It is not sufficient to focus on how political institutions constrain or empower presidents who desire to take over political regimes. Instead, we also need to understand what it is that individual presidents can gain or lose, in or out of political office.[52]

Baturo's core argument is that "contemporary Caesars will attempt to stay in office if the stakes of losing are too high." He contends, in substance, that "monetary and personal motives to remain in office—the value of holding political office for individual presidents—depend on the income-generating capacity of that office, in contrast to potential income after leaving it, as well as on personal concerns over future immunity and status."[53] A president is thus more likely to try to personalize his or her regime and extend tenure if the spoils from political office are plentiful and the probability to keep these spoils and enjoy personal immunity after leaving office is rather low.

Unlike presidents in more mature democracies who have limited opportunities for personal enrichment while in office and look forward to "start making some real money," as George W. Bush once put it, after leaving office; many of their counterparts in Africa and other unconsolidated political regimes around the world enjoy plenty of opportunities to enrich themselves beyond measure while in office, and thus treat that office as a personal property and source of income for themselves as well as their families and clients. When faced with term limits, these leaders are often unable to depart and will resort to all types of prolongation subterfuges to stay. Rent-seeking in presidential regimes and concerns over immunity status (especially criminal) represent, Buturo argues, the key motivators of a president's personal decision to hang on to power, often at any cost for the country he or she claims.[54]

The rent-seeking framework of analysis helps explain why, among other things, the value of holding presidential office in Botswana for example, a country with a vibrant private sector, is much lower than in many African countries where the magnitude of spoils is immensely larger and grand corruption and theft is often institutionalized at the highest level of the state. The post-presidency of Botswana's former leaders resembles, for the most part, that of other presidents in more mature democracies who pursue various income-generating activities in the private sector and in the international arena. While the office of the US presidency did not present President Barack Obama with any spoils and the latter enjoyed very limited income-generating opportunities during his eight years in office, it is safe to say that the former president's income-generating capacity has astronomically increased since leaving office mainly through book deals and his grand entrance into the lucrative public speaking circuit.[55] Speaking about African leaders' tendency to cling to power, Barack Obama, in his address to the African people from the podium of the African Union in Addis Ababa on July 28, 2015, said—sometimes mockingly—to a big applause from the audience,

> Africa democratic progress is also at risk when leaders refuse to step aside when their term ends. Let me be honest with you. I don't understand this. I am in my second term. It has been an extraordinary privilege for me to serve as President of the United States. I can't imagine a greater honor or a more interesting job. I love my work. But, under our Constitution, I can't run again (…) I am looking forward to life after being President. I won't have such a big security detail all the time. It means I can go take a walk. I can spend time with my family. I can find other ways to serve (…)Nobody should be president for life. And your country is better off if you have new blood and new ideas. I'm still a pretty young man, but I

know that somebody with new energy and new insights will be good for my country. It will be good for yours too, in some cases.[56]

The establishment of the Mo Ibrahim Prize for African Leadership in 2006 was intended, in part, to reward democratic governance and encourage power alternation by offering generous financial incentives to leaders who govern well and voluntarily step down at the expiration of their term. By guaranteeing financial security in retirement to African leaders as an alternative to the lures of the spoils of office, the latter could be persuaded to move away from rent-seeking practices and respect constitutionally mandated term limits rules.[57] In most countries, however, especially the ones endowed with abundant natural resources and weak institutions, the magnitude of spoils is just so large that the Prize seems to have not really curbed leaders' tendency to seek to subvert the constitution in order to pursue their grand theft and ensure their own political survival and that of their coterie of clients.

The case of President Joseph Kabila of the Democratic Republic of the Congo offers a vivid illustration of Baturo's thesis. The magnitude of the spoils of office and concerns over immunity are thought to be the primary drivers in Kabila's attempt to cling to power in flagrant violation of DRC's constitution. Possibly one of the most endowed countries on the planet in terms of natural resources, the DRC is also a country with some of the weakest institutions in the world and a state that has miserably failed in some of its core functions. This lethal combination (abundant wealth and weak institutions) means that the spoils of office in the DRC are amongst the largest in the world. By some conservative estimates, Kabila is believed to have accumulated an estimated $15 billion during his time in office mainly through mining deals and other grand theft schemes making him, by all accounts, one of the wealthiest African presidents.[58] He also notoriously engaged in gross violations of human rights and other atrocities to suppress popular dissent and silence political opponents. Nearing toward the end of his second term, Kabila became seriously concerned about his ability to keep his spoils and retain his immunity after exiting office.[59] His desire to cling to power and subvert Congo's constitution was however met with strong popular opposition and a concerted effort on the part of the international community not to see him run again, especially in light of his disastrous economic and political record. In the end, Kabila was forced to bow to pressure and not seek another term, he managed however to engineer a post-electoral political situation that makes him, in the eyes of many observers of Congo's politics, a de facto president of the country, thus guaranteeing personal immunity and untouchability of spoils for himself and his supporters.[60]

This Book's Added Value and Structure

The discussion of scholarship on term limits in the preceding sections has provided important insights into the variables affecting both a leader's personal decision to stay in power beyond the constitutionally mandated term limits and the outcomes of the term prolongation bids. This discussion has also underscored the centrality of informal institutions in African politics. While the quantitative analysis undertaken in leading studies on presidentialism and term limits helps explain the relationship between a range of formal institutions and the outcomes of bids to temper with term limits, it does not provide for an assessment of the effects of a number of potentially influential, yet difficult to quantify, informal institutions, such as the extent of patronage and the use of violence, that play a critical role in presidential term limits and succession behavior in Africa.

The in-depth investigation of case studies within the single framework of this volume offers the benefits of maximizing the analytical leverage in ways that provide a holistic understanding of the term limits phenomenon as it has unfolded within the real-life context of six African countries included in this volume. The case study methodology and approach adopted in this book adds value to the study of term limits through a rich and deep contextual data exploration of the causal mechanisms identified in larger analytical studies, and the specific local environments in which they are activated. This in-depth contextual exploration is enriched by a cross-case comparison that highlights important findings and conclusions that tend to escape the radars of large quantitative analyses.

To ensure scholarly cohesion, all contributors in this volume have been instructed to take stock of the current literature on term limits, and address the following points in the case study chapters:

- An overview of the historical and political context surrounding the attempt to change the presidential term limits.
- A snapshot of the main political actors (parties, civil society organizations) in favor or opposed to the president's attempt to change term limits.

- A discussion of the main arguments in favor of or against the constitutional change both in the national parliament and in the broader society.
- International actors (foreign donors, AU) involvement in this debate (stated v. real position, pressure and sanctions).
- A discussion of the strategies used by each side to achieve its goal.
- The factors explaining the outcome of the bid to change term limits (success or failure).
- The key lessons stemming from this experience.

This volume is structured in two parts. The first part includes case studies from three countries (Rwanda, Gabon, and Uganda) where presidents succeeded in subverting the constitution and extending their term in office. The second part includes case studies from three countries (Burkina Faso, Nigeria, and Zambia) where attempts at *continuismo* failed. A concluding chapter will provide a cross-case comparison and discuss the main findings.

Notes

1. David E. Kiwuwa, "Democracy and the Politics of Power Alternation in Africa," *Contemporary Politics* 19, no. 3 (2013): 263.
2. See Boniface Dulani, "Personal Rule and Presidential Term Limits in Africa," Doctoral Dissertation in Political Science (Michigan State University, 2011), 116. The author compiled his data from the US Department of States Country Profile, Comparative Constitutions Project.
3. See Alexander Baturo, *Democracy, Dictatorship, and Term Limits* (Ann Arbor: The University of Michigan Press, 2014), 1.
4. See Theodor Mommsen, *The History of Rome* (London: Richard Bentley and Son, 1894).
5. See Christian Meier, *Caesar: A Biography* (New York: Basic Books, 1997).
6. See Baturo, *Democracy, Dictatorship, and Term Limits*, op. cit., 22–23.
7. Ibid., 23.
8. See Paul Sondrol, "The Presidential Tradition in Latin America," *International Journal of Public Administration* 28 (2005): 517–530.
9. For an overview of the historical development of the institution of term limits between the end of WWII and the end of the Cold war, see Baturo, *Democracy, Dictatorship, and Term Limits*, op. cit., 30–32.
10. See Dulani, "Personal Rule and Presidential Term Limits in Africa," op. cit., 106.

11. See Peter Von Doepp, "Party Cohesion and Fractionalization in New African Democracies: Lessons from Struggles over Third-Term Amendments," *Studies in Comparative International Development* 40 (2005): 65–87.
12. See *Democracy, Dictatorship, and Term Limits*, op. cit., 32.
13. Ibid., 33.
14. Data compiled by Dulani, "Personal Rule and Presidential Term Limits in Africa," op. cit., 106.
15. Quoted in Roberta Sigel and D. J. Butler, "The Public and the No Third Term Tradition: Inquiry into Attitudes Toward Power," *Midwest Journal of Political Science* 8, no. 1 (1964): 39.
16. Gary King and Andrew Gelman, "Systemic Consequences of Incumbency Advantage in U.S. House Elections," *American Journal of Political Science* 35, no. 1 (1991): 110–138.
17. See Steven Levitt and Catherine Wolfran, "Decomposing the Sources of Incumbency Advantage in the U.S. House," *Legislative Studies Quarterly* 22, no. 1 (1997): 45–60; Stephen Ansolabehere and James Snyder, "The Incumbency Advantage in U.S. Elections: An Analysis of State and Federal Offices, 1942–2000," *Election Law Journal* 1, no. 3 (2002); 315–336.
18. See Gideon Maltz, "The Case for Presidential Term Limits," *Journal of Democracy* 18, no. 1 (2007): 128–142; Sigel and Butler, "The Public and the No Third Term Tradition," op. cit.
19. See Maltz, "The Case for Presidential Term Limits," op. cit.
20. Ibid.
21. Staffan Lindberg, *Democracy and Elections in Africa* (Baltimore: John Hopkins University Press, 2006), 42.
22. See Devra Moehler and Staffan Lindberg, "Narrowing the Legitimacy Gap: The Role of Turnovers in Africa's Emerging Democracies," *Journal of Politics* 71, no. 4 (2009): 1448–1466.
23. Letter to Vermont State Legislature, December 10, 1807, quoted in Charles Stein, *The Third-Term: Its Rise and Collapse in American Politics* (Westport, CT: Greenwood Press, 1943), 38.
24. See Juan Linz, "The Perils of Presidentialism," *Journal of Democracy* 1, no. 1 (1990): 51–69.
25. Putin's Russia, Erdogan's Turkey and Maduro's Venezuela are often cited as examples of electoral authoritarianism.
26. Preamble to Amendment 73 to the Arkansas State Constitution, November 3, 2002.
27. See Napoleon Bamfo, "Term Limits and Political Incumbency in Africa: Implication of Staying in Power Too Long with References to the Cases of Kenya, Malawi and Zambia," *African and African Studies* 4, no. 3 (2005): 327–356; Alexandre Baturo, "The Stakes of Losing Office, Term

Limits and Democracy," *British Journal of Political Science* 40, no. 3 (2010): 635–662.
28. See Cynthia Farrar, "Power to the People," in Kurt Raaflaub, Josia Ober, and Bobert Wallace (eds.), *Origins of Democracy in Ancient Greece* (Los Angeles: University of California Press, 2007), 170–189.
29. Te Mann, "Congressional Term Limits: A Bad Idea Whose Time Should Never Come," in Edward Crane and Roger Pilon (eds.), *The Politics and Law of Term Limits* (Washington, DC: The CATO Institute, 1994), 94.
30. Ibid.; Mark Petracca, "Restoring the University in Rotation: An Essay in Defense of Term Limitation," in Edward Crane and Roger Pilon (eds.), *The Politics and Law of Term Limits*, op. cit.
31. Juan Linz and Arturo Valenzuela (eds.), *The Failure of Presidential Democracy: Comparative Perspectives* (Baltimore, MD: Johns Hopkins University Press, 1994).
32. See Gideon Doron and Michael Harris, *Term Limits* (New York: Lexington Books, 2001); Timothy Besley and Anne Case, "Does Electoral Accountability Affect Economic Policy Choices? Evidence from Gubernatorial Term Limits," *Quarterly Journal of Economics* 110, no. 3 (1995): 769–798.
33. See Bruce Cain, "Term Limits: Not the Answer to What Ails Politics," in Edward Crane and Roger Pilon (eds.), *The Politics and Law of Term Limits*, op. cit.
34. Eastland Staveley, *Greek and Roman Voting and Elections* (Ithaca, NY: Cornell University Press, 1972), 55.
35. Alexander Hamilton, *The Federalist Papers* [1788] (Charleston, SC: Forgotten Books, 1999), 412.
36. Victor Kamber, *Giving Up on America: Why Term Limits Are Bad for America* (Washington, DC: Regnery Publishing, 1995), 83.
37. See Andreas Schedler, *Electoral Authoritarianism: The Dynamics of Unfree Competition* (Boulder, CO: Lynne Rienner Publishers, 2006).
38. Alexander Hamilton, *The Federalist Papers* [1788], op. cit., 410.
39. See Victor Kamber, *Giving Up on America: Why Term Limits Are bad for America*, op.cit.; Bruce Cain, "Term Limits: Not the Answer to What Ails Politics," op.cit.
40. See Eastland Staveley, *Greek and Roman Voting and Elections*, op. cit.
41. James March and Johan Olsen, "Elaborating the 'New Institutionalism'," in R. A. W. Rhodes, Sarah Binder, and Bert Rockman (eds.), *The Oxford Handbook of Political Institutions* (Oxford: Oxford University Press, 2006), 3.
42. See Gretchen Helme and Steven Levitsky, *Informal Institutions and Democracy: Lessons from Latin America* (Baltimore, MD: John Hopkins Press, 2006).

43. See Jean-Francois Bayart, Stephen Ellis, and Beatrice Hibou, *The Criminalization of the State in Africa* (Oxford: James Currey, 1999); Michael Bratton and Nicholas van de Walle, *Democratic Experiments in Africa: Regimes Transitions in Comparative, Perspectives* (Cambridge: Cambridge University Press, 1997); Patrick Chabal and Jean-Pascal Daloz, *Africa Works: Disorder as Political Instrument* (Bloomington: Indiana University Press, 1999).
44. Beatrice Hibou, "The Social Capital of State as an Agent of Deception," in Jean-Francois Bayart, Stephen Ellis, and Beatrice Hibou, *The Criminalization of the State in Africa*, op. cit., 88–91.
45. See BBC News, "No Third Term for Nigerian Leader," May 16, 2006, available online at http://news.bbc.co.uk/2/hi/africa/4986904.stm.
46. See, among others, Daniel Posner and Daniel Yong, "The Institutionalization of Power in Africa," *Journal of Democracy* 18, no. 3 (2007): 126–140.
47. See Jean-Francois Bayart, Stephen Ellis, and Beatrice Hibou, *The Criminalization of the State in Africa*, op. cit.; Michael Bratton and Nicholas van de Walle, *Democratic Experiments in Africa: Regimes Transitions in Comparative*, op. cit.; Patrick Chabal and Jean-Pascal Daloz, *Africa Works: Disorder as Political Instrument*, op. cit.
48. Nicholas van de Walle, "Presidentialism and Clientelism in Africa's Emerging Party Systems," *Journal of Modern African Studies* 41, no. 2 (2003): 310.
49. James March and Johan Olsen, "Elaborating the 'New Institutionalism'," op. cit.
50. Daniel Posner and Daniel Yong, "The Institutionalization of Power in Africa," op. cit.
51. Daniel Vencovsky, "Presidential Term Limits in Africa," *Conflict Trends* 2 (2007): 19.
52. Baturo, *Democracy, Dictatorship, and Term Limits*, op. cit., 6.
53. Ibid.
54. Ibid., 7.
55. Former President Barack Obama and First Lady Michelle Obama signed book deals with the publisher Penguin Random House for a staggering $60m. See https://www.theguardian.com/books/2017/mar/01/barack-michelle-obama-book-deals-penguin-random-house.
56. Remarks by President Obama to the People of Africa, Addis Ababa, July 28, 2015, available online at https://obamawhitehouse.archives.gov/the-press-office/2015/07/28/remarks-president-obama-people-africa.
57. Recipients of the Ibrahim Prize receive an award of five million dollars over ten years, and a lifetime grant of two hundred thousand dollars annually. Another two hundred thousand dollars is given annually if they establish a charitable foundation. See Ken Auletta, "The Dictator Index," *The New*

Yorker, March 17, 2011. In the article, Mo Ibrahim is quoted saying, "European leaders can become rich after leaving office. African leaders don't have that option."

58. See Michael Kavanagh and Dan MacCarey, "All the President's Wealth: The Kabila Family Business," *Congo Research Group*, July 20, 2017, available online at https://pulitzercenter.org/reporting/all-presidents-wealth-kabila-family-business.
59. See Chris Phiri, "Why DR Congo's Kabila Cling to Power," *Zambia Reports*, April 20, 2017.
60. All serious and impartial observers of the 2018 presidential elections in the Congo concluded that Mr. Fayulu, the opposition candidate, won handily. Despite a majority of the population favoring a clear break from his regime, Mr. Kabila struck a deal with Felix Tshisekedi, the opposition candidate who came in third, to hand him power because he was concerned that Mr. Fayulu would protect neither his immunity nor his spoils. Legislative and regional elections were also rigged to ensure a commanding majority to Kabila's political coalition in both the parliament and the senate. Moreover, before leaving office, Kabila appointed his allies to key positions in the army and the security services, thus ensuring that he will control key levers of power even after leaving office. See Robbie Gramer and Jefcoate O'Donnell, "How Washington Got on Board with Congo's Rigged Election," *Foreign Policy*, February 1, 2019.

PART I

J'Y Suis, J'Y Reste[1]

---

[1] "Here I am, here I'll stay," legendary words of Field Marshall MacMahon during the siege of Sabastopol in 1855 who went on to become President of France, but turned out to be a mediocre politician. His famous quote has often been echoed during the term limits debate in reference to African presidents who cling to power *manu military* and at any cost.

CHAPTER 2

The Battle for Term Limits in Rwanda

David E. Kiwuwa

INTRODUCTION

At the dawn of the Cold War, many authoritarian regimes in Africa found themselves under pressure to undergo what was deemed then as transformative democratic political reforms.[1] This meant the strengthening and institutionalisation of democratic norms and their constitutional entrenchment. Owing to the painful legacies of military coups, authoritarian strongmen, civil war and general instability along with new pressures from former patron states and donor agencies, many of these countries embarked on wide-ranging liberal reforms. Additionally, they pursued a constitutional experiment of limiting their political executives to time-bound tenures. This gave rise to the phenomenon of term limits in the region.[2] To date, while some countries have retained this executive check many others, approximately fourteen, have successfully sought to remove this on account of shifting priorities or change in circumstances that precipitated term limits in the first place.[3] Rwanda like its neighbours Uganda, Burundi, Congo and potentially DRC has recently seen the suspension of term limits to allow the Rwanda Patriotic Front (RFP) long

D. E. Kiwuwa (✉)
School of International Studies,
University of Nottingham Ningbo China, Ningbo, China
e-mail: david.kiwuwa@nottingham.edu.cn

© The Author(s) 2020
J. R. Mangala (ed.), *The Politics of Challenging Presidential Term Limits in Africa*, https://doi.org/10.1007/978-3-030-40810-7_2

term chairman and current president Paul Kagame run for office in 2017. After being very adamant that he will respect the constitutional term limits and showing disdain for the common weakness that long afflicted African governance, why then did Kagame succumb to the same shortcoming that he so often despised? This paper attempts to interrogate the lifting of term limits in Rwanda, examining what led to this change, what forces informed this process, the strategies used and implications thereof.

The crafters of Rwanda's democracy experiment were cognisant of the lessons of weak democratic institutionalisation and long term incumbency both at home and in their neighbourhood. This awareness was also driven by the lessons of the genocide and the ensuing bitter civil war that had cost over eight hundred thousand lives.[4] As a result, they sought broad political reforms and safeguards against dictatorship, democratic reversal and the plague of personalistic patronage politics. They did so through partly instituting constitutional term limits for the country's presidency, at the time a general trend in sub-Saharan Africa. For instance, in the nineties, thirty-three of the forty-eight African constitutions adopted presidential term limits.[5] However, this political safety pin has increasingly become dislodged casting a dark shadow over the continent's substantive democratisation credentials.[6] With the over centralisation of political power in the office and person of the presidency, the all too powerful executive with ever weaker checks and balances became a strong addiction that confounded optimists. In the late eighties, Uganda's Museveni once beseeched his peers that "no African leader should stay longer than ten years". To date, he has since changed both his mind and the constitution to frustrate regular power alternation in the event racking up 32 years of incumbency and counting. While the nineties crop of new leaders (freedom fighters) espoused fighting dictatorship as their raisons d'être, they too have succumbed to the "sit tight" syndrome. They have been unwilling to surrender political power by resorting to unlimited tenure thus creating a kind of democratic deficit.[7]

The focus on term limits has become all the more important given the fact that a general lack of leadership alternation has encouraged the entrenchment of personalistic politics. Consequently, this increases the risk of political instability with challengers seeking extra-constitutional means to access the levers of power as recently evidenced by events in Burundi, Burkina Faso and DRC. It is demonstrable that manipulation of term limits has a detrimental effect on the health of democracy often occurring in highly patrimonial and personalistic regimes with political elite having a vested interest in staying in power for continued financial benefit.[8] For both the very destiny of the patronised and the patron are hereof interlinked. As a consequence, the ability to control the administrative apparatus, the coercive instruments of force and state resource provides ample opportunity to remove any potential hindrances to perpetuation of the incumbent's rule and limitation to their all too pervasive power.

Undeniably, there have been some notable cases of leadership alternation elsewhere in Africa though there is also clearly a steady roll back of various constitutional safeguards that were initially intended to precipitate peaceful leadership transfer across a number of African countries for various reasons.[9] For instance, Chad's Idris Derby's argument was centred on the need for continued stability, Burundi's Pierre Nkurunziza on a divine right to rule, Gambia's Jammeh going on record pledging to uplift Gambian lives even if it took him "one billion years" while Congo's Sassou-Nguesso's allies argued that the current constitution passed in 2002 had "had its day". This leadership mentality is precisely why Africa still grapples with the phenomenon of the "imperial presidency" where leaders have ruled for a very long period of time. Evidently, Paul Biya of Cameroon, Robert Mugabe of Zimbabwe, Eduardo dos Santos of Angola, Yoweri Museveni of Uganda and until recently Blaise Compaore of Burkina Faso and Teodoro Nguema of Equatorial Guinea have collectively ruled their countries for 194 years. The continent's five longest presidencies stretch between 29 and 36 years, adding to a cumulative 170 years while Gabon's Omar Bongo (for a none monarchy) had been president for an unbelievable 41 years when he died in office at the age of 73 in 2011.

Interrogating the case for term limits within a specific political context is warranted. Evidently, where there is regular leadership alternation, political stability, democratic habituation and political institutionalisation emerge. This also ensures the periodical creation of elite coalitions that act as check and balance to the existing status quo. On the flip side, the absence of periodical leadership turnover dis-incentivises building of strong institutions, locks out elites who are out of the power loop, has a tendency to promote personalistic politics by way of putting a premium on loyalty and sees a growth of unconstitutional means of challenging for power.[10] Within societies that are characterised by ethnic cleavages, leadership alternation ensures the possibility of building of coalitions by elites across ethnic strata to challenge for office and the equitable distribution of economic opportunities and resources.[11] As such, the recent Afrobarometer survey[12] has indicated that term limits even in countries without them are still very popular (75% supportive) but if this is the case, what then explains this rush of constitutional revisions to expunge term limits in general and more specifically suspend them in Rwanda?

Setting the Stage for Constitutional Reforms: Temporary Repeal of Article 101

It is perhaps difficult to pinpoint exactly when this effort to repel was launched. However, there is no doubt that post-2010 presidential elections that President Kagame overwhelmingly won by 93.08% of the vote also signalled the closing stages of his constitutionally mandated tenure.[13] As such, mutterings soon picked steam as to who was to fill his big shoes if at all, the high stakes at play, the very future of Rwanda and if Rwanda was ready for a post-Kagame era. Within both diplomatic and government circles this was not a subtle conversation with many keenly aware of the lack of a clear successor to Kagame post 2017 (Personal observation 2010). But to the coterie increasingly nursing the idea of Kagame's continued tenure, it was the complexity of overcoming Article 101 without portraying Kagame as another African despot unwilling to unclench his fist from the presidential chair that stood in their way. In fact, citing weariness in being compared to such despots Kagame noted at the time that "I do not want to destroy the political capital that I have carefully built over the years".[14] That notwithstanding, a coalition of party enablers was assembled one which was initially to gauge the public appetite for Project 2017 and where necessary to shape public discourse through the media. In earnest, the debate on a possible third term for Kagame started after a meeting on 8 February 2013 in which Kagame asked the ruling RFP party members (approximately 2500 delegates) to devise a formula that ensures change, stability and continuity beyond 2017. For him, "there needs to be continuity and stability. Therefore the challenge is how to organise this change while at the same time ensuring continuity of what we have achieved and also retaining the stability of the country".[15] At a glance, these two tasks appeared to be irreconcilable and at odds. Nevertheless pro-regime media led by the government New Times, Rwanda Radio, columnists and pro-regime cadres within civil society, the political and business elite class set about shaping the tone of the debate and making a forceful albeit persuasive case for retaining Kagame beyond 2017. It was notable that the general narrative constructed to support the repeal was the indispensability and uncertain risky future post Kagame. For a war-weary populace, this posed a very existential conundrum. Writing in the government *New Times* daily on 19 January, Fred Mufulukye opined that the Rwandan people had "anxiety, fear and uncertainty" over what may happen after 2017. "In view of our recent history where everyone has been affected in one way or another, Rwandans recognize President Kagame as their source of security, comfort and the father of Rwanda". Writing in the same newspaper on 9 February, Joseph Karemera too extolled that "Rwanda was blessed to have a great and visionary leader in President Paul Kagame" warning that "we cannot afford to mess around with achievements we have made under Kagame's leadership". Anticipating international criticisms, On 11 February, Rtd Captain Frank Mugisha wrote in the same paper that western nations should not impose their values on Rwanda, asking: "where were they when the genocide was taking place?...we certainly can't take a gamble, not with our future. We shall not allow him (Kagame) to abandon us come 2017". The former Prime Minister of Rwanda (7th October 2011–24th July 2014), Pierre-Damien Habumuremyi commenting in the same newspaper on 12 March cautioned that the people faced a choice between a "performing Rwanda as a nation with its leader who embodies it and an uncertain future that may fall prey to political opportunism". On 23 March, columnist Emmanuel Nibishakas argued that "leaders like Kagame are very rare!...It will even be irrational and dangerous to embark on an uncertain path in trying a new leader, unsure that they will keep the legacy of their predecessor in fostering unity, peace and prosperity". This doomsday chorus continued with Nshuti Manasseh warning in a commentary in the same newspaper on 19 June that the reconciliation that started after the 1994 genocide "will regress on his departure with consequences we can't afford to underwrite....President Paul Kagame is the only guarantor of our security amidst serious national threats and we Rwandans are aware".[16]

Such was the generally apocalyptic tone that fed into the mostly elite public discourse that sought to shape and ensure public consensus as to the merits of Kagame's continued leadership. While there was undeniably some public uncertainty as to the merits of the case, this was never strongly and overtly voiced or at least not within the public domain. For to do so, would attract possible censure and unwarranted state attention with unknown repercussions. As such, the very public discourse appeared to point to a seemingly agreeable and universal consensus that Kagame's continued leadership was merited and certainly indispensable for Rwanda's transformation and its present context.

The Public Debate

Beyond the prompting from pro-regime cadres, what has been the case for suspending terms limits in Rwanda for Kagame's explicit benefit? The argument for Kagame's continued stay in office has admittedly hinged around the country being too fragile to withstand leadership alternation. As we argued earlier, while Kagame has not always been the president, it is largely acknowledged that during the time as vice president (1994–1999), he was the man in charge. To supporters and critics alike, he was credited for leading the RPF stop of the genocide carnage and rebuilding Rwanda after an almost total collapse of the state apparatus and the dismemberment of society.[17] For that reason Rwanda's very existence today as a functional state is in no small measure attributed to Kagame's single-mindedness and iron-fisted leadership. As a historical figure, many reasons have been given to account for the 2017 project among which is nostalgia for a powerful leader, reward for leadership sacrifice, absence of alternatives, realisation and consolidation of regime gains to mention but a few.[18]

More specifically, there is no doubt that Rwanda under Kagame has experienced tremendous transformation underpinned by a foundation of order and security. For the past decade, its economic growth has averaged around 7–8% per year, maternal and child mortality fallen by more than 60% and achieved an African rarity—near universal health coverage. According to the International Monetary Fund, the country with gross domestic product per head of $732 last year is also now considered one of the safest and least corrupt in sub-Saharan Africa having the seventh "cleanest" politicians in the world. There has also been tremendous progress in education with primary school enrolment standing at 92%, the highest in the region according to the United Nations.[19] Rwanda also uniquely stands out in the world of gender equity with its parliament posting the highest proportion of female representation in the world—women hold 55% of seats.[20] And in just three years, the percentage of people living in poverty dropped from 44.9% in 2011 to 39.1% in 2014 thanks to a successful government programme of one cow per poor family, the creation of agricultural cooperatives and increased use of fertilisers to increase farm yields. Increasingly lauded as one of the best places to do business in emerging economies and in the world, registering a business for example only takes 24 hours. This is all attributed to cutting of red tape, crackdown on corruption, an investor-friendly attitude and fast-tracking the implementation of information and communication technology within its governance structures. Signalling this transformation in 2012, Rwanda became the world number two reformer in the five year period between 2006 and 2011. Underpinning such progress is the yearly ambitious performance contracts, known as *imihigo* signed between cabinet ministers, leaders of Rwanda's 30 districts with the president with failure to meet their targets in a range of development indicators opening one to potential dismissal.[21] To Kagame's supporters these achievements are no mean fit given their post-genocide near failed state status and as long as he is still delivering, term limits only become a tool of academic debate. Unverifiable government surveys pointed to Rwandans opinions for their petition to amend Article 101 to allow President Kagame to run for another term citing several reasons. These included infrastructure, social benefits like health insurance, one-cow-per family, monthly stipends to the poor, education for all, security among others. These opinions clearly resonate with the case for both pro-third term supporters and paradoxically the few who are against while acknowledging government achievements. Within Rwanda and across a number of public forums public debates have raged over the term limit issue particularly on Kinyarwanda and English private radio stations, social and print media and private and public spaces. Through these discourses, there was a broad supportive spectrum of opinion that acknowledged Rwanda's great strides and Kagame at the head of this transformation.

THE RPF AND THE MAINTENANCE OF THE STATUS QUO

Research has demonstrated elsewhere that leaders of revolutionary, liberation or independence movements and those who came to power via coups were often more susceptible to seeking extended tenures than those who came to power through elections.[22] This therefore makes the RPF a case of no exception. Since the genocide, the RPF has been the dominant party in Rwanda and the party in government heading a ruling coalition composed of allied "opposition" parties. Many observers agree that the RPF has had a monumental stranglehold on Rwanda's politics having far-reaching influence within the social and financial sphere with a sophisticated and deeply rooted network.[23] Perhaps Rwanda's nature of politics can be understood as different given its historical context specifically underscored by its genocide legacy. The RPF conscious of the country's fragile nature notably its socio-political fabric prioritised non-confrontational politics. It privileged consensus over adversarial governance and as such claims to rule in concert with other parties. Chapter 3 Article 10 enshrines power-sharing in the constitution thereby moving away from zero-sum politics but inadvertently or otherwise also precipitating a less than critical political scape. The implication is that most of the decisions reached thereof are consensual and follow inter-party consultation through the National Forum for Political Organisation though the perception of RPF dominance still persists.

The RPF decision to support its chairman continued incumbency was perhaps not unexpected as Kagame has long been a very dominant figure within the party hierarchy by virtue of his very position and historical leadership.[24] Within intraparty politics, it has been alleged that Kagame didn't appreciate any semblance of critical questioning of his leadership or its potential continuity within the party nor elsewhere and any such pretensions are often easily snuffed out through political demotions, disciplinary action or systematic sidelining. As a consequence, there was an increase in internal political tensions within the ruling party characterised by defections and purges of regime elites like the former speaker of parliament, army chief of staff, the intelligence chief, attorney general, ex-ambassador to the US to mention but a few.[25]

Within the broad political spectrum, human rights activists and organisations have alleged a persistent trend of systematic domestic repression and in particular an emerging disquiet within the RPF ranks occasioned by Kagame's perceived iron-fisted leadership and now the 2017 project.[26] In the cabinet, it is alleged that Kagame stymied any direct ministerial challenges to the prospect of a third term, as witnessed by the sacking of minister of justice, Tharcisse Karugarama, and cabinet affairs minister, Protais Musoni, in 2013.[27] Karugarama was sacked days after giving an interview to Chris McGreal of the *Observer* in which he criticised Kagame's planned changes to the constitution and repeating such concerns in a cabinet meeting. Musoni a long leading RPF ideologue alongside the likes of Tito Rutaremara was reportedly sacked because of ailing health though insiders intimate that he jeopardised his position by openly supporting Karugarama on the issue of presidential term limits. In this very rare and somewhat open instance of internal discord, Kagame was more belligerent in respect to his justice minister's views chiding him "why don't you tell him to step down himself? All those years he's been there, he's not the only one who can be the justice minister...In the end we should come to a view that serves us all. But in the first place I wonder why it becomes the subject of heated debate".[28] It should be remembered that both Karugarama and Musoni played important roles in the creation and running of the Rwandese Alliance for National Unity [RANU] that became the RPF *Inkotanyi* in 1987. With the later becoming RANU Secretary General in 1983 and remaining in that post until December 1987 when RANU transformed into the RPF in Kampala. He subsequently became a general coordinator during the RPF war. In a further sign of some internal RPF tensions, 07 September 2014, Senator Tito Rutaremara complained that a group of women comprising of former state chief Protocol Col Rose Kabuye was undermining the party progress and forming negative solidarity. Addressing the issue, Kagame called these disgruntled RPF members "deviants". Prior to this internal discord, many more RPF cadres had long come into conflict with the RPF itself in general and Kagame in particular and consequently escaped into exile prominent of whom were Rwanda's former parliament president Joseph Sebarenzi, former intelligence chief, Patrick Karegeya (murdered), Chief of Staff Kayumba Nyamwasa, its secretary general, Prosecutor General to mention but a few all accusing Kagame of growing intolerance, dictatorship and human rights abuse. These have since formed a new political party in exile known as the Rwanda National Congress (RNC).[29] But while these might be read as internal RPF party tension and disagreement occasioned by the third term debate among other issues, on the whole these were not game-changing cracks but marginal fissures and ultimately easily suppressed and papered over to ensure party unity and continued party dominance and consequently realisation of the 2017 project.

The momentum for extending Kagame's tenure or push for constitutional revision was officially not to be seen as having started from within the RPF camp. Nevertheless, it was long known within that a broad constitutional revision was increasingly likely to be absent of any appetite to change political leadership within the RPF ranks. In fact, it was officially a party allied with the RPF led by Sheikh Harelimana that called for a reconsideration of the constitutional limits and its revision to allow for the stewardship of Kagame to continue. The argument was that "his services were most acutely needed to consolidate the gains of the post-genocide regime and ensure that the genocide ideology is completely eradicated and development consolidated".[30] While this pronouncement did not meet so much as a general uproar from both civil society and the official opposition, it pointed towards a tacit agreement or machination from within the RPF camp. It should be noted that Kagame often asked if this was something he would consider, routinely retorted that it was not a pressing matter and that it was for Rwandans to decide their own political destiny. During his party retreat to deliberate on the matter at Rosororo, Gasabo District, Kagame noted that "what we shall decide shall be dependent on solid principles and not people's prejudices and fears".[31]

However, with 2017 drawing ever closer and the domestic and international chorus seeking clarity about post-2017 Kagame and the succession status growing louder and more urgent, President Kagame called an extraordinary meeting of the RPF politburo and later appointed a committee of three RPF "sages" Tito Rutaremara, Joseph Karemera and Antoine Mugesera to look into the transition issue and deliver the party roadmap leading up to and beyond 2017. At its core was ensuring a transition formula that guaranteed both change and continuity.[32] Following a 600 member party convention, the RPF delegates backed the lifting of term limits for Kagame and by extension Kagame's stewardship of the country. "Considering the wishes of many Rwandans and those of members of the RPF, we support the proposed amendment of Article 101 of the constitution and any other provisions in the law that need modification", they proclaimed.

The Unconventional Alliance: Opposition Support

It is largely acknowledged that democracies are often only as good as their institutions as the performance of a political system is considered a direct function of its institutions.[33] Hence, where there is a high degree of institutionalisation of democratic ethos, then their durability is bound to withstand relatively well systematic encroachment. In this context, opposition parties are considered crucial as not only governments in waiting but equally a medium for checks and balance, mechanism for accountability and political expression. But for this to be realised it will often depend on the degree of party institutionalisation; the ability of the party to be distinct and act relatively independent of undue influence from especially the party in power.[34] In Rwanda's case however, the role of the main and old opposition political parties; Social Democratic Party (PSD) and the Liberal Party (PL) appears rather "unconventional" for lack of a better reference. While in other countries opposition parties and civil society put up spirited resistance against repeal of presidential term limits, here nine out of the eleven recognised opposition parties Liberal Party (PL), Union Démocratique du Peuple Rwandais (UPDR), Ideal Democratic Party (PDI), Social Democratic Party (PSD), Parti du Progrès et de la Concorde (PPC), Centrist Democratic Party (PDC), Parti Socialiste Rwandais Party (PSR), Solidarity for Solidarity and Progress Party (PSP) backed the lifting of term limits for Kagame with the exception of Social Party Imberakuri (PS—Imberakuri) and the Democratic Green Party of Rwanda (DGPR). "We need Article 101 to be amended because in a democratic society people have powers to choose leaders of their own choice", Sheikh Musa Fazil Harelimana, Minister of Internal Security argued.[35] Perhaps we should be mindful that these parties are allied opposition parties in a coalition governance structure with the RPF. To many observers, Rwanda's political opposition has always been considered more or less an extension of the RPF in all but name given their lack of ability to bring to account or act as a counterweight to RPF dominance. Perhaps giving some credence to this, Francois Ngarambe, secretary general of the ruling RFP noted that political parties have a responsibility to respect the voice of the approximately four million Rwandans who have petitioned parliament calling for scrapping of term limits. It was notable too that the second biggest party in Rwanda and in parliament by way of numbers, the PSD with 11 members of Parliament in the House of Deputies equally supported the lifting of term limits through its two-day consultative national convention. The 800 strong delegates signalled a no-objection to the lifting of term limits and subjecting the decision to a national referendum. Like the other parties, the PSD party too is part of the RPF governing coalition with two cabinet members. The PSD president and cabinet member Hon Vincent Biruta argued that since their own internal party term limits had been removed for various positions, this logic was extended to national politics and hence:

> "we have agreed that we are going to field our candidate. We removed term limits in our internal elections, we have removed that principle, (and) the same has dictated to us to remove the term limits for any other elections,"... "If they want to keep the same leaders, they should be allowed

to do so, and that is democracy". "If the people are happy with the leaders, they should be able to elect them, if they are not happy, they should exercise their right to remove them".[36]

Mr Biruta, a former president of the senate and ex-lower chamber speaker, said it is not a conspiracy of the ruling party and PSD to keep Mr Kagame in power, but that his party has to respond to the mood in the country. The political mood in Rwanda is charged to have Mr Kagame return, even when the president in public argues that he "must be convinced". Likewise, the opposition leader from Rwanda's People's Party appeared to curiously echo a consistent RPF mantra that people "…need to understand that term limits and other issues are not as important as a nation's social and economic emancipation. Democracy is about the people holding their leaders' accountable, the right to elect and to remove their leaders on the basis of their conduct in office. Democracy has nothing to do with term limits. Those who want term limits on President terms; want to see African leaders continue obeying the orders of some foreign governments, companies and agencies that have continued to unleash intolerable and unjust miseries on the continent and its people….[37] In an interview published by The Chronicles, Mr Harerimana, the leader of the opposition Idealist Democratic Party (PDI) but working under Mr Kagame, argued that a third term for Mr Kagame "would be very good for Rwanda". "The constitution should be amended so that people can decide. If Kagame stood again, we would vote for him".

While the above demonstrates general opposition parties' acquiescence for the third term project, there was some marginal opposition from a smaller opposition party. Frank Habineza, leader of the country's perceivably only independent opposition party, the Democratic Green Party of Rwanda expressed strong criticism of the third term project going as far as seeking legal redress from the high and supreme court. There has reportedly been internal debate and dissent within some of the traditional allies of the RPF. For instance, at the March PSD party congress, some members walked out in protest while some senior members including Dr Jean Damascene Ntawukuriryayo a former President of the upper house (senate) and Marc Rugenera lost their positions in the party for potentially being reluctant to tow the preferred position of backing the RPF position. In addition, there have been alleged attacks on critical press and activists.[38] For instance, Jean-Leonard Rugambage, an independent journalist was mysteriously murdered while Jean Bosco Gasasira, senior editor of the local-language tabloid Umuvugizi alleges that "People are forced to keep quiet. That is not peace...all independent voices in the country have been shut down", and has since fled Rwanda for Uganda after his colleague was shot dead.[39]

In many countries, opposition political parties would act as a check on executive excesses including leading strong opposition to constitutional revision that seeks to entrench incumbents in power. In, DRC, Burundi, Uganda, Nigeria, Zambia, Congo, Burkina Faso, opposition political parties have been central to organising anti-third term protests and resistance in and outside parliament. In Rwanda's case, the very acquiescence of the official opposition parties to the dominant party agenda brings into question the very role of the opposition in Rwanda and their capacity and efficiency to act as a counterweight to RPF dominance and play an oversight role of government initiatives that are considered crucial to the very health of the country's democracy.

"Africa Doesn't Need Strongmen. It Needs Strong Institutions"

In the summer of 2009, President Barack Obama while in Ghana opined about African democracy, in which he noted that "history is on the side of brave Africans...not with those who use coups or change constitutions to stay in power. Africa doesn't need strongmen. It needs strong institutions".[40] These words of caution came against a visibly growing trend of African incumbents unwilling to vacate office once their constitutional terms end. Most recently, the US has been at the forefront of chastising DRC's Kabila, Burundi's Nkurunziza, Burkina Faso's Campoare's against pursuing an unconstitutional extension of tenures. In reference to events afoot in Kigali, the US government was "deeply disappointed" by Kagame's decision to run for re-election in 2017 and expressed concern about attempts to tinker with the constitution seeing this as unhelpful in ensuring stability and democratic consolidation in the region. "With this decision, President Kagame ignores an historic opportunity to reinforce and solidify the democratic institutions the Rwandan people have for more than twenty years labored so hard to establish", State Department spokesman John Kirby noted in a statement.[41] "The United States believes constitutional transitions of power are essential for strong democracies and that efforts by incumbents to change rules to stay in power weaken democratic institutions,...we are particularly concerned by changes that favour one individual over the principle of democratic transitions" the statement noted. "President Kagame has an opportunity to set an example for a region in which leaders seem too tempted to view themselves as indispensable to their own countries' trajectories". Maintaining the critical rhetoric, the US UN ambassador, Samantha Power also noted that despite "parliamentary manoeuvrings" which led to amendment of constitution to allow President Kagame to seek another term, he had to step aside for "nobody is indispensable...we expect President Kagame to step down at the end of his term in 2017".[42] Elsewhere, the European Union too echoed its displeasure in a statement warning Kagame to keep his promise;

> The reform of a Constitution is a transformative process engaging all interests in society, which adjusts norms and rules with the aim of strengthening and adapting institutions to meet contemporary challenges. It is a legitimate expectation of a country to revise its governance. However, the adoption of provisions that can apply only to one individual weakens the credibility of the constitutional reform process as it undermines the principle of democratic change of government enshrined in Article 23 of the African Charter of Democracy, Elections and Governance. The amendments to the Rwandan constitution recently approved by Parliament – if confirmed by referendum – would give rise to this situation.[43]

The EU was equally unsatisfied with the handling of the referendum noting that the speed was way too fast to enable a careful interrogation of the merits and demerits of the case and make an informed judgement let alone allow those opposed to the scheme time to formulate and have an organised response and campaign to make their case to the wider electorate.

On the whole, while overt criticism both in private and public was evident in similar cases across Africa, the criticism from the international community in Rwanda's case was relatively muted and largely private perhaps the usual donor partners having been cowed from harsh open criticism of Rwanda and Kagame in particular given their own deficiency in responding to the genocide.[44] The US in this case was the exception maybe unafraid of Kigali's wrath being that it is without doubt, Kagame's staunchest ally eager to maintain Rwanda as a strategic partner with a powerful army in mineral-rich eastern Africa.

In the region the only notable criticism came from Kenyan opposition leader and twice-failed presidential candidate Oraila Odinga who noted that Rwanda, Burundi and Uganda's presidents ought to leave the stage for others to lead instead of prolonging their tenure. His argument was that constitutional change to remove term limits was not only selfish on the part of leaders but it was also setting a dangerous precedent notwithstanding the various dubious justifications for continued tenure. "Kagame is a protégé of Museveni and he has learnt very well from him. He is leading a campaign that says nobody else can hold Rwanda together, that Rwanda situation is unique and therefore should stay in office".[45]

Given his unique circumstances, Kagame has been more sophisticated in courting the right supporters for his regime from the international community. He has retained the advisory services of former British Prime Minister through his firm Africa's Governance Initiatives, former US assistant representative for Africa Rosa Whitaker, Bill Clinton with Clinton Foundation, Bill Gates with the Bill and Melinda Gates Foundation and George Soros to mention but a few. These have been instrumental in building up his image as a transformative leader irrespective of the shortcomings in specific reference to the political space so often a source of criticisms.[46] To Tony Blair he is a "visionary leader", further arguing that "we've got to be cognisant of the fact that Rwanda has been through these immense difficulties (genocide). They are not going to develop a western-style democracy in a short period of time. But if you look at the way it is as a society today, where there are people of all sorts of ethnicities in the government, I think there is a lot to commend".[47] Bill Clinton too saw Kagame as "one of the greatest leaders of our time", Clare Short, former British Secretary for International Development holding him in the highest regard and Howard Schultz, chief executive of Starbucks, convinced enough to invest in Rwanda. Elsewhere, world-famous American investment guru and philanthropist Howard Buffet voiced his support of the African leader's governance noting that "If I didn't think president Kagame was going to be here for another seven years, we wouldn't even consider doing some of the things we're trying to do", imploring outsiders to let Rwandans be as they know better what they want for the future. With an investment in the Agricultural industry to a tune of $500m, this was a strong endorsement to Kagame's leadership.

> Let's not think we know better than Rwandans what they want for the future. Let's look at the result, let's not put form before substance. This is not my or your future, this is the Rwandans future. It is imperative that they drive what will achieve success.[48]

The former US Secretary of State, Hillary Clinton pointed to this transformation when she too noted that:

> ...progress sometimes comes so slowly. But in a country that had been ravaged by genocidal conflict, the progress is amazing. It has one of the fastest growing economies in Africa, even in the midst of the global recession. Health indicators are improving. The Rwandan people believed in themselves. And their leaders, led by President Kagame, believed in policies based on evidence and measurable results, including a nationwide emphasis on family planning, cross-cutting partnerships with donors and NGOs, a greater premium on professionalism in the government and the health sector.[49]

Perennially, Rwanda's Human Rights record, civil rights and political openness have been a constant concern for the international community.[50] For many in the international community and democracy activists, "alongside Rwanda's remarkable development progress, there have been equally consistent efforts to reduce space for independent voices and to diminish the ability of the media, opposition groups and civil society to operate", Deputy Assistant Secretary of State Steven Feldstein said in testimony to a US House of Representatives subcommittee on Africa. Repressive actions by the Rwandan government are setting "a disturbing precedent for the region and continent," he warned. "Other countries are carefully watching Rwanda's model of economic liberalisation and political repression. In my discussions, counterparts frequently point to Rwanda and question whether protecting the rights of their citizens matters if they can achieve substantial economic development".

To say that Rwanda has pushed back against international criticisms is an understatement. Kigali has distinguished itself with being very acerbic with international interference in its internal affairs in as far as its political governance is concerned for they argue these don't have any moral authority to do so.[51] As such, the international community has had a tiptoed attitude towards Kigali post-genocide mostly owing to its inaction and failure to intervene during the tragedy. Hence, Kigali has since seen no reason to take lessons or criticisms however justified from the international community.[52] Even though they have largely lauded Rwanda's progress as a rising star in social and economic development constantly named as one of the best places to do business in Africa, ranking no 44 by Doing Business Index, Transparency International consistently ranking it as one of the least corrupt countries in Africa they are also not oblivious to the less than acceptable progress largely within the parameters of civil liberties, human rights and political competitiveness. For democratic advocates and observers, the third term project signals a significant setback to democratic deepening and habituation but it is an irritation that Kigali is unapologetic for.

Kagame: The "Uninterested" Beneficiary

There is something conspicuously familiar with the term limits debate and their beneficiaries. Chiluba of Zambia, Museveni of Uganda, Obasanjo of Nigeria, Nujoma of Namibia all initially feigned a disinterest and detachment from the clamours to change the constitutional provisions limiting their tenures.[53] All often argued that this wasn't a priority for them and that they were more focused on the task at hand. Kagame was equally no exception. Flashback to 2008, Kagame had been explicitly asked if he saw himself as extending his tenure as many other African leaders were beginning to do notably his mentor Museveni of Uganda. "I have not asked anyone to change the constitution and I have not told anybody how or what to think about 2017", Kagame then noted. He later told delegates at an RPF conference that his inability to groom a successor and create "capacity for a post-me Rwanda" would represent a "personal failure". "People say that I should stay because there is no one to replace me…but if in all these years I have been unable to mentor a successor or successors that should be the reason I should not continue as president. It means that I have not created capacity for a post-me Rwanda. I see this as a personal failure".[54] In fact as recent as 2011, he butted away suggestions of a potential third term arguing that

> Just look at me, I don't need it. I don't do this job I am doing as a job for being paid, or as something that benefits me (…) I am not the person who needs the third term…I want to do my business for which the Rwandans entrusted me to do and when am done I will be done… I can continue to serve my country in very many different ways…Personally I don't want to be involved in or changing the constitution so that I stay in power and particularly changing the constitution for that purpose. I would hate it.[55]

These protestation and signals of disinterest perhaps marked a deeper desire to safeguard a carefully crafted legacy but at the same time a genuine anxiety as to the future of Rwanda.

Fast forward to 2014/2015, when these clamour for constitutional change began to gain momentum, Kagame started singing a different tune arguing that while he was not personally invested in the scheme, he also acknowledged the right of Rwandans to make their own choices and choose their own political destiny without regard to foreign interference and prompts. Asked what he thought about a perceived mass and popular campaign to have him retained, he argued that "what is more important to me …is not that people want something for the sake of it. It is because of the benefit. This person maybe has delivered something. You saw the women and men talk about their journey in their lives". Still, the only person in Rwanda who regularly and publicly professed not to have made up his mind about a third term was Kagame. He says—in a way that recalls Shakespeare's Caesar, repeatedly refusing the crown, but each time more gently—that he needs to be persuaded of the argument though for many years he was adamant that he would step down. To hold on to power, he noted, "would be a personal failure". However, while successions are long and carefully choreographed rituals, by design or default, nothing of this sort had happened in Rwanda and therein was the fundamental problem.

For a while, Kagame continued to insist that he was a reluctant convert to the third term project arguing that "By the way, I didn't ask for this thing. I was actually trying to tell my people: 'You know what, there's room - can't you find someone else? You need to take a risk and look for someone else,…' And they kept saying 'No. We are not ready to take risks. We want you to stay.' I said, 'But I'm having difficulties staying'".[56] Between 2013 and 2015, there was a marked increase in the public campaign calling for the review of the constitution with a package of reforms principle of which was the revision of the term limits. In this scheme there was a marked co-option of civil society, political parties and the mass public all calling for the amendment of the constitution.

Removing Term Limits

As previously noted, Article 101 of the Rwanda constitutional limited the country's president to two seven-year terms.[57] Kagame as the sitting president was in his last term of office having run for two constitutionally mandated terms due to expire in 2017 having been re-elected in 2010 with a resounding mandate. On 8 October 2015, Rwanda's Supreme Court ruled the constitutional amendment efforts valid dismissing the opposition Democratic Green Party's lawsuit challenging any amendment to Article 101 on presidential two term limits. The referendum that followed saw the decision to suspend term limits and thereby clearing the way for Kagame run for re-election resoundingly approved by an enviable 98.3% of the vote. During November 2015, Rwandan Parliament (both the lower house and senate) voted in support of changes to 32 articles and formatting changes to 16 others, and in the event clearing President Kagame run for a third term of office. These changes also reduced the presidential tenures and suspended terms limits for the incumbent president. The new and modified constitutional amendment was for the President of the Republic's election for a five (5) year term, down from seven. He or she may be re-elected once.[58] This vote was in response to a petition of more than 3.7 million Rwandans or 72% of those on the electoral roll asking parliament to lift presidential term limits. Ladislas Ngendahimana, a spokesperson for the Ministry of Local Government, called it a "spontaneous initiative from the population", adding that his ministry has "no idea how it happened". Nkusi Juvenal, a member of parliament from the PSD, noted after parliament unanimously passed the vote that "3.7 million Rwandans from different constituencies and walks of life have spoken, we are their representatives here, we have no option but to... listen to their pleas".[59] This was later to be followed by a national referendum for a popular decision on the matter.

The campaign leading to the national referendum was notable for its lack of critical interrogation of the merits and demerits of the constitutional repeal and more profoundly the almost complete absence of the no-campaign. Following, a short campaign period, on 18 December 2015, a constitutional amendment referendum was held asking voters to signal their intention as to the constitutional amendments. With 97% turnout, there was a resounding win for the "Yes" campaign approving the changing of presidential terms from seven to five years, renewable only once (in agreement with East African Community norms), but with Mr Kagame allowed one transitional seven-year term from 2017 to 2024. The amendment does not discontinue the principle of term limits, but rather makes an exception for the man accredited with ending the Rwandan genocide in 1994 and driving the country's strong record of economic development. "The electoral commission declares in public that 98.3 percent of voting Rwandans accepted the constitution as amended in 2015", National Electoral Commission chairman Kalisa Mbanda informed a news conference after Friday's vote with ten dissenters in the whole country.[60] The amendments passed retained two-term limits for the presidency and shortened terms from seven to five years. They also explicitly stated, however, that the current president is eligible for a seven-year term following his current term, after which he may run for two five-year terms.

The Triple Barrel Strategy

Often the strategy for a successful constitutional revision to repeal term limits hinges on a number of calculations. When the regime has an insurmountable majority either on its own or in coalition with other parties in parliament, the route for repeal has been legislative. Equally, when the courts are deemed regime friendly owing to the mode of their appointment and previous behaviour that has pitted the regime against the opposition or critics, a constitutional or judicial referral has been the preferred approach. In a few cases where the regime was uncertain as to its ability to control and dictate proceedings in parliament or gamble on judicial proceedings they have sought a popular referendum but also in as much as they are sure to influence the workings of the Electoral Commission.

The strategy to amend the constitution and remove term limits in Rwanda was more sophisticated and meticulously choreographed than any other similar effort on the continent. In Rwanda's case, all the above were deployed; popular demand through a petition, that was then subject to a court process challenging the constitutionality of the amendment, a parliamentary debate and approval and a referendum. This triple barrel approach provided a semblance of procedural robustness and popular legitimacy of the reform process that was meant to dampen specifically international criticism that was expected. The successful repeal of Article 101 was, by and large, a foregone conclusion. Not only was there almost no visible and appreciable resistance to the repeal but the tactic to pursue a triple barrel approach, popular petition and referendum, constitutional court interpretation and parliamentary support I argue further ensured the perception of the broadest consensus and consultation providing a firm mandate for Kagame's continued leadership. Peculiarly, while the RPF maintained a very dominant position in the lower house and senate the regime allowed the opposition challenge to the repeal to proceed to the high and later constitutional court. This is a case they could have so easily thwarted given the fact that the courts are seen as being staffed by regime cadres and as such regime friendly.

Following the referendum and the attendant processes, Kagame was to deliver his anticipated formal response to the succession debate. In his 2016 new year's message to Rwandans, he noted: "You clearly expressed your choices for the future of our country (in the referendum) ... You requested me to lead the country again after 2017. Given the importance and consideration you attach to this, I can only accept".[61] This pronouncement on 1 January 2016 that Kagame had after careful consideration and listening to the great call of the people was after all going to avail himself to continue in the service of the people was not only expected but was to set the tone for Rwanda's 2020 strategic transformation and continuity. The events that followed largely signalled by a general consensus, muted opposition to the constitutional reforms and ultimately reaffirmation of Kagame as the oversized figure of Rwanda's politics for a while to come was as expected. This was a culmination of post-genocide political machination a carefully calibrated political scheme that ensured the entrenchment of the RPF as the dominant political force in Rwanda, the attempt at social re-engineering and establishment of a new political ideology defined and implemented by the RPF and the expected acquiescence from society.

Ultimately, project 2017 is firmly on course and there is no doubt that Kagame will emerge triumphant and continue leading Rwanda for the foreseeable future. What this means to democratic deepening in Rwanda is perhaps best captured by two critical reviews. Thierry Vircoulon of the International Crisis Group's project director for Central Africa has noted that "He (Kagame) is popular because of his record on economic and social delivery but the Rwandan political system is also a one-man show. There's no space for opposition or protests", while Charles Onyango Obbo a Ugandan commentator has noted that "Generals like Kagame can build prosperous economies, roads, hospitals, and fight Aids", "What they cannot do is build liberal democracies" and therein lies the paradox.[62]

Conclusion

As we have observed, Rwanda is not an anomaly but a growing trend in much of Africa where as noted many long-serving leaders have sought to entrench their leadership and at worst create "imperial presidencies". At Tuft University in Boston in 2014, Kagame noted:

"I think at some point we need to leave countries and people to decide their own affairs...why I'm saying that is because I'm asked when and whether I plan to leave office...". "There is a new democratic fundamentalism that values form over substance...If it is inherently undemocratic to amend constitutions, why do they contain provisions for doing so everywhere?"[63]

On the surface these observations have a degree of validity in as much as democracy at its core is about the will of the people to decide their own destinies. However, it is the systematic weakening of the institutions that underpin the people's supremacy that often characterises this illusion for many a regime there is absence of both form and substance. While longevity of tenure or even issue of term limits may on the surface not look fundamental to the broader challenges of governance as some of these African leaders rightly point out, it is the failure to realise promised transformation, perpetuation of political malfeasance, the narrowing of the political space and the growing perception that the incumbents hold the only key to unlock their country's fortunes that makes their protestation ring hollow. Evidently, across Africa much like DRC, Burkina Faso, Congo and Burundi there is a significant disconnect between longevity of the presidency with the quality of leadership and transformative governance. Instead these countries with Rwanda (in part) the exception, are among the world's poorest, least developed, corrupt and worst governed. When their leaders say that they must remain in office, they make no case for what good they will do, no connection between their interest in power and the public interest. While there can evidently be merit in Rwanda's case, its success to expunge term limits from the constitution appears to signal a general victory for leaders who argue that they should be judged on their record, not on their longevity. However, what is least said is not only the abysmal record they stand on but also the fundamental weakness of the institutions they superintend over, the failure to abide by the rules of the game as long as they don't suit their political playbook and the very systematic manner in which they seek to subvert political accountability and responsive governance the longer they retain the ever so powerful presidencies.

Specifically for Rwanda, joining other African countries in expunging term limits from its constitution and allowing Kagame to continue unchecked leadership is without a doubt a two-edged sword. Rwanda's leadership was once seen as the "new breed" of leaders who were to deliver Africa from its incessant wars, human rights abuse and wanton political malfeasance. Today, Rwanda is considered as having treaded an all so familiar path of African political leadership alternation or precisely lack of the repercussions of which is yet unknown in this case. While supporters do point to the fact that elections will act as a check and balance to leaders who don't deliver to expectations forget to note that incumbents in Africa rarely lose elections as long as they maintain disproportionate levers of power to influence the performance of the institutions and mechanisms that are designed to check their very leadership. As such the only guarantee that there would be leadership alternation as mandated by term limits provisions is not only rendered useless but points to the broader challenge of designing institutions that can withstand a wilful and systematic attempt to bend them to their leaders will. Deepening democracy and government accountability are embedded in the economic and development and poverty reduction strategy, Musoni the Local government minister of Rwanda once noted. How this constitutional amendment to remove term limits speaks to deepening democracy may provide sceptics reason to doubt Rwanda's very commitment to realise genuine and far-reaching institutional transformation.

NOTES

1. Michael Bratton and Nicholas van de Walle, *Democratic Experiments in Africa: Regime Transitions in a Comparative Perspective* (Cambridge: Cambridge University Press, 1997); B. Baker, "The Class of 1990: How Have Autocratic Leaders of Sub-Saharan Africa Fared Under Democratisation?" *Third World Quarterly* 19, no. 1 (1998): 113–125.
2. Gisbert H. Flanz, *Constitutions of the Countries of the New World* (Dobbs Ferry, NY: Oceana Publications, 1995); Baker 1998: 119; Daniel Vencovsky, "Presidential Term Limits in Africa," *Conflict Trends*, no. 2 (2007): 15–21.
3. Boniface Dulani, "African Publics Strongly Support Term Limits, Resist Leaders' Efforts to Extend Their Tenure," Afrobarometer Dispatch No. 30 (2015); Njunga M. Mulikita, "A False Dawn?" *African Security Review* 12, no. 4 (2003): 105–115, p. 108; L. Diamond, "Progress and Retreat in Africa: The Rule of Law Versus the Big Man," *Journal of Democracy* 19, no. 2 (2008a): 138–149; L. Diamond, "The Democratic Rollback: The Resurgence of the Predatory State," *Foreign Affairs* 87, no. 2 (2008b): 36–48; E. Gyimah-Boadi, "Africa's Waning Democratic Commitment," *Journal of Democracy* 26, no. 1 (2015): 101–113.

4. Mahmood Mamdani, *When Victims Become Killers: Colonialism, Nativism, and the Genocide in Rwanda* (Princeton, NJ: Princeton University Press, 2001).
5. David E. Kiwuwa, "Democracy and the Politics of Power Alternation in Africa," *Contemporary Politics* 19, no. 3 (2013): 262–278, p. 263; Lonel Zamfir, "Democracy in Africa Power Alternation and Presidential Term Limits," European Union Policy Briefing, European Parliament (2016).
6. D. Posner and J. Young, "The Institutionalization of Political Power in Africa," *Journal of Democracy* 18, no. 3 (2007): 126–140; P. Smith, "Africa's Year of Democratic Reverses," *The BBC News*, December 29, 2005; Nancy Bermeo, "On Democratic Backsliding," *Journal of Democracy* 27, no. 1 (2016): 5–19.
7. B. Baker 1998; B. Baker, "Outstaying One's Welcome: The Presidential Third Term Debate in Africa," *Contemporary Politics* 8, no. 4 (2002): 285–303; N. Bamfo, "Term Limits and Political Incumbency in Africa: Implication of Staying in Power too Long with References to the Cases of Kenya, Malawi and Zambia," *African and Asian Studies* 4, no. 3 (2005): 327–356; G. Maltz, "The Case for Presidential Term Limits," *Journal of Democracy* 18, no. 1 (2007): 128–142.
8. A. Baturo, "The Stakes of Losing Office, Term Limits and Democracy," *British Journal of Political Science* 40, no. 3 (2010): 635–662.
9. Baker 2002; Rachel B. Riedl, *Authoritarian Origins of Democratic Party Systems in Africa* (Cambridge: Cambridge University Press, 2014); Adeolu Durotoye, "Resurgent Backsliding and Democracy in Africa," *International Journal of African and Asian Studies* 18 (2016).
10. M. Bratton, "The 'Alternation Effect' in Africa," *Journal of Democracy* 15, no. 4 (2004): 147–158.
11. Zeric Kay Smith, "The Impact of Political Liberalisation and Democratisation on Ethnic Conflict in Africa: An Empirical Test of Common Assumptions," *Journal of Modern African Studies* 38 (2000): 22, 26.
12. Dulani 2015; Simon Maina, "Voters Standing up for Term Limits in Africa," *The East African*, May 4, 2015.
13. Hilde Coffe, "The 2010 Presidential Elections in Rwanda," *Electoral Studies* 30, no. 3 (September 2011): 581–584.
14. Andrew Mwenda, "Kagame's Retirement Plan: Becoming the 1st Revolutionary Leader to Leave Voluntarily," *Umuvugizi*, March 4, 2013, https://umuvugizi.wordpress.com/2013/03/04/kagames-retirement-plan-becoming-the-1st-revolutionary-leader-to-leave-voluntarily/.
15. Associated Press, "Kagame's Headache: To Bow Out or Hang On?" *The Daily Monitor*, Uganda, March 10, 2013.
16. Manasseh Nshuti, "The Ideal Change Is No Change at All," *The Rwanda New Times*, February 23, 2015.

17. Colin M. Waugh, *Paul Kagame and Rwanda: Power, Genocide and the Rwandan Patriotic Front* (McFarland & Co, 2004); Timothy Longman, "Limitation to Political Reforms," in Scott Straus and Lars Waldorf (eds.), *Remaking Rwanda: State Building and Human Rights After Mass Violence* (Madison: University of Wisconsin Press, 2011), 25–47.
18. Ibid.
19. Jordy Clarke, "Rwandan Leader Fails to Quell Despot Fears," *The Financial Times*, August 7, 2010.
20. Swanee Hunt, "The Rise of Rwanda's Women," *Foreign Affairs* 93, no. 3 (2014): 150–156.
21. Filip Reyntjens, "'I Will Also Fight with You': President Kagame, Rwanda's Berater-in-Chief," 2018, https://africanarguments.org/2018/03/13/i-will-also-fight-with-you-president-kagame-rwanda-berater-in-chief/, accessed March 20, 2018.
22. Bireete Sarah, "The Politics of Term Limits in Africa—Case of Uganda," February 16, 2015, https://www.linkedin.com/pulse/politics-term-limits-africa-case-uganda-sarah-bireete, accessed June 12, 2015.
23. Filip Reyntjens, "Rwanda's Progress or Powder Keg," *Journal of Democracy* 26, no. 3 (July 2015): 19–33.
24. Waugh 2004.
25. Ted Dagne, "Rwanda: Background and Current Developments," *Current Politics and Economics of Africa* 4, no. 1 (2011); Mireille Mutima, "Is Third Term Push Behind Paul Kagame's Decision to Sack Karugarama?" 2013, http://rwandinfo.com/eng/is-third-term-push-behind-paul-kagames-decision-to-sack-karugarama/.
26. L. Waldorf, "Censorship and Propaganda in Post-genocide Rwanda," in Allan Thompson (ed.), *The Media and the Rwandan Genocide* (London: Pluto Press, 2007), 404–416; Jonathan W. Rosen, "Ahead of Vote on Term Limits, Rwandans Worry About Presidential Power Grab," December 16, 2015, http://america.aljazeera.com/articles/2015/12/16/paul-kagame-rwandas-president-for-life.html.
27. Edmund Kagire, "Kagame Drops Last Two RPF 'Historicals'," *The East African*, Saturday, June 1, 2013.
28. Kagire 2013.
29. Reyntjens 2004, 2015: 25; Danielle Beswick, "Managing Dissent in a Post-genocide Environment: The Challenge of Political Space in Rwanda," *Development and Change* 41, no. 2 (2010): 225–251, p. 242; Filip Reyntjens, "Rwanda, Ten Years On: From Genocide to Dictatorship," *African Affairs* 103, no. 4 (2004): 177–210.
30. Ignatius Ssuuna, "Rwanda at the Crossroads over Lifting of Term Limits," *The Daily Monitor*, Uganda, February 15, 2015.
31. Henry Mukasa, "Kagame to Decide on Third Term After Referendum," *The New Times*, Tuesday, December 8, 2015.

32. Mwenda 2013.
33. G. Sartori (ed.), *Comparative Constitutional Engineering: An Inquiry into Structures, Incentives and Outcomes* (New York: New York University Press, 1994); Markus M. L. Crepaz, Thomas A. Koelble, and David Wilsford (eds.), *Democracy and Institutions: The Life Work of Arendt Lijphart* (University of Michigan Press, 2000); Robert A. Dahl, "What Political Institutions Does Large-Scale Democracy Require?" *Political Science Quarterly* 120, no. 2 (2005): 187–197.
34. Shaheen Mozaffar and James R. Scarritt, "The Puzzle of African Party Systems," *Party Politics*, 11, no. 4 (2005): 399–421; Michelle Kuenzi and Gina Lambright, "Party Systems and Democratic Consolidation in Africa's Electoral Regimes," *Party Politics* 11, no. 4 (2005): 423–446; Staffan I. Lindberg, "Institutionalization of Party Systems? Stability and Fluidity Among Legislative Parties in Africa's Democracies," *Government and Opposition* 42, no. 2 (2007): 215–241.
35. Imirasire, "Rwanda Opposition Backs New Plan to Lift Presidential Term Limits," 2015, http://eng.imirasire.com/news/all-around/in-rwanda/article/rwanda-opposition-backsnew-plan.
36. Mike Segawa, "Rwanda Opposition Backs Lifting Term Limit," *The Daily Monitor*, Uganda, May 25, 2015.
37. The Insider, "Rwanda Opposition Figure Cheers Lifting Term Limits," Uganda, January 6, 2016.
38. Anjan Sundaram, "How President Paul Kagame Crushed Rwanda's Free Press," *The Guardian Sunday*, January 3, 2016.
39. Clark 2010.
40. The White House, "Remarks by the President to the Ghanaian Parliament," Office of the Press Secretary, Accra International Conference Center, Accra, Ghana, July 11, 2009.
41. Kevin Kelley, "US 'Deeply Disappointed' with Kagame's Third Term Bid," *The East African*, Sunday, January 3, 2016.
42. AFP, "We Expect You to Go in 2017, US Tells Rwanda's Kagame," *Mail and Guardian*, Africa, 2015. http://mgafrica.com/article/2015-12-02-we-expect-you-to-go-us-tells-rwandas-kagameus-says-kagame-should-go-when-term-ends-in-2017.
43. European Council of the European Union, "Declaration by the High Representative Federica Mogherini on Behalf of the EU on Constitutional Review in Rwanda," December 3, 2015, http://www.consilium.europa.eu/en/press/press-releases/2015/12/03-hr-declaration-on-constitutional-review-in-rwanda/.
44. Peter Uvin, "Difficult Choices in the New Post-conflict Agenda: The International Community in Rwanda After the Genocide," *Third World Quarterly* 22, no. 2 (2001): 177–189.

45. Jeremiah Kiplang'at, "Raila Odinga Criticises Paul Kagame, Yoweri Museveni over Term Limits," 2015, http://www.theeastafrican.co.ke/news/Raila-Odinga-criticises-Kagame-Museveni-over-term-limits/-/2558/2857282/-/y0wqudz/-/index.html.
46. Richard Grant, "Paul Kagame: Rwanda's Redeemer or Ruthless Dictator?" *The Telegraph*, July 22, 2010.
47. IGHE Reporter "Blair: Cutting Aid to Rwanda Is Counter-Productive," http://www.bbc.co.uk/news/world-africa-21608731, accessed May 8, 2016.
48. PH, "'Right Time for a Leader to Leave Office Is Determined by the People'—Rwandan President, Paul Kagame," https://howafrica.com/right-time-for-a-leader-to-leave-office-is-determined-by-the-people-rwandan-president-paul-kagame/, accessed May 3, 2017.
49. Hillary Clinton speech, August 2009, Africa Growth and Opportunity Act (AGOA) Forum in Nairobi, Kenya.
50. Reyntjens 2015; Human Rights Watch, "Rwanda: Eights Years Sentence for Opposition Leader," October 30, 2012.
51. Chris McGreal, "Is Kagame Africa's Lincoln or a Tyrant Exploiting Rwanda's Tragic History," *The Observer*, Saturday, May 18, 2013.
52. Peter Uvin 2001; Jennie Burnet, "Gender Balance and the Meanings of Women in Governance in Post-genocide Rwanda," *African Affairs* 107, no. 428 (2008): 361–386, p. 366; Grant 2010.
53. Momba 1999.
54. AP 2013.
55. Emmanuel Gyezaho, "Cheerleaders Want Kagame Third Term," *The Daily Monitor*, Uganda, Friday, November 11, 2011.
56. Reuters, "I Didn't Want Third Term, Says Rwanda's Kagame," 2016, http://www.dailymail.co.uk/wires/reuters/article-3585334/I-didnt-want-term-says-Rwandas-Kagame.html#ixzz4Qolqg5H0.
57. Republic of Rwanda Constitution, "Official Gazette n° Special of 24/12/2015," 2015, http://www.parliament.gov.rw/fileadmin/Bills_CD/THE_CONSTITUTION_OF_THEREPUBLIC_OF_RWANDA_OF_2003_REVISED_IN_2015.pdf.
58. Ibid.
59. Stephanie Aglietti, "Rwanda Parliament Votes in Support of Kagame Third Term," AFP, July 15, 2015.
60. Clement Uwiringiyimana, "Rwandans Approve Extension of Presidential Term Limits," *The Daily Mail*, December 19, 2015, http://www.dailymail.co.uk/wires/reuters/article-3366880/Rwandans-approve-extension-presidential-term-limits.html, accessed June 17, 2016.
61. Reuters, "Rwandan President Paul Kagame to Run for Third Term in 2017," *The Guardian*, Friday, January 1, 2016, https://www.

theguardian.com/world/2016/jan/01/rwanda-paul-kagame-third-term-office-constitutional-changes, accessed May 5, 2016.
62. Clark 2010.
63. David Smith, "Paul Kagame Hints at Seeking Third Term as Rwandan President," *The Guardian*, UK, April 24, 2014.

CHAPTER 3

The Making of a Monarchical Republic: The Undoing of Presidential Term Limits in Gabon Under Omar Bongo

Daniel Mengara

INTRODUCTION

The year 1989 marked, for Gabon, the beginning of months of socioeconomic and political unrest that, ultimately, forced Omar Bongo to agree not only to the holding of a National Conference on March 23–April 19, 1990 but also to the framing of a new constitution reinstating multiparty politics in the country. This change intervened after decades of dictatorship under the one-party system that then named Albert-Bernard Bongo had forced upon the nation on March 12, 1968, just a few months after his rise to power on December 2, 1967. This was before Bongo converted to Islam in 1973 and took on the Muslim name of El Hadj Omar Bongo. Later, in a bid to finally acknowledge his patronymic ties with his late father, Bongo changed his name once again in 2004 to become El Hadj Omar Bongo Ondimba.

D. Mengara (✉)
Montclair State University, Montclair, NJ, USA
e-mail: mengarad@montclair.edu

© The Author(s) 2020
J. R. Mangala (ed.), *The Politics of Challenging Presidential Term Limits in Africa*, https://doi.org/10.1007/978-3-030-40810-7_3

The reintroduction of multiparty politics did not, however, translate into factual and effective democracy for Gabon. By the two decades that followed the National Conference (1990–2009), Omar Bongo had managed to reverse and even undo most of the political gains derived from the Conference, including the term-limit provision that had been adopted as part of the 1991 constitution.[1] Omar Bongo was thus, paradoxically, able to survive another nineteen years in office until his unexpected death on June 8, 2009. At the time of his death, Omar Bongo was the longest-serving head of state in the world and his grip over the country had actually strengthened, paradoxically. He left behind a forty-two-year-old regime that was stronger than ever thanks to the complex and intricate political system that he had manufactured. His regime relied upon a ruthless, yet subtly organized system in which a savant interplay of political corruption, geo-tribal politics and patronage, socioeconomic coercion, and a massive electoral fraud apparatus combined with a repressive police state to ensure his complete political supremacy, and suzerainty, over the nation. As Philippe Bernard from *Le Monde* newspaper put it, Omar Bongo was indeed a "despot oscillating between a clientelist bonhomie and an iron grip in his country."[2] The result, consequently, was the emergence of "a nominal multiparty system,"[3] that is, a political system that, on the surface, acknowledged multiparty politics, but nevertheless constituted an adulterated model that, in reality, did not allow for any sort of alternation of power through elections. There was, indeed, multipartyism in Gabon, but without the democratic practice and spirit that go with it. In the Gabonese case, adversarial and even seemingly competitive elections were held, but were never truly transparent nor really truly sufficiently free and fair to allow for alternation. Since the National Conference of 1990, Gabon has held five presidential elections (1993, 1998, 2005, 2009, and 2016) and six legislative elections (The transitional one in 1990, then the regular ones under the new 1991 constitution and its subsequent iterations in 1996, 2001, 2006, 2011, and 2018). All were, one might argue, fraudulently won by Omar Bongo and his regime. Hence the question that Sory Baldé posed when he wondered whether the "National Conference that took place in this state truly fulfilled its role" and whether this role was "to achieve democratic alternation or [merely] to sketch [an elusive] liberalization of political life" (My translation).[4]

In the case of Gabon, this quasi-impossibility of alternation inspired, but also provided, a political framework that has ensured the unobstructed continuity of the Bongo regime. It also naturally paved the way for Omar Bongo's son, Ali Bongo Ondimba, to succeed his father upon his death in June 2009. This process of dynastic succession in the context of a republic is, itself, a paradoxical trend that stood out in the past decade or so as a truly African political innovation that appeared to find some favor among a number of African regimes in such countries as the Democratic Republic of the Congo, Togo, Gabon, Libya, Egypt, and Senegal, where dictators sought to groom their sons for dynastic successions in the context of republics.[5] Although these attempts did fail in Libya and Egypt (due to the ousting of Muammar Gadhafi and Hosni Mubarak in the aftermath of the Arab Spring), but also in Senegal (the Senegalese took to the streets to prevent this), they did succeed in the Democratic Republic of the Congo, Gabon, and Togo, where sons of presidents—Joseph Kabila, Ali Bongo Ondimba, and Faure Gnassingbé respectively—took over through sham elections and/or extra-constitutional arrangements. This phenomenon of dynastic successions in the context of republics was so remarkable that it prompted Andy Moses to consecrate a whole volume on the subject. His book, which addresses the particular case of Gabon, was, thus, aptly entitled *La République monarchique* (The Monarchical Republic).[6] One thing remains clear though, when it comes to Gabon's political trajectory: Gabon is now, arguably, the only so-called Republic, that is, the only officially non-monarchical system in the world to have been ruled not only by the same family, but also by the same regime, for fifty-three years (and counting).

To begin to answer the question as to what led to the political upheavals of the 1990s in Gabon and why and how, after a new constitution instituting term limits was promulgated in 1991, Omar Bongo was able to roll back such term limits as well as other democratic gains the country had managed to secure, one must first look at the general political and economic landscape of the preceding decades in Gabon; this landscape, in turn, will help to illuminate the aftermath of Gabon's National Conference and clarify the circumstances and factors that enabled Omar Bongo to set Gabon on a course that allowed his antidemocratic ethos to prevail for more than half a century.

Setting the Stage: Gabon's Political and Economic Landscape Prior to the National Conference of 1990

Gabon's road to democracy has not been easy. The roots of its failed democratic transition of the 1990s go back to the 1960s. In 1967, Albert-Bernard Bongo inherited power from the country's first postindependence president, Léon Mba, in a controversial manner that has been widely attested not only in a number of books by French investigative journalists such as Pierre Péan[7] and Glaser and Smith[8] but also in the seminal writings of French activist François-Xavier Verschave.[9] Various interviews of the main artisan of the "Françafrique" system himself,[10] the now deceased, yet very enigmatic and secretive Jacques Foccart,[11] have also come to complete the picture. What transpires from these accounts is that France, through the work of Foccart, but also with the direct benediction and involvement of then French President Charles de Gaulle,[12] had basically taken advantage of President Mba's illness—an alleged cancer—and hospitalization in Paris, to propel Bongo to the presidency of Gabon after carefully plotting an amendment to the Gabonese constitution. This constitutional amendment, in Jacques Foccart's own account, was basically commandeered from Paris, where President Mba was hospitalized in August 1966 and remained for more than a year until his death in 1967. The purpose was to introduce a position of vice president that was specifically tailored for Albert-Bernard Bongo. The intent, in Foccart's own words, was to ensure an American-style automatic succession.[13]

Although president Mba did already, from his hospital bed in Paris, appoint Albert-Bernad Bongo "vice president of the government"[14] as of November 14, 1966, in replacement of Paul-Marie Yembit, the constitutional reform of February 1967 formalized this status, but with a twist. It created a formal post of "vice president of the Republic" and introduced provisions that ensured that Bongo would automatically become president should President Mba die. The early presidential and legislative elections that were held on March 19 of the same year under the new constitution saw Léon Mba literally run for president from his hospital bed in Paris, with the Mba-Bongo ticket eventually earning more than 99% of the vote.[15] This was, however, an election in which the Mba-Bongo ticket ran unopposed due to the repressive climate that had developed in the country following the 1964 coup that had briefly deposed President

Léon Mba. It is interesting that, in order to prevent the possibility of such automatic successions in the future, Omar Bongo himself ended up suppressing the position of vice president in 1975, replacing it with that of prime minister. He did not apparently want to feed any appetite for power around him. This move, however, was already a strong indication of Omar Bongo's psychology and mentality. It clearly illuminated, at this very early stage of independent Gabon's history, the assertive antidemocratic tendencies that would become the hallmark of his presidency for 42 years. It remains, thus, that from its independence on August 17, 1960 to the fatidic year of 1967, Gabon had a rather painful and tumultuous, if not illusive, road toward democracy. Throughout these years, Léon Mba, first as prime minister (1957–1961) and later as president (1961–1967), already displayed despotic tendencies that resulted in his spearheading a constitutional amendment effort that ended up transforming his presidency into a "hyper-presidency" as early as February 21, 1961.[16] This came after plot allegations he probably invented allowed him to repress and imprison his political opponents on November 16, 1960, just three months after Gabon's proclamation of independence.[17] Léon Mba's gradual drift toward despotism and autocracy began to show the limits of Gabon's earlier experimentation with democracy. This drift inevitably led to a military coup by a group of Gabonese soldiers on the night of February 17–18, 1964.[18] By February 20, the 2000 French troops who were dispatched to Gabon from Dakar and Brazzaville in the night of February 18–19 by French President Charles de Gaulle had quelled the revolt and restored President Mba.[19] At least one French soldier and some twenty-five Gabonese military were reportedly killed during this rescue and restoration operation.

The rapid reinstatement of President Léon Mba by Charles de Gaulle paved the way for two factors that were going to fundamentally shape the political course of the young nation over the next five decades. The first factor was a general trend toward the overall limitation of the democratic rights and aspirations of the Gabonese people, often with France's complicity and, for that matter, initiative; the second was France's neocolonialistic meddling as the incontrovertible kingmaker in Francophone African and, therefore, Gabonese politics.[20] After the still-seen-as-mysterious death of President Léon Mba from cancer in Paris in 1967 and the easing of Omar Bongo into power, it was just a matter of time before the dictator, as he himself obliquely acknowledges in interviews published by Airy Routier in 2001, used the argument of ethnic and tribal divisions to justify the banning of political parties and the imposition of the one-party system on March 12, 1968.[21] It was not until the appearance of the first clandestine political party, the *Mouvement de Redressement National* (MORENA), in 1981, and the subsequent arrests of its local leaders following an unauthorized public rally in the Gare Routière district of Libreville the same year, that the debate about Gabon's need for democracy rekindled. This rekindling was occurring at a time when Gabon's economic trajectory began to show signs of faltering after being greatly enhanced by the oil boom the country experienced in the 1970s. This faltering was caused by the oil crisis resulting from the fall in oil prices and the weakening of the dollar that occurred in the mid-1980s.[22] It eventually turned into a full-fledged economic crisis toward the end of the decade,[23] thus paving the way for the political upheavals that saw the MORENA reemerge in 1989, both nationally and in exile, as a major challenger to the monopolistic supremacy that the state party, the *Parti Démocratique Gabonais* (PDG), had enjoyed since its creation in March 1968.

The economic crisis itself had brought forth the various managerial shortcomings of the Omar Bongo regime, which had proven incapable of satisfying the basic needs of the Gabonese people. In spite of presiding over the destiny of a country abundantly rich in various types of minerals and natural resources (uranium, oil, manganese, iron, timber, etc.)—a country that, moreover, boasted a population count that, at the time, was estimated at just about a million souls, if not less—wealth redistribution was unequal and a majority of the people still lived under the poverty line. In fact, the World Bank, even as late as 1997 before the PPP (Purchasing Power Parity) system began to be more universally used to measure poverty line and per capita GDP, was still estimating that at least 62% of Gabon's population lived under the poverty line in 1994.[24] This percentage, which is again cited in a study conducted in 2002 by the African Development Bank (ADB) and the Organization for Economic Cooperation and Development (OECD),[25] had even worsened in a World Bank report published in 2000. This report pegged at 83% the population of Gabon living under the poverty line[26] and this despite Gabon boasting a nominal per capita GDP of $3700,[27] one of the highest in Africa at the time. In fact, around 1989–1990, Gabon still had one of the highest per capita income levels in Africa. And despite being almost cut in half due to a weak dollar and the drop in oil prices of the mid-1980s, Gabon's per capita GDP was still around three thousand US dollars, which still made it one of the richest countries in Africa at the time.[28] It is this paradox between a high per capita income and the economic disparities observed in the country that, ultimately, constituted the principal hallmark of Omar Bongo's managerial disaster for forty-two years.

By 1989, thus, the general dissatisfaction with the regime was such that the political debate that Omar Bongo wanted to keep under the rug had become inevitable. The underlying political and socioeconomic pressures even caused the klepto-despotic leader to begin to develop a certain level of paranoia. For instance, following the 1982 trial which saw the regime send thirteen of the forty presumed MORENA conspirators to jail for a duration of twenty years (although Bongo did offer them amnesty in 1986), the Gabonese authorities announced in 1985 that they had "uncovered" a plot against the regime. On October 3, 1989, the regime again claimed to have "uncovered" another plot aiming at assassinating the president.[29] The subterfuge did not work, however, because neither the popular pressure nor the economic downfall relented. Omar Bongo nevertheless remained defiant. During his tour of the hinterland in 1989, he was still, at least publicly, defiantly rejecting the possibility of returning the country to multiparty politics. In a speech delivered on November 1989 in the town of Bitam in Gabon's northern province of Woleu-Ntem, he proclaimed that as long as he was in power, the country would never see a return to multipartyism. But the pressures brought upon him by the economic and political circumstances of the time were such that he secretly began negotiations with the leaders of the still clandestine opposition party, the MORENA. In 1989, Paul Mba Abessole, a Catholic priest who was also the president of the exiled branch of the MORENA, returned to Gabon from his thirteen-year exile in France to begin overt political negotiations with the regime. The year 1989, as a result, marked a turning point in the regime's attitude, especially because, going forward, a number of factors, some internal, others external, played a pivotal role in the precipitous fall of the one-party system. In addition to the economic crisis and the political debate triggered in 1981 by the "Gare Routière events," four other factors were going to play a major role in this fall, namely the "wind from the East" that, in 1989, blew over from the crumbling fragments of the Soviet Union, the various popular insurrections that this wind inspired in several Francophone African countries in the 1989–1993 period, the student revolts of the 1989–1990s in Libreville, and the various union strikes that came to complicate things for the regime around the same period. These factors combined to lead to a general state of unrest in the country and Omar Bongo was left with no choice but to agree to the holding of the National Conference that the people and the still illegal political opposition were now clamoring for.

There is no doubt that Benin's 1990 National Conference had a precursory and even primordial influence not only on the one held in Gabon on March 23–April 19, 1990, but also on the several others that were held in the 1990s to bring the wind of democracy into such other Francophone, sub-Saharan African countries as Congo-Brazzaville, Togo, Mali, Niger, Zaïre, and Chad. When looked at in strict chronological order based on when the conference began as opposed to when it ended, one can clearly see the line or sequence of succession: Benin (February 19–28, 1990), Gabon (March 23–April 19, 1990), Congo (February 25–June 10, 1991), Togo (July 8–August 28, 1991), Mali (July 29–August 12, 1991), Niger (July 29–November 3, 1991), Zaïre (August 7, 1991–March 17, 1993), and Chad (January 15–April 7, 1993).[30] A truly African political innovation spearheaded and inspired by Benin,[31] the national conferences of the 1990s seem to have mostly remained a Francophone African phenomenon.[32] And only Benin can claim to be the best, if not the only true success story of them all.

How Benin came to represent one of the shining examples of Africa's ability to produce sound and resilient democratic systems is itself the story of a miracle. In the 1980s, Benin, which had been a Marxist–Leninist state under Mathieu Kérékou's despotic rule since 1972, was mired in an economic crisis that eventually led to socioeconomic and political troubles. As early as the early months of 1989, with the Soviet Union and communist regimes crumbling in Eastern Europe, Kérékou understood his regime had become unsustainable. In an unexpected move, he announced the liquidation of his regime's long-standing Marxist–Leninist orientation. He also agreed without too much resistance to the holding of a National Conference whose goal was to usher in a new era of democratic ethos for Benin. The Conference began on February 19, 1990 and a new multiparty constitution was promulgated by referendum on December 2, 1990. Multiparty elections were held on March 21, 1991, which Kérékou lost to Nicéphore Soglo, who won 67.7% of the vote. Since then, Benin has held five other presidential elections (1996, 2001, 2006, 2011, and 2016). Overall, power has changed hands four times in Benin since 1991 (Nicéphore Soglo, 1991–1996; Mathieu Kérékou, 1996–2006; Yayi Boni, 2006–2016; and Patrice Talon, 2016–present). Most elections in Benin since 1991 have been won only in the second round after a run-off between the two candidates who survived the first round. Only Yayi Boni was able, in the 2011 election, to win an outright majority of 53% in the first round. A clear sign that Benin's democracy has been both sound and resilient for the past twenty-nine years.

That the Beninese National Conference process and experiment greatly influenced the political discourse and process in Gabon therefore leaves no doubt. Internationally, the Benin experiment was invariably hailed in the media as a remarkable feat that had a profound impact on French-speaking Africa:

> An instant media event throughout Francophone Africa, the story of Benin was carried live on Benin radio, rebroadcast on national television, given prominent international coverage on Radio France Internationale (RFI), reported and analyzed by the government media and the independent press in every Francophone African country, and held up as a model of political reform by the Paris-based journal, *Jeune Afrique*. The text of this political drama was preserved by the Benin government news agency, which produced a two-hour videotape of conference highlights. Over 400 copies of the video had been sold by the end of 1991, and untold numbers of pirated copies began to circulate. The lessons of Benin's National Conference were not lost. Between March 1990 and August 1991, the rulers of Gabon, Congo, Mali, Togo, Niger, and Zaire faced the demands of pro-democracy forces and convened national conferences.[33]

In demanding the holding of a National Conference in the midst of the political unrests of the early months of 1990, the Gabonese opposition was inspired by the rather positive and deliberate way in which the Beninese process had unfolded. And this helped to exert political pressure on the Bongo regime. Omar Bongo's forced acceptance of the principle of a National Conference in Gabon had seemed, at first, to carry the promise of a process that would lead to the untethered democratization of the country. Held mostly between March 23 and April 19, 1990, the Conference saw the participation of more than two thousand delegates from civil society and political organizations that had quickly formed in order to secure representation at the Conference. The Conference's mission was rather vague: its goal was to "seek the ways ... towards multiparty democratization."[34] On April 19, that is, at the very conclusion of the Conference, Omar Bongo finally officially pronounced the instauration of multipartyism in Gabon, a process that was followed on May 22 by the adoption of a transitional constitution that became the basis for the legislative elections that were held on September 1, 1990. These elections saw the ruling party, the PDG, win the absolute, albeit weak, parliamentary majority. Paradoxically, even if recognized, none of the opposition parties that took part in the election were officially legalized. This legalization came only in January 1991 when the newly elected multiparty National Assembly unanimously voted to formalize their existence under the new constitution. The new Assembly also officially promulgated the new constitution in March 1991. This is the constitution that was the basis for the 1993 presidential elections, the first under the new multiparty system. Omar Bongo won that election with 51% of the vote amidst allegations of widespread fraud.

Gabon's National Conference and Its Aftermath

Gabon's democratic experiment was, in reality, rather short lived. While the country's multiparty system was never really put into question again, the way the whole process unfolded lacked sincerity and never really held the promise of true democratic change. Unlike Benin's Mathieu Kérékou who somewhat willingly, although hesitantly, accompanied the process, promising the delegates that their conclusions would be his,[35] Omar Bongo only grudgingly agreed to the National Conference and this only after the backlash that followed the brutal repression of student demonstrations in January 1990 pressured him into it. The unrest that indeed ensued caused the various unions that represented the sectors of water and electricity, health, and education to launch general strikes and, consequently, join the chorus of those who saw a National Conference such as was being organized in Benin as the only way out of the country's political and socioeconomic quagmire.[36]

Gabon's experience therefore shows that Omar Bongo had, in fact, sought to stonewall the process every step of the way. His main attempt at sidetracking the democratic aspirations of the Gabonese people dated back to a secret agreement he had allegedly, the rumors go, reached with the leader of the MORENA, father Paul Mba Abessole, shortly after his return from exile in September 1989 and well before the calls for a National Conference had become inevitable.[37] Both leaders had reportedly agreed to convince the country of the need to delay full plurality and to adopt, instead, a transitional model under the umbrella of the *Rassemblement Social-Democrate Gabonais* (RSDG). The RSDG was, thus, to be some sort of an all-inclusive grand movement that would allow for a certain degree of freedom and plurality in the form of political currents, but without totally suppressing the one-party system formula itself. The RSDG was thus to simply replace the state party, the PDG, which was therefore to be dissolved.[38] Omar Bongo would remain president above all political currents and was therefore never to be subjected to adversarial elections. Even though, on the surface, Omar Bongo and his allies—among whom Paul Mba Abessole and Pierre-Claver Maganga Moussavou—presented the RSDG as the transitional instrument that would prepare the country for full multipartyism after an agreed-upon transitional period, the real intent was probably elsewhere. And so, even after he was pressured into accepting the holding of the National Conference, Omar Bongo was still expecting the conference delegates to give a stamp of approval to the RSDG proposal.[39] But things were not necessarily going to move in that direction due to a number of unforeseen circumstances, one of which was the unexpected crumbling of the Bongo-Mba Abessole alliance.

What caused the alliance to falter was the result of two interrelated factors. The first was the political weakening of Paul Mba Abessole after he joined the "presidential majority" that emerged out the RSDG negotiations in January 1990. He thus became an official ally and partner of the Omar Bongo regime. This "betrayal" caused the founding fathers of the MORENA to exclude him from the party. In response, Mba Abessole created his own party, which he called *MORENA-Bûcherons* (MORENA-Woodcutters).[40] But the political powerhouse that the MORENA was before the split was no more and neither Paul Mba Abessole nor his old MORENA companions fully recovered from the split. The second factor resided in the circumstances and dynamics of the National Conference itself. These dynamics had naturally led to the formation of two factions: a pro-RSDG faction that included, among others, the ruling party (PDG), Mba Abessole's MORENA-Bûcherons and Pierre-Claver Maganga Moussavou's Parti Social-Démocrate (PSD), and an anti-RSDG faction, led by Jean-Pierre Nzoghé Nguéma of the MORENA (original branch) and Pierre-Louis Agondjo Okawé's Parti Gabonais du Progrès (PGP).[41] No one had really fully anticipated that the opposition delegates, against all expectations, would, in the various speeches given at the Conference, take the courage to defy Omar Bongo openly and demand an integral and untethered multiparty system. Their insistence, under the leadership of figures such as Jean-Pierre Nzoghé Nguéma and Pierre-Louis Agondjo

Okawé, that the Conference moved away from the RSDG project and, instead, laid the groundwork for integral multiparty democracy is what, ultimately, caused the agreement between Paul Mba Abessole and Omar Bongo to fall through.[42] In his very much-anticipated conference speech, Paul Mba Abessole, acknowledging this reality, declared that the RSDG project was now null and void. He chose instead to side with the rest of the opposition delegates because, in his view, the very fact that the Conference had given birth to a pro-RSDG camp and an anti-RSDG camp meant Gabon was now a de facto democracy.[43] In some paradoxical way, this reversal may have also been what ultimately saved Mba Abessole's political career, propelling him into the enviable position of leader of the Gabonese opposition until his electoral "defeat" in the 1993 presidential elections.

While the constitution that came out of the National Conference process had indeed held the promise of real democratization, the first two electoral tests of 1990 (transitional legislative elections) and 1993 (presidential elections) under the new political arrangements, in fact, revealed the limits of Gabon's National Conference. Not only were the 1990 legislative elections "won" by the ruling party, Omar Bongo himself also managed, unexpectedly, to "win" the 1993 presidential election, albeit amidst accusations of rampant fraud on both counts. French investigative journalist Pierre Péan, who was Mba Abessole's point man and an eye witness in the Mba-Bongo-France negotiations that followed the 1993 elections, testifies to how France and Bongo played Mba Abessole to proclaim Bongo the outright winner when, in fact, all had agreed to a run-off that Mba Abessole was expected to win.[44] In retrospect, it now appeared that Gabon's opposition delegates made a number of "rookie mistakes" along the way that allowed the Bongo regime to gradually empty the newly formulated Gabonese electoral process of its democratic substance. This inevitably resulted in a system whereby several political parties were allowed to compete, but with no real chance of power alternation through the voting booth. Further, the various provisions that had been adopted and inserted into the 1991 constitution to guarantee term limits—the president could now stay in power only for a maximum of two consecutive terms of five years each as opposed to seven years previously—had all been undone by the 2005 presidential election. Even the principle of run-off elections, which required an absolute majority of over fifty percent to win any type of election in Gabon, was rolled back to a simple majority process, meaning that a president could now be elected in the Gabonese republic with just five percent of the vote so long as these five percent represented more votes than what the closest challenger received. This was clearly neither the spirit nor the intent of the 1990 National Conference in Gabon. In fact, as Sory Baldé put it, Gabon's National Conference and its aftermath had suddenly become a counter-model to the Beninese one:

> Opposite the Beninese version of the institution that causes fright in palaces now exists a "Gabonese conference technology" that fascinates because it permits "a decompression perfectly mastered by those in office. [Thus] during the year 1990, the oppositions that demand a national conference certainly have in mind the Beninese precedent, but the dictators that are going to end up accepting it in 1991 have in mind the Gabonese model. (...) The principal vector of this national conference model, thus, resides in its ambiguity." (My translation)[45]

What had happened? The answer to this question is to be traced back, first and foremost, to both the National Conference of 1990 itself and the subsequent 1991 constitution.

WHAT TERM LIMITS? BONGO'S ENTRENCHMENT AND THE FAILURE OF GABON'S DEMOCRATIZATION PROCESS

The overarching element that led to the failure of the Gabonese democratization process single-handedly and squarely resides in one prominent shortcoming: The National Conference's lack of sovereignty.[46] What the Beninese did, but that the Gabonese delegates failed to emulate, was to assert the sovereignty of their Conference. The Beninese process made the decisions and resolutions emanating from the delegates compulsory and binding upon all, including the incumbent president. The Gabonese process did not. Gabon's failure to render its National Conference sovereign therefore meant that the Conference's resolutions were not binding and the president retained a great deal of control over the process.[47] Omar Bongo thus had the ability to accept the Conference's resolutions or reject them. This fact alone deeply weakened the Conference's resolutions, thereby making it fundamentally flawed from the outset.[48]

The 1991 constitution, on the other hand, also came with its own lot of flaws. Its design and implementation occurred in a context of extreme euphoria and naïveté that seemingly compromised the ability of the political actors to foresee the inadequacies that would later compromise Gabon's democratization process. In other words, the general state of euphoria that seized not only the political class, but also the entire country in the pre- and post-Conference period led to a certain level of credulity that mistakenly convinced the various political and civil society actors that Omar Bongo had been dealt an irreparable blow. This blow was assumed to have also weakened him politically, which, to many, ensured an outcome that left no doubt. This naïveté may have also been somewhat amplified by the riots of May 23, 1990. These riots erupted following the alleged assassination of Joseph Rendjambé, whose deceased body was found in a hotel room at a time when the National Conference euphorias were still obscuring the thought process of many a politician (Rendjambé was one of the leading opposition figures and a member of Agondjo Okawé's PGP party). These riots almost caused the fall of a Bongo regime that survived only thanks to a French military intervention that, under the guise of protecting the security of the French nationals residing in Gabon, indirectly, and perhaps also directly so, contributed to the restoration of peace and, therefore, the survival of the Bongo regime. Another factor that contributed to this collective delusion was that Omar Bongo was, at the time, perceived as so unpopular that very few analysts saw him surviving the process, let alone surviving the next presidential election. Where the delegates and country should have, for instance, attempted to bar him from running, or maybe tried to subject him to a special one-term limit after the National Conference, no such idea emerged. Such protection mechanisms, it seems, may have appeared as unnecessary at a time when everybody thought that Bongo was essentially done. A fourth element that contributed to this euphoria may have been, paradoxically so, the Beninese National Conference itself. In other words, Benin's experience may have indirectly influenced the Gabonese into thinking that Omar Bongo would also end up giving up, especially after the May riots. As a consequence, the Gabonese political class never thought of inserting into the 1991 constitution the types of failsafe measures that would have prevented or, at least, complicated any attempt to undo the democratic provisions enshrined in the document. Such failsafe measures as, for instance, the imposition of a constitutional moratorium that would have prevented any modification of the term limits for, at least, the next one hundred years, and/or an edict that would have, for example, required the term-limit provisions to be amendable only by a ninety percent majority vote in a referendum, could have gone a long way reducing the risk of reverting back to the old ways of the Bongo system. Yet, it is this very failure to insert failsafe measures into the 1991 constitution that made it possible for Omar Bongo, as early as 1994, to begin the process of dismantling all the provisions that could have barred him from remaining in office beyond 2003.

Although various aspects of the 1991 constitution—some good and some questionable—were amended in 1994 (as a result of the "Paris Accords" of 1994), but also in 1995, 1997, 2000, 2003, 2011, and 2018, the most significant changes to the 1991 constitution under Omar Bongo in the 1991–2009 period came on April 22, 1997[49] and August 19, 2003 when Articles 4, 9, and 11 were amended for the specific purpose of rolling back key democratic features of the fundamental law of 1991.[50] For instance, the first paragraph of Article 11, which was amended as early as April 22, 1997, now stipulated that "the term of office of the President of the Republic begins on the day of his taking the oath and ends upon the expiration of *the seventh year* [emphasis added] following his election" (my translation),[51] as opposed to "the fifth year" previously.[52] This amendment was echoing and completing the one that was inserted in the first paragraph of Article 9, which was also amended on April 22, 1997. This Article now specified that "the President of the Republic is elected for *seven years* [emphasis added] by direct universal suffrage. He is *reelected once* [emphasis added]" (my translation).[53]

The major change here, thus, had to do with the fact that, in the previous version of the constitution, the president was "elected for five years" as opposed to the seven years instituted in the 1997 version.[54] So, here already, the term of office was being extended from five to seven years, which means it was being restored to its pre-National Conference duration. It is worth noting that while this first batch of reversals had indeed achieved the effect of prolonging the duration of the term of office from the 1991 limit of five years to the 1997 limit of seven years, it did not yet, however, undo the overall term-limit infrastructure. The president could still be reelected only once, which effectively limited his/her presidency to a maximum of two consecutive terms of seven years each, hence a maximum possible total of fourteen years in office, as opposed to ten years previously. It is also worth noting here that this initial batch of antidemocratic changes came at a time when a debate over the right of Omar Bongo to run for president again began to heat up. The unresolved and unfinished debates of 1990 and 1991 had thus, ironically, spilled over to 1997. This was because, precisely, 1998 was going to be a presidential election year and, one would suspect, Omar Bongo wanted to give himself some more time in power if he won in 1998. But what these 1997 changes were also aiming for, strategically, had to do with a stratagem that many dictators in Africa had become adept at using to prolong their reigns. The stratagem consisted in simply initiating a constitutional amendment that would "reset the clock" on term limits, thus making the new duration both the new norm and the new beginning. In the specific case of Gabon, Omar Bongo was, in some cunning way, reserving himself the right to argue that 1998 was a new beginning for him since, by changing the length of the term, the constitutional clock on term limits was also, perforce, reset. Based on this argument, a term of five years was not the same as a term of seven years, and so the two contradictory terms could not be counted as part of the same legal or constitutional process. In other words, since the 1991 constitution, technically, defined two consecutive terms of five years each, and not one term of five years and one term of seven years, it was impossible to abide by both constitutions at the same time. And since the regime had a majority in parliament, the change was easily rubberstamped and the amendments promulgated. The 1998 presidential election thus marked the beginning of a presidential term that was now going to last seven years, with the potential for Omar Bongo being reelected for an additional seven years in 2005, at which time he could theoretically change the duration of the term back to five years again in order to, once again, "reset the clock," if he so desired. This "game" could theoretically go on and on, ad infinitum. But while such a stratagem could potentially pave the way for a life presidency, it still comported too much political risk because of the national debates that each such change tended to trigger. It was therefore just a matter of time before the regime came up with a better and simpler idea, an idea that ultimately found substance in the second round of major constitutional changes that intervened in 2003: Omar Bongo simply got rid of the term-limit provisions altogether.

In other words, the second batch of major reversals, as stated earlier, came on August 19, 2003 when, this time, Articles 4 and 9, among others, were affected. The first noticeable change that came out of the 2003 amendments had to do with the voting procedure. Article 9, in the 1991 and 1997 versions of the constitution, stipulated that, "the President of the Republic is elected by an *absolute majority* [emphasis added] of the suffrages expressed. If such a majority is not obtained in the first round, a *second round* [emphasis added] is organized on the Sunday after next. Can compete in the second round only the two candidates who received the most votes. In the second round, the election is won by relative majority" (my translation).[55] This older version of Article 9, as can be seen, essentially provided for the possibility of run-off voting if none of the candidates managed to win an outright, absolute majority in the first round. This provision was, however, split and redistributed between Articles 4 and 9 in the 2003 version of the constitution: Article 4 now specified that "All political elections follow the *one-round* [emphasis added] voting system" (my translation) and Article 9 completed and complemented this provision by stating that "the election is won by the candidate who received *the most votes* [emphasis added]" (my translation).[56] This change essentially meant that a candidate could now win a presidential election in Gabon after receiving only five percent of the suffrages if these five percent represented "the most votes" against candidates who received less than five percent. One can surmise, at this juncture, that Omar Bongo, faced with growing unpopularity, devised this stratagem as a way of securing "easy" victories for himself. The idea behind the stratagem consisted, as practice later confirmed, in "dividing" the opposition by secretly financing several allied candidates who could split the opposition's votes, thereby giving Bongo a relative advantage in a one-round, relative-majority electoral system.

But Article 9 as changed in 2003 contained an additional modification that, basically, sealed Gabon's political fate and definitively crushed the hopes of those who would have wanted to see an end to the Bongo regime. This single article—which now was stipulating that "the President of the Republic is elected for a seven (7) year term by direct universal suffrage. *He can be reelected* [emphasis added]" (my translation)[57]— essentially rolled Gabon's democratic process back to what it was prior to 1991. Whereas the 1997 version of the constitution still used the adverb "once" to indicate a term limit whereby the president could be reelected only one additional time after completing the first term, the 2003 version of the constitution deleted the adverb "once," thus making it possible for the incumbent president to seek reelection ad infinitum. Gabon was now primed for the possibility of being encumbered by the same president for life.

These constitutional moves were, in some canny way, Omar Bongo's response not only to the massive voter defections that had come to typify Gabon's elections over the years but also to the uncertainties arising from the increasingly deteriorating political atmosphere in the country. But, at the same time, these changes naturally paved the way for a presidency for life for Omar Bongo. Ironically, the dictator did end up dying in office in 2009, just four years after he had—fraudulently according to the opposition—won the 2005 election using the 2003 version of the constitution as the basis for his reelection. While Omar Bongo is said to have won the 2005 election with a comfortable, albeit deemed fraudulent score of 79.2% in a context in which voter turnout was only around 20–30% (see Table 3.1), his son was declared a winner in 2009 with just 41.79% of the vote in the context of a 54% abstention rate.[58] The very fact that only 46% of the electorate voted in 2009 and that, of those 46%, only 41.79% voted

Table 3.1 Presidential elections results and turnout, 1993–2016

Presidential elections		
Year	Ali Bongo score (%)	Voter turnout (%)
2016	49.80–50.66	48/57/59.46
2009	41.79	46
	Omar Bongo score (%)	Voter turnout (%)
2005	79.18	20–30
1998	66.88	46
1993	51.18	88.08

Sources Matsiegui (Matsiegui Mboula, *Elections politiques*, 99–100); OIF 1998; OIF 2001; IZF; AFP ("Près de 56% d'abstention pour le premier tour des législatives au Gabon," December 14, 2001, *AFP*, as republished by *Bongo Doit Partir*, accessed October 18, 2007, http://www.bdpgabon.org/articles/categories/politique/EpplFZupFlHEXBWPYI.shtml); Midepani; Diop (Omar Diop, *Partis politiques et processus démocratiques en Afrique noire: Recherches sur les enjeux juridiques et sociologiques du multipartisme dans quelques pays de l'espace francophone* (Paris: Editions Publibook, 2006), 566; see also Omar Diop, "Participation électorale en Afrique noire," in Jean-Pierre Vettovaglia, Jean Du Bois de Gaudusson, Albert Bourgi, and Christine Desouches (eds.), *Prévention des crises et promotion de la paix, Volume 2: Démocratie et Elections dans l'espace francophone* [Bruxelles: Bruylant, 2010], 302–325); France Diplomatie; *L'Union* ("Législatives partielles: Une nouvelle configuration à l'Assemblée nationale," *L'Union*, June 19, 2007, last accessed October 18, 2007, as republished by *BDP-Gabon Nouveau*, http://www.bdpgabon.org/archives/content/view/4762/42/)

for Ali Bongo while the clear majority of 58.21% voted against him, has raised the question of Ali Bongo's legitimacy as the president of Gabon.

But other questions do come to mind, however, that need clarifying. For instance, what other factors, beyond the inability of the 1990 opposition delegates to secure constitutional safeguards, made it so easy for the Omar Bongo regime to undo the 1991 consensus and, thus, pave the way not only for his life presidency but also for the dynastic succession that saw his son so easily succeed him upon his death in 2009? And how do such factors help to explain why Omar Bongo, and later his son, were able to reassert and reconsolidate the stranglehold of the regime over the nation, and this after the dictator had appeared to falter in the early 1990s?

The answers to these questions are rather complex, mostly because of the multitude of factors that could be evoked to explain the very particular idiosyncrasies of Gabon's failed democratic experiment. The various elements that, however, do come into play more prominently in the context of this question range from such obvious nepotistic considerations as Omar Bongo appointing his own mistress (and mother of two of his children), Marie-Madeleine Mborantsuo, to the presidency of the Constitutional Court—thus guaranteeing that all the electoral processes and recriminations would always result in the Court proclaiming the victory of the ruling party and, thus, Omar Bongo himself—to the very intricacies that came to build themselves into the way Omar Bongo managed to indoctrinate the Gabonese elite into believing in the power of money and political appointments. This indoctrination does have a name: political corruption and, therefore, patronage; it also has a process: absence of accountability. Corruption, arbitrariness, and the absence of the rule of law have, thus, in Gabon, resulted in a form of statelessness which has used a heteroclite assortment of tools such as political corruption, electoral fraud, bait-and-switch development projects that never really lead to real development, human rights violations, socioeconomic coercion in the form of employment blackmail, erosion and suppression of political, civil, and press freedoms, and, last but not least, police brutality and military "boogiemanship." All these anachronicities have, in Gabon, contributed to the subjection of the people. They have also led to a stalemate of despair.

The direct result of all these factors is that Gabon's so-called "democracy" has, in reality, built itself into a very paradoxical and very peculiar system over the years. This system constitutes a strange assortment of undemocratic practices asserting themselves within the confines of an undemocratic pluralistic system, practices that have combined with methods of government so anachronistic that the result has been the systemic and systematic violation of human and civil liberties at all levels of the nation's social, cultural, economic, and political life. Yet, the system has also been able to maintain a sufficient, albeit misleading, illusion of democratic plurality. The manifestations of this *trompe-l'oeil* plurality have at times been confused with democratic practice.

While the Gabonese constitution, on paper, does guarantee the right of association as well as freedoms of expression, and laws do exist, on paper, that purport to protect civil and political liberties, combat corruption, and assert the rule of law, the reality is far from the truth: The antidemocratic and coercive methods used by Omar Bongo, but also now his son, to stay in power have, over the years, significantly weakened political opposition and civil society.[59] A strong and hyper-presidency combined with the extreme weakness of the legislative and judiciary branches of government are features that further conspired to enable Omar Bongo to reign relatively unchallenged for forty-two years.[60] The ten years since Ali Bongo took over have seen a similar trend toward further restrictions to, and erosion of, public liberties. Gabon is, thus, essentially, now, a "bananized" failing state.[61]

But there are a number of other subtle elements, many of which intervene at the psychological level, that have also played in favor of the Bongo regime: one of these is a form of voter disaffection that has stemmed from political lassitude, another is time. In other words, because the passing of time has not brought the truly democratic changes that the Gabonese people were expecting, a certain fatigue and discouragement has led to the electorate deserting the voting booth. This desertion, in turn, has naturally advantaged the regime.

As noted previously, Gabon has held five presidential elections since the reinstatement of multiparty politics in 1990. The Bongos have "won" all five presidential contests: Three were won by Omar Bongo himself (1993, 1998, and 2005) and two were won by his son Ali Bongo (2009 and 2016). These "victories" occurred amidst controversy and accusations of massive fraud by both opposition parties and independent observers. Following the first multiparty presidential elections of December 5, 1993, for example, post-electoral violence erupted after Omar Bongo claimed 51% of the vote to declare himself the winner over twelve other candidates. This result led to a political stalemate that was resolved only a year later with the signature of the *Accords de Paris* (Paris Accords) in October

1994 under French mediation. The agreement that was brokered between the regime and opposition leaders provided a framework that, on paper, was supposed to enable such positive advances as more transparency in the electoral process, better voter registration handling, biometric voter ID, the affirmation of the rule of law, security, and stability, and a more asserted freedom of the press, among other demands. However, none of the clauses set forth in the Paris agreements truly found concrete application on the ground. Granted, most of the provisions emanating from the 1994 Paris Accords were inserted into the constitution in 1994 and subsequently promulgated by the Gabonese people in a referendum that was held on July 23, 1995. But, in concrete terms, these provisions were cosmetic in nature and did not bring any real improvement to Gabon's lackluster democratic process. In fact, just two years after this referendum, the regime began to undo the term-limit provisions that would have, at least, guaranteed the possibility of power alternation in Gabon. Without the possibility of power alternation through free and fair elections, the Gabonese democratization process could not thrive.

The disaffection of the electorate and, perhaps, its resignation to the idea that democratic change would never come through the voting booth, thus, became a natural consequence of the democratic deficit that gradually became the norm not only in the 1990–1997 period but also later. This disaffection, in turn, emboldened the regime, comforting it in the belief that the Gabonese people would never take to the streets in any massive way that could affect the regime's ability to perpetuate itself. If anything, political corruption and electoral fraud accentuated and caused the snowball effect of further massive voter defections. The result was the development of a crisis of confidence between the political elite and the Gabonese people that slowly but surely drove the Gabonese people away from the polls over the years.[62]

What Tables 3.1 and 3.2 show, thus, is an interesting correlation between electoral fraud, the impossibility of power alternation via the voting booth, and voter defections not only during the Omar Bongo era but also in the Ali Bongo era. After the high hopes reflected in the 88% voter turnout of the first presidential election of 1993, voter participation went downhill. In subsequent elections under Omar Bongo, voter disaffection reached endemic proportions and the higher the scores obtained by Bongo and his ruling party were, the lower voter turnout became. What this meant was that Omar Bongo's legitimacy as president of Gabon became increasingly undermined, and questioned, due to lack of voter

Table 3.2 Legislative elections results and turnout, 1990–2018

Legislative elections—national assembly

Year	Seats by ruling coalition (PDG and Presidential majority parties)	Independents & others (Usually affiliated with ruling party)	Opposition	Voter turnout (%)
Under Ali Bongo				
2018	115 out of 143 (PDG, 98)	8 (independents)	20	20–59
2011	114 out 120 (PDG, 114)	4	2	34.28
Under Omar Bongo				
2006	102 out of 120 (PDG, 83)	5	13	20–38.90
2001	96 out of 120 (PDG, 86)	2	12	20–38.54
1996	97 out of 120 (PDG, 91)	7	16	35.2
1990	66 out 120	N/A	54	N/A

Sources Matsiegui (Matsiegui Mboula, *Elections politiques*, 99–100); OIF 1998; OIF 2001; IZF; AFP ("Près de 56% d'abstention"); France Diplomatie; *L'Union* ("Législatives partielles: Une nouvelle configuration"; see also "Législatives partielles: Taux de participation toujours en chute libre," *L'Union*, June 20, 2007, http://www.bdpgabon.org/archives/content/view/4757/42/); *Encyclopedia Universalis* ("29 décembre 1996: Gabon. Victoire du parti du président Omar Bongo aux élections législatives," *Encyclopaedia Universalis*, accessed October 6, 2015, http://www.universalis.fr/evenement/29-decembre-1996-victoire-du-parti-du-president-omar-bongo-aux-elections-legislatives/). 2018 Results

turnout. His 2005 score of 79.2%, for example, is built upon the meager 20–30% participation rate that was recorded in the 2005 presidential election. Similar inferences can be surmised from the scores obtained by the ruling party, the PDG, in various parliamentary elections over the same period (see Table 3.2).[63] The trend of electoral fraud, which includes the secret financing of pseudo opposition parties meant to later reinforce the "presidential majority,"[64] seems to have continued under Ali Bongo.

Indeed, two presidential elections and two legislative elections have been held in Gabon since the death of Omar Bongo in 2009. Ali Bongo has directly presided over three of these elections: One presidential election in 2016 and two legislative elections (see results of the 2018 legislative elections in Table 3.2[65]). In the 2009 early election that saw the son succeed his father, only a dismal voter turnout of 46% was recorded.

And these were probably manipulated figures anyway. Nevertheless, Ali Bongo "won" that election with 41.79% of the votes, against Pierre Mamboundou and André Mba Obame, who received 25.64 and 25.33% of the votes respectively. The one-round electoral system that was instituted in 2003, in this case, marvelously paid off for the Bongo regime. In other words, if one, indeed, added up the votes received by Ali Bongo's two main opponents, one would see that the majority of the Gabonese people (51%) actually voted for his opponents. But because the electoral system was now based on a relative majority, one-round voting configuration, Ali Bongo "won," technically.

This "victory," however, was marred by accusations of vote manipulation. In fact, various French sources, including various French government personalities, have attested to the fact that those results may have, in fact, been "reversed" and that the true winner was, in fact, André Mba Obame. According to Olivier Piot,

> ... several inquiries testified that the results had been rigged. In a documentary broadcast on the France 2 TV channel in December 2010, Mr. Michel de Bonnecorse, former Africa advisor to President Jacques Chirac, accredited this version of events (3). A few months later, in February 2011, the WikiLeaks cables confirmed it: "*October 2009, Ali Bongo reverses the count of votes and declares himself president*," wrote the US ambassador to Paris, Mr. Charles Rivkin, in a telegram sent in November 2009 to Secretary of State Hillary Clinton, who immediately advised Mr. Barack Obama not to recognize the victory of Mr. Bongo (4) ... Without success. The US president even received his counterpart in 2011. This January 16, on the set of the show "On n'est pas couché" (France 2), Prime Minister Manuel Valls inadvertently let go that in 2009 Mr. Bongo was not elected "as one would understand it" ...[66]

As expected, Ali Bongo's controversial "win" in 2009 was indeed facilitated by the fact that his father, fearing his own inability to obtain an absolute majority in future elections, changed the constitution in 2003 to allow for an outright victory by relative majority via a unique round of elections. This served Ali Bongo well in 2009 since the official results of the August 30, 2009 election declared him the winner with only 41.73% of the votes, and this after he had inflated vote counts in his provincial fief of Haut-Ogooué. Except that the results had simply been reversed in a way that deprived the alleged real winner, André Mba Obame, of his victory.[67] Thus, under the very eyes of the Gabonese people, the Gabonese republic was being transformed into a quasi-hereditary monarchy.[68] In this monarchical republic, elections were now being transformed into a meaningless formality in which the Bongo clan could decide to ignore with the greatest impunity the real results from the voting booth and proclaim, as they did in 1993 and probably in all subsequent elections, arbitrary results that had nothing to do with how the people actually voted. The turnout seems to have, however, improved slightly in the 2016 presidential election, but the available statistics have been highly unreliable and have ranged from the low end of 48% to the high end of 59.46%. These figures' unreliability was exacerbated by the fact that massive frauds were witnessed that totally compromised any attempt at establishing reliable results. In reality, there was a mathematical impossibility for Ali Bongo to win the 2016 presidential election in Gabon. Fact is that Ali Bongo actually lost the vote not only in the diaspora, but also in seven out of the nine provinces of Gabon, including the provinces of Estuaire (where Libreville, the capital city, resides), Ogooué-Maritime (the oil capital of Gabon) and Woleu-Ntem (reputed to be hostile to the Bongo clan). The regime itself acknowledged this massive loss. In order to secure his fraudulent win, however, Ali Bongo had to concoct himself a Stalinian score in his provincial bastion of Haut-Ogooué. There, a miraculous 99.93% of the people recorded on the electoral ledgers voted. Out of these, of course, 95.46% allegedly voted for him. However, according to the European Union's observer mission, "Without the results from the Haut-Ogooué province, Jean Ping has 59,396 more votes than Ali Bongo Ondimba, with a participation rate of 54.24%. With the results of Haut-Ogooué, Ali Bongo Ondimba leads Jean Ping by 5,597 votes."[69] A clear sign, thus, that without such vote manipulations and the subsequent arbitrary invalidation of unfavorable results in twenty-one stations in the Estuaire province by the Constitutional Court,[70] Ali Bongo would have mathematically lost the election in 2016. The consequence, of course, was that Ali Bongo's very "mother-in-law" and Constitutional Court president Marie-Madeleine Mborantsuo was effectively able to arbitrarily increase his victory from the initial count of 49.80% to a final count 50.66% (see Table 3.1), thus saving Ali Bongo and his regime from a humiliating loss.

No reliable voter participation figures have been published yet for the 2018 legislative election, but various reports have alluded to a turnout that may have been as low as 20%[71] and as high as 59%.[72] In all cases, however, initial reports have alluded to a massive abstention rate in both the first[73] and second rounds[74] that seems to belie the 41% that the government appears to have been pushing. What the massive voter defection statistics provided in Tables 3.1 and 3.2 ultimately suggest, however, is that the Gabonese people, at some point, stopped believing in the credibility of their country's electoral process. This is confirmed in a 2005 report by the regional bureau of the African Development Bank (ADB), which found voter defection to be a problem in Gabon.[75] Most Gabonese, therefore, have simply often chosen to stay home because, as they often put it, "Why vote? The results are always known in advance" and in Gabon, "the Tower of Pisa [Gabon's Constitutional Court] always leans towards on one side."[76] But, at the same time, this disaffection, which itself stems from the Gabonese citizens' increasing state of disillusionment and discouragement, has paradoxically helped the Bongo regime ease the political pressures that have often threatened to destabilize it. It has also enabled it to more comfortably resist the wind of change.

Political corruption and the practice of an excessively clientelist patronage system in Gabon is yet another factor that has influenced the Bongos' ability to resist change while at the same time weakening political opposition in the country. The practice has contaminated virtually all levels of Gabonese society. Omar Bongo, for instance, systematically used the national coffers not only to finance the corruption of his political opponents, but also to reward all those who, in the country, had helped to ensure the survival of the regime in both electoral and non-electoral situations. In fact, as early as 1990, Omar Bongo instituted a system of financing political parties that enshrined his patronage system as a most efficient tool for the preservation of political power. As a way of "aiding" their participation in the 1990 legislative elections, for instance, the government gave each of the 74 still-unrecognized "political parties" that had taken part in the National Conference in March–April 1990 a whopping 20 millions CFA francs (US$34,000) as an election-participation allocation.[77] This practice of *Franc electoral* (electoral Franc, that is, electoral financing), which continued to be the norm in future elections although increasingly with some restrictions, has been used by some political leaders as a way of simply getting easy and free money even when one's party had no real political viability.[78] Omar Bongo, thus, seems to have understood the power that Gabon's oil money conferred upon him and he used this power profusely to reduce his opposition into impotence. Bongo, ultimately, became an expert in the "carrot and stick" game, distributing money to "soften" his staunchest opponents, and while he did so, he would temporarily agree to reforms that, a few years later, he would simply roll back once he felt that the leaders he had corrupted no longer posed a threat. Omar Bongo had apparently understood that a corrupt opposition would become a weak opposition and a weak opposition, in essence, could not mount the types of sustained protests that could force the regime to democratize. A case in point was his rumored allocation of 11.3 billion CFA francs (US$19.4 million) to Pierre Mamboundou—leader of the *Union du Peuple Gabonais* (UPG) party and the country's main opposition figure for the 1998–2009 period—on the pretext that he was helping him with a program aimed at developing Ndendé, Mamboundou's hometown located in the south of Gabon. But, as was suggested in an AFP release of July 2, 2007, most Gabonese suspected that the monies may have been disbursed to secure the opponent's abandonment of his 2005 electoral victory claim as well as his long-standing radical political stance.[79] With such strategies, that is, when he did not simply appoint his opponents to ministerial positions in the government, such as happened with virtually all the leaders of the splintered branches of the historical MORENA between 1990 and 2009, Omar Bongo concentrated on instigating a crisis of confidence between the opposition leaders and their militants. This subterfuge, in turn, affected their credibility and, therefore, their ability to mobilize for change. In some cunning way, Omar Bongo understood that the fact that he himself and his regime had lost the confidence of the people did not mean he could not discredit the opposition and lead to a crisis of legitimacy for both camps. In the long run, this situation was always bound to benefit the regime and ensure its longevity.

The distribution of food, t-shirts, monetary, and material gifts has also fueled political corruption in the direction of the populations themselves. This practice became so pronounced and pervasive over the years that both the IMF and the World Bank had a hard time getting Gabon under Omar Bongo to stick with the requirements of the structural adjustment programs negotiated with the international banking institutions. In a 1999 report to the Permanent Subcommittee on Investigations of the Committee on Governmental Affairs of the United States Senate, the IMF noted that "Gabon was spending money in ways not specified in its official budget and that $62 million of these 'extrabudgetary expenditures' in

1997 and 1998 had caused the IMF to cut off further loans to the country pending an independent review of its spending."[80] Jan-Peter Olters, et al. of the IMF further revealed the devastating consequences that the regime's tendency to use the national treasury as a source of electoral funds during presidential elections had on capital spending:

> Despite an abundance of fiscal resources through the years, Gabon has to date had little success in raising growth and reducing poverty. Real per capita non-oil growth has been negative in every year from 1998 through 2003 and has been close to zero since then. This poor performance is particularly surprising given large budgetary appropriations for the public investment program (PIP). Over the last 15 years, Gabon's public investment program has averaged 5 percent of GDP. Capital spending exceeded 10 percent of GDP in the late 1990s during presidential elections.[81]

This exponential increase in spending at election time was directly related to the political corruption stemming from the regime's need to finance its electoral campaigns as well as its bait-and-switch development projects. In the context of these endeavors, poorly planned projects were launched that, officially, aimed at bringing much needed development to the nine provinces of the country. But the initiatives were either abandoned soon after the election was over or simply stopped midway altogether. This is because the regime had developed cunning bait-and-switch strategies that aimed at launching development projects at election time as a means of luring the electorate into voting for Omar Bongo and his cronies. But once the election was over, the projects were forgotten and abandoned. At other times, the funds allocated to various projects would simply "vanish" into complex networks of misappropriation. Such was the case with the notorious *Fêtes tournantes* (Rotating Feasts) projects initiated by Omar Bongo in 2002.[82] These "fêtes," alongside other factors such as electoral fraud and the financing of political parties by the government—some of which were fabricated by the regime itself as a way of manufacturing "plurality" and the apparent, therefore misleading, "credibility" of the electoral process—simply became conduits for political corruption in Gabon.[83] As a result, billions of government monies ended up, over the years, lost into the vast networks of failed "investments" and outright misappropriations. And with no checks and balances as to how these monies were spent and for what purposes, these types of dubious government investments could only be seen as subtle misappropriation and corruption strategies. Over time, with no real concrete results seeming to emanate from the *Fêtes tournantes* program, many Gabonese ended up considering the whole thing to be an elaborate government sham, and scam.[84] This explains why the *Fêtes tournantes* project, whose purpose was to inject a whopping 25 billion CFA francs (US$43 million) into one or two provincial economies each year, failed to deliver the promised development.[85] In fact, an audit published in 2011 did reveal the extent of the disaster for the 2005, 2006, 2007, and 2008 periods: The *Fêtes tournantes* ended up benefiting only members of the Bongo regime themselves.[86] Most had simply used the projects attached to the "fêtes" as fronts that allowed them to engage in massive misappropriations schemes. Even after the IMF strongly recommended that the Gabonese government put an end to these *Fêtes tournantes* and, additionally, asked that in "the 2007 budget the fêtes tournantes [be] folded into the PIP [public investment program],"[87] Omar Bongo did not yield. In fact, after a brief period of hesitation, he incorrigibly announced that the *Fêtes tournantes* would continue. He did go ahead and organize one on August 17, 2007 on the occasion of the nation's 47th independence anniversary. Yet, according to *L'Union*, the government's own newspaper, the *Fêtes tournantes* programs had, by then, already swallowed up a whopping 310 billion CFA francs (US$535 million) in just five years,[88] without any real sign of durable development emerging in any of the provinces that had been targeted for these investments.

The Omar Bongo regime also developed a weapon in the form of socioeconomic coercion and pauperization. Various forms of pressures, intimidations, oppressions, and repressions by the regime made it virtually impossible for most politically "dangerous" Gabonese to hold a job in the government or in the private sector while remaining visible and vocal opponents to the Omar Bongo regime. The prospect of losing one's job led to many Gabonese preferring to avoid open opposition to the Bongo regime altogether, for fear of becoming *fichés* (having a political record with the repressive Gabonese secret service). This situation basically amounted to a strategy of socioeconomic and psychological terror that became so pervasive that it indeed managed to keep many Gabonese in check politically. It also discouraged from diasporic political engagement and activism the students who relied on government-sponsored scholarships abroad. The strategy of the regime therefore consisted in building, around any person openly engaged in opposition politics, a precarious environment that would eventually bring such persons to "better sentiments" once their ability to earn a living or provide for their families became irremediably compromised. One such victim of the system was Grégory Ngbwa Mintsa, a Gabonese activist who was well known nationally and internationally as one of the leaders of Gabonese civil society. He had indeed reported that his salary had been cut by Omar Bongo in a bid to punish him not only for his radical opposition but also for his joining a Transparency International lawsuit against the despot in 2008.[89] He allegedly remained without a salary until his death from a cancer of the liver on April 10, 2014.[90] Many in Gabon were subjected to the same treatment.

In the end, because of the inability of Gabonese citizens to engage in credible opposition politics without being confined to precarity and pauperization, they have often been unable to mount a serious threat or challenge to the despotic supremacy of Omar Bongo's regime. As a result, Gabonese politics have, as the Gabonese like to put it, turned into a mere *mangeoire* (eatery), that is, a system which everybody understands is impossible to change or reform, but which one nevertheless enters for the sole purpose of getting to "eat" one's share like everybody else. Better yet, many Gabonese have engaged in "auction politics," that is, a method whereby a Gabonese with some name recognition ups the antics by declaring radical opposition to the Bongo regime as a way of calling attention to himself and getting noticed, but with the firm intention of eventually selling his "silence" or public "regrets" to the dictator. Such was the case with now defunct Pastor Ernest Tomo who announced his candidacy for president with great pump in 2005 as an opponent to Omar Bongo, just to "wake up" one day with a prophetic message that God had given him in some dream, a message that told him it was useless for him to continue his bid for president because he, God, had already decided that Bongo will win. Opposing Bongo, therefore, was tantamount to opposing God himself, pastor Tomo argued.[91] A rumor has it that pastor Tomo may have secretly received a few billion CFA francs for this "prophecy." These types of behaviors have naturally given birth to a pervasive and rampant culture of political corruption in Gabon.

Investing so much of Gabon's wealth on its political survival was bound to have a negative impact on the overall ability of the regime to govern effectively. It would seem that the regime invested much more of its time and effort artificially buying its way out of political collapse than initiating productive and sustainable development policies. While the political evolution of Gabon did enable Omar Bongo to stay in power for forty-two years without discontinuity, this longevity had the adverse effect of weakening the powers of the state while reinforcing the arbitrary powers of the presidency. This situation, in turn, undermined all efforts aimed at asserting the rule of law and promoting responsible management in a way that could lead to sustained economic growth and progress. Gabon's apparent political stability has therefore always been artificial, misleading, and paradoxical. Underneath the surface, the country under Omar Bongo was actually always ruled by a ruthless mafia state in which corruption, the deficit in the rule of law, and the absence of sustainable democracy compromised the ability of the government to effectively operate in a transparent, responsible, and accountable manner. Under Omar Bongo,[92] as well as later under Ali Bongo,[93] Gabon has continued to vegetate on the verge of total collapse.[94]

If anything, the situation of Gabon has worsened, especially with the debt level now hitting 50% of the country's GDP and debt service increasing by 190% according to the IMF.[95] On the political front, Ali Bongo has tightened his grip. His unilateral amendment of the constitution by decree in 2011 began the process of turning him into a hyper-president. With the amendments of 2018[96], he became a monarchical president who, as a consequence, could no longer be tried for crimes he may have committed before, during, and after his presidency.[97] And while the 2018 amendments to the constitution brought back the two-round, run-off electoral system that had been abolished in 2003, they left untouched the provisions that allow Ali Bongo, just like his father before him, to continue to run for reelection for life, with no term limits to stop him. As such, Ali Bongo has, in his own way, reinforced the dictatorial tendencies of the Bongo clan. It is therefore an implicit contention of this paper that, today, Gabon's political and socioeconomic landscape presents, as can be seen in so many other African countries with aborted democracies, a number of characteristics that are consistent with those of a failing, if not an already-failed state. Dictatorship, corruption, human right abuses, and rampant and ruthless criminality have simply been too pervasive in Gabon and, thus, have led to the irrecoverable inability of the Bongo regime to create an atmosphere conducive to sustainable development in a context effectively supported by sound democratic institutions. This situation, ultimately, has led to the belief that nothing good will happen in

Gabon so long as the Bongo family is in power and that only a popular revolution such as happened in Tunisia or Burkina Faso could bring about the change that the Gabonese people are seeking.

Conclusion

What we have ultimately been able to establish in this study of Gabon's failed democratic experiment is that it is through a savant dosage of both electoral fraud and constitutional manipulation that Omar Bongo was able to prolong his regime's lifespan. His ability to manipulate the constitution in ways specifically tailored to both his person and his parliamentary majorities was a determining factor. The controversial constitutional amendments voted into law on August 19, 2003 therefore had the dual effect of allowing him to recover politically while reinforcing the powers of the presidency that had been taken away from him in the original 1991 constitution. This allowed him, now that he felt unshackled by term limits, to also regain the ability to exercise coercive control not only over the legislative and judicial branches but also over the whole state apparatus. This coercive control often took the form of political and economic intimidation, nepotism, and political corruption. The combination of all these factors may have ultimately had a "pacifying" effect on the populace which allowed the regime under Omar Bongo to continue in all impunity to empty state coffers to "win" elections, lead the high life, and subdue the dictator's political opponents. But these same factors also ruined the country economically and permanently brought it to the brink of bankruptcy. Such was the ultimate cost of removing the term limits that could have allowed Gabon to regenerate itself through new generations of leaders with new ideas on how to modernize the country and lead it to a sustained prosperity that would be supported by truly democratic institutions.

Whether the Gabonese people will, someday, be able to emulate the revolutionary experiences of countries such as Benin, Tunisia, and Burkina Faso in a way that would allow them to successfully put an end to their plight remains to be seen. And so while the political debate in Gabon in the 1990–2009 period may have indeed revolved around the naïve expectation that Omar Bongo would willingly, as Mathieu Kérékou had done for Benin, engage the country on a peaceful path toward consensual democracy, the debate awaiting the Gabonese people under Ali Bongo will ultimately revolve around their ability to come to the crude realization that the only way for democracy to prevail in the country may well end up hinging upon their own willingness to impose the democratic institutions they seek via what I call the "democratic force of the street." In view of the political system that Omar Bongo left behind, a system that has been hyper-presidentialized and monarchized by Ali Bongo over the past 10 years, they probably have no choice.

A number of doubts, however, do make a change via popular insurrection in Gabon almost illusory in view of the political indolence that seems to have become the nature of the Gabonese populace. These doubts are clearly supported by recent developments. One such development was when, on October 26, 2018, Ali Bongo experienced a stroke in Riyadh, Saudi Arabia's capital.[98] He was hospitalized in total opacity outside of the country with no real clarity as to what he was really suffering from.[99] In addition, no photos of him on his hospital bed in Riyadh or during his transfer from Saudi Arabia to Morocco were released, which led to widespread speculations and rumors that he may have, in fact, died.[100] Yet, despite a prolonged absence that left the country leaderless until March 2019 and in utter confusion as to who was actually ruling it, no one in Gabon's opposition seized this opportunity to force an ouster that could have ridden the country of the Bongo dynasty once and for all. Another discouraging development came on January 2019 when five young soldiers from the presidential guard attempted an improvised coup that was met with total popular indifference. The coup failed within hours.

Worse still, in order to give Ali Bongo time to recover from his illness, the Constitutional Court itself felt obligated to violate the constitution. Not only did the high court circumvent the mandated transition that Article 13 of the constitution is supposed to trigger to prevent situations of power vacuum, it also in November 2018 arbitrarily and illegally inserted into the constitution a provisional clause that provided for a temporary indisposition of the president where the constitution as written never defined such a clause.[101] Here too, no political leader in Gabon's opposition dared to challenge the arbitrariness of the measure and lead the people to liberation. Compare this to Burkina Faso where the mere intent by dictator Blaise Compaoré to modify an article of the constitution that would have allowed him to prolong his rule triggered a revolution that led to his ouster by the people in a matter of days in 2014.[102] The Gabonese people, as someone put it to me recently, are so indolent that they could be led even by the cadaver of Ali Bongo.

Ali Bongo eventually returned to Gabon to assume office in March 2019, but, in view of what now looked like a heavy physical handicap resulting from his Riyadh stroke and months of care in Morocco hospitals, doubts have continued to linger as to his ability to return to full mental and physical capacity. But the very fact that the country remained surprisingly calm not only before and since Ali Bongo's return but also after young presidential guard soldiers attempted a failed coup in January 2019—and this after the Constitutional Court itself butchered the constitution in November 2018 to accomplish what in the eyes of the opposition amounted to a "constitutional coup"[103]—is, perhaps, a sign that the Bongo dynasty may still have, as the French often say, "beautiful days ahead of it," unless the people finally decide to wake up in order to thwart the dynastic ambitions of the Bongo clan, once and for all.

Notes

1. "Gabon: Constitution du 26 mars 1991" (Initial version), *Digithèque MJP*, accessed October 2, 2015, http://mjp.univ-perp.fr/constit/ga1991i.htm.
2. Philippe Bernard, "Omar Bongo, président du Gabon," *Le Monde*, June 9, 2009, accessed October 5, 2015, http://www.lemonde.fr/afrique/article/2009/06/09/omar-bongo-president-du-gabon_1204722_3212.html.
3. Central Intelligence Agency, "Introduction: Gabon," *The World Factbook*, accessed October 5, 2015, https://www.cia.gov/library/publications/the-world-factbook/geos/gb.html#Intro.
4. Sory Baldé, *La convergence des modèles constitutionnels: études de cas en Afrique subsaharienne* (Paris: Editions Publibooks, 2011), 132–133.
5. Daniel Mengara and Jack Mangala, "Digne fils de son père: Joseph Kabila, Faure Eyadema et Ali Bongo: Réflexions sur les récentes successions filiales du pouvoir en Afrique," Joint paper presented at the annual meeting of the Canadian Association of African Studies (CAAS), Carleton University, Ottawa, Canada, May 5–7, 2010.
6. Andy Moses, *La République monarchique* (Paris: EdiLivres, 2015).
7. Pierre Péan, *Affaires africaines* (Paris: Fayard, 1983); *L'argent noir* (Paris: Fayard, 1988); *L'Homme de l'ombre: éléments d'enquête autour de Jacques Foccart, l'homme le plus mystérieux et le plus puissant de la Ve République* (Paris: Fayard, 1990); *Nouvelles affaires africaines: Mensonges et Pillages au Gabon* (Paris: Fayard, 2014).
8. Antoine Glaser and Stephen Smith, *Comment la France a perdu l'Afrique* (Paris: Calmann-Lévy, 2005).

9. François-Xavier Verschave, *La Françafrique: Le plus long scandale de la République* (Paris: Stock, 1998; reprint Paris: Stock, 1999); see also François-Xavier Verschave, *Noir silence: Qui arrêtera la Françafrique?* (Paris: Les Arènes, 2000).
10. The "Françafrique" is France's neocolonialist system, which François-Xavier Verschave expounds greatly upon in his seminal *La Françafrique: Le plus long scandale de la République*; as his title indicates, he sees the Françafrique system as the longest scandal of the [French] Republic, a scandal built upon a criminal system put into place toward the end of the 1950s by Charles de Gaulle and Jacques Foccart. This system has resulted not only in France continuing to determine the political and economic course of its former colonies even after independence, but also in very ruinous and bloody situations for Francophone African countries, situations that have France's commandeering hand all over them. He defines it, specifically, as "a nebula of economic, political and military actors in France as well as in Africa who are organized into networks and lobbying groups bent on appropriating two sources of funds: natural resources and public development aid. The logic of this drain is to prevent any sort of initiative outside of the circle of the initiates. This system, which is self-regulating, recycles itself into criminalization. It is naturally hostile to democracy" (My translation, p. 175).
11. Philippe Gaillard, *Foccart Parle: Entretiens avec Philippe Gaillard*, vol. 1 (Paris: Fayard/Jeune Afrique, 1995).
12. Philippe Bernard, "Omar Bongo, président du Gabon"; see also Yves-Laurent Ngoma, "Léon Mba le président qui ne voulait pas de l'indépendance du Gabon," *RFI*, August 16, 2010, last modified August 23, 2010, accessed October 5, 2015, http://www.rfi.fr/afrique/20100816-leon-mba-le-president-voulait-pas-independance-gabon.
13. Gaillard, *Foccart parle*, 275–281.
14. "Paul-Marie YEMBIT, homme politique (1917–1978): De la province au palais," *L'Union*, January 1, 1999, accessed September 9, 2017, http://www.union.sonapresse.com/personnalites-gabonaises/paul-marie-yembit-homme-politique-1917-1978-de-la-province-au-palais-12947.
15. Ngoma, "Léon Mba"; Gaillard, *Foccart parle*, 275–281.
16. Moïse N'Solé Biteghe, *Echec aux militaires au Gabon en 1964* (Paris: Editions Chaka, 1990), 46.
17. Ngoma, "Léon Mba."
18. N'Solé Bitegue, *Echec aux militaires*.
19. Ngoma, "Léon Mba"; Gaillard, *Foccart parle*, 275–281.
20. Daniel Mengara, "Gabon and the Enduring Legacies of France's Françafrique System in Francophone Africa," *EuropeNow* 15 (March 2018), https://www.europenowjournal.org/2018/02/28/sarko-viens-

chercher-ali-gabon-and-the-enduring-legacies-of-frances-francafrique-system-in-francophone-africa/.
21. Omar Bongo and Airy Routier, *Blanc comme nègre: Entretien avec Airy Routier* (Paris: Grasset, 2001).
22. Martin Edzodzomo-Ela, *Mon projet pour le Gabon: Comment redresser un pays ruiné par trois décennies de mauvaise gestion* (Paris: Karthala, 2000), 186.
23. Sven Wunder, *Quand le Syndrome Néerlandais rencontre la French Connection: Pétrole, Macroéconomie et Forêts au Gabon* (Bogor Barat [Indonesia]: Center for International Forestry Research, 2003), 15–21.
24. Edzodzomo-Ela, *Mon projet*, 186.
25. Banque Africaine de Développement and OCDE, *Perspectives économiques en Afrique, 2001/2002* (Paris: OCDE, 2002), 366.
26. Caroline Damour, Michael Marx and Gilles de Pas, *Evaluation de la coopération française dans le secteur santé au Gabon (1990–2001)* (Paris: Direction Générale de la Coopération et du Développement, Ministère des affaires étrangères, 2002), 13, accessed October 5, 2015, http://www.diplomatie.gouv.fr/fr/IMG/pdf/Evaluation_de_la_cooperation_francaise_dans_le_secteur_sante_au_Gabon.pdf.
27. Damour, Marx and de Pas, 13.
28. Aristide Mba, "Gaspillages et gabégies au Gabon," *Le Monde diplomatique* (April 1990): 10, accessed October 5, 2015, https://www.monde-diplomatique.fr/1990/04/MBA/42516.
29. "Quarante ans de pouvoir," *RFI*, May 22, 2009, accessed October 5, 2015, http://www1.rfi.fr/actufr/articles/113/article_81266.asp.
30. Robert Buijtenhuijs, *La Conférence nationale souveraine du Tchad: Un essai d'histoire immédiate* (Paris: Karthala, 1993).
31. F. Eboussi Boulaga, *Les Conférences nationales en Afrique noire: Une affaire à suivre* (Paris: Karthala, 2009).
32. Pearl T. Robinson, "The National Conference Phenomenon in Francophone Africa," *Comparative Studies in Society and History* 36, no. 3 (July 1994): 575–610.
33. Robinson, "National Conference," 576.
34. "Quarante ans de pouvoir."
35. Philippe David, *Le Bénin* (Paris: Karthala, 1998), 69–70.
36. Baldé, *Convergence*, 131.
37. Daniel Mengara, *Le Gabon en danger - Du devoir de réforme au devoir de violence: Autopsie d'une République monarchique "bananisée" en état de déliquescence* (Paris: L'Harmattan, 2019).
38. Wilson-André Ndombet, *Renouveau démocratique et pouvoir au Gabon (1990–1993)* (Paris: Karthala, 2009).
39. Baldé, *Convergence*, 131.

40. Baldé, 129; note also that in 1991 Mba Abessole changed his party's name again and called it *Rassemblement National des Bûcherons* (RNB), which, following another split in 1998, became *Rassemblement National des Bûcherons*-Rassemblement pour le Gabon (RNB-RPG) following a split with Professor Pierre-André Kombila—who led the dissident faction—before, again, becoming simply Rassemblement pour le Gabon (RPG) in 2000.
41. Ndombet, *Renouveau démocratique*, 120.
42. Ndombet, 146.
43. Paul Mba Abessole, *Discours lors de la plénière de la Conférence Nationale*, April 4, 1990.
44. Pierre Péan, *Nouvelles Affaires Africaines*, 77–92.
45. Baldé, *Convergence*, 132.
46. Robinson, "National Conference," 579–580.
47. Robinson, 580.
48. Ndombet, *Renouveau démocratique*, 112.
49. "Gabon: Constitution du 26 mars 1991" (2000 version), *Digithèque MJP*, accessed October 2, 2015, http://mjp.univ-perp.fr/constit/ga2000v.htm.
50. "Constitution de la République gabonaise," *Assemblé Nationale Gabonaise*, last modified March 6, 2014, accessed October 2, 2015, http://www.assemblee-nationale.ga/object.getObject.do?id=188.
51. "Gabon: Constitution du 26 mars 1991" (2000 version).
52. "Gabon: Constitution du 26 mars 1991" (Initial version).
53. "Gabon: Constitution du 26 mars 1991" (2000 version).
54. "Gabon: Constitution du 26 mars 1991" (Initial version).
55. "Gabon: Constitution du 26 mars 1991" (Initial version).
56. "Constitution de la République gabonaise," *The World Bank*, accessed October 2, 2015, http://publicofficialsfinancialdisclosure.worldbank.org/sites/fdl/files/assets/law-library-files/Gabon_Constitution_1991_(as%20amended%202003)_fr.pdf.
57. "Constitution de la République gabonaise."
58. Lévi Martial Midepani, "Pratiques électorales et reproduction oligarchique au Gabon. Analyses à partir des élections législatives de 2006," *Politique africaine* 115 (March 2009): 47–65, par. 48, accessed October 2, 2015, http://www.cairn.info/revue-politique-africaine-2009-3-page-47.htm, https://doi.org/10.3917/polaf.115.0047.
59. Ndombet, *Renouveau démocratique*, 113–114, 122–128, 164–166, 171–172.
60. Ndombet, 156–160.
61. Daniel Mengara, *Le Gabon en danger*.
62. Fortuné Matsiegui Mboula, *Les Elections politiques au Gabon de 1990 à 2011* (Paris: L'Harmattan, 2015), 97.

63. See also "Gabon/Législatives: L'appel au boycott n'a pas mobilisé grand-monde," *AFP*, December 23, 2011, as republished by Bongo Doit Partir, accessed October 6, 2015, http://www.bdpgabon.org/articles/2011/12/23/gabonlegislatives-lappel-au-boycott-na-pas-mobilise-grand-monde/.
64. "Élections 2018: les sigles inconnus sont dans la place," *Gabon Review*, 21 septembre 2018, consulté le 25 septembre 2018, http://gabonreview.com/blog/elections-2018-les-sigles-inconnus-sont-dans-la-place/.
65. "Second tour des législatives: La CGE a sorti les résultats," *Le Défi Gabon*, October 30, 2018, accessed November 25, 2018, http://ledefigabon.com/2018/10/30/elections-legislatives/.
66. Olivier Piot, "Au Gabon, la mécanique du népotisme s'enraye," *Le Monde diplomatique* (octobre 2016): 4, accessed October 25, 2017, https://www.monde-diplomatique.fr/2016/10/PIOT/56406.
67. Péan, *Nouvelles affaires*, 167–169.
68. Andy Moses, *La République monarchique* (Paris: EdiLivres, 2015).
69. Mission d'observation électorale de l'Union européenne au Gabon, *Rapport final - République gabonaise: Election présidentielle 27 août 2016*, December 12, 2016: 31, accessed June 4, 2017, https://eeas.europa.eu/sites/eeas/files/gabon_moe_rapport_final_0.pdf.
70. "Gabon: 'Tournons la page' satisfait de la publication du rapport de l'OIF sur la présidentielle," *VOA*, June 22, 2017, accessed December 1, 2018, https://www.voaafrique.com/a/gabon-tournons-la-page-satisfait-de-la-publication-du-rapport-de-l-oif-sur-la-presidentielle/3911989.html.
71. "Gabon-Elections: Taux de participation faible, percée de l'UN dans le nord, le PDG résiste à Mouila," *Africa Post News*, October 6, 2018, accessed December 1, 2018, https://www.africapostnews.com/gabon-elections-taux-de-participation-faible-percee-de-lun-dans-le-nord-le-pdg-resiste-a-mouila/.
72. "Élections - Gabon: ce que cache le 'raz-de-marée' en faveur du pouvoir," *Le Point*, October 14, 2018, accessed December 1, 2018, http://afrique.lepoint.fr/actualites/elections-gabon-ce-que-cache-le-raz-de-maree-en-faveur-du-pouvoir-14-10-2018-2262894_2365.php.
73. "Législatives au Gabon: forte abstention et 'raz-de-marée' pour le parti au pouvoir, *Jeune Afrique* with AFP, October 8, 2018, accessed December 1, 2018, https://www.jeuneafrique.com/641601/politique/legislatives-au-gabon-forte-abstention-et-raz-de-maree-pour-le-parti-au-pouvoir/.
74. "Législatives 2018: Vers un taux d'abstention record," *Gabon Review*, October 28, 2018, accessed December 1, 2018, http://gabonreview.com/blog/legislatives-2018-vers-un-taux-dabstention-record/.

75. Banque Africaine de Développement, *République Gabonaise: Profil de gouvernance-pays*, African Development Bank Group, October 2005, accessed October 6, 2015, http://www.afdb.org/fileadmin/uploads/afdb/Documents/Project-and-Operations/ADB-BD-IF-2005-229-FR-GABON-PROFIL-GOUV-PAYS-17-OCT-2005-FINAL.PDF.
76. "Gabon: des voix s'élèvent contre la présidente de la Cour constitutionnelle," *TV5 Monde*, November 17, 2018, accessed December 1, 2018, https://information.tv5monde.com/afrique/gabon-des-voix-s-elevent-contre-la-presidente-de-la-cour-constitutionnelle-271761.
77. Ndombet, *Renouveau démocratique*, 114, 126.
78. Banque Africaine de Développement, *République Gabonaise: Profil*.
79. "Gabon: 'Les milliards de Mamboundou,' ou l'embarras de l'opposant radical," July 2, 2007, *AFP*, as republished by Bongo Doit Partir, accessed October 18, 2007, http://www.bdpgabon.org/archives/content/view/4815/72/.
80. Permanent Subcommittee on Investigations, *Private Banking and Money Laundering: A Case Study of Opportunities and Vulnerabilities, United States Senate*, November 9–10, 1999, accessed October 18, 2007, http://frwebgate.access.gpo.gov/cgi-bin/getdoc.cgi?dbname=106_senate_hearings&docid=f:61699.pdf.
81. Jan-Peter Olters et al., *Gabon: Selected Issues*, June 20, 2006 (Washington, DC: International Monetary Fund, 2006), 54, accessed October 23, 2007, http://www.imf.org/external/pubs/ft/scr/2006/cr06232.pdf.
82. "Gabon: Des fêtes tournantes pour le développement de l'arrière-pays," *PANA*, August 22, 2002, accessed October 3, 2015, http://www.panapress.com/Gabon---des-fetes-tournantes-pour-le-developpement-de-l-arriere-pays--13-603254-17-lang4-index.html.
83. Jan-Peter Olters et al., *Gabon: Selected Issues*, 58.
84. Fred Ntoutoume, "Les fêtes tournantes de l'Indépendance au Gabon: une escroquerie à l'échelle nationale?" *Bongo Doit Partir*, August 26, 2008, accessed October 3, 2015, http://www.bdpgabon.org/articles/2008/08/26/les-fetes-tournantes-de-lindependance-au-gabon-une-escroquerie-a-lechelle-nationale-par-fred-ntoutoume/.
85. Jan-Peter Olters et al., *Gabon: Selected Issues*, 58.
86. "Gabon: BGFIBank et les 26 milliards des Fêtes tournantes," *GabonEco*, July 18, 2011, accessed October 3, 2015, http://www.gaboneco.com/nouvelles_africaines_23123.html.
87. Jan-Peter Olters et al., *Gabon: Selected Issues*, 59.
88. "Fêtes tournantes: une formule à revoir?" *L'Union*, June 25, 2005, as republished by Internet Gabon, accessed October 18, 2007, http://www.internetgabon.com/Actualites/Actus-Juin2007/m-actu-25062007c.htm.

89. "Hommage à Grégory Ngbwa Mintsa," *Transparency International*, April 16, 2014, accessed October 3, 2015, http://www.transparency.org/news/feature/hommage_a_gregory_ngbwa_mintsa/.
90. "Décès de l'activiste gabonais Grégory Ngbwa Mintsa," *RFI*, April 11, 2014, accessed October 2, 2015, http://www.rfi.fr/afrique/20140411-deces-activiste-gabonais-gregory-ngbwa-mintsa/.
91. "Le pasteur Ernest Tomo se retire de la présidentielle," *PANA*, October 23, 2005, as republished by Bongo Doit Partir, accessed October 23, 2007, http://www.bdpgabon.org/archives/content/view/2390/72/.
92. "Gabon: En cessation de paiement…" *La Lettre du Continent* 323 (February 18, 1999).
93. "Finances de l'Etat: le Gabon en récession, en cessation de paiement ou insolvable?" *Gabon Review*, October 13, 2014, accessed December 1, 2018, http://gabonreview.com/blog/finances-letat-gabon-en-recession-en-cessation-paiement-insolvable/.
94. Bertrand Feumetio, *Le Gabon, un pays si riche… mais très pauvre: Décryptage d'un authentique paradoxe socio-économique* (Paris: Publibook, 2008).
95. Mays Mouissi, "Gabon: La dette transmise aux générations futures," *MaysMouissi.com*, April 13, 2016, last updated June 26, 2018, accessed August 12, 2018, https://www.mays-mouissi.com/2016/04/13/gabon-reporter-dette-generations-futures/.
96. "Gabon: la révision constitutionnelle adoptée par le Congrès," *Jeune Afrique*, January 11, 2018, accessed January 12, 2018, http://www.jeuneafrique.com/509042/politique/gabon-la-revision-constitutionnelle-adopte-par-le-congres/.
97. "Gabon: que pensez-vous des mesures proposées dans la réforme de la Constitution?" *Jeune Afrique*, November 17, 2017, accessed August 8, 2017, https://www.jeuneafrique.com/494064/politique/gabon-que-pensez-vous-des-mesures-proposees-dans-la-reforme-de-la-constitution/.
98. "Le président gabonais Ali Bongo hospitalisé en Arabie saoudite," *RFI*, October 26, 2018, last modified October 27, 2018, accessed December 1, 2018, http://www.rfi.fr/afrique/20181026-le-president-gabonais-ali-bongo-hospitalise-arabie-saoudite.
99. "Ali Bongo poursuit sa convalescence au Maroc," *AFP*, November 29, 2018, accessed December 1, 2018, https://www.voaafrique.com/a/gabon-le-president-ali-bongo-a-quitte-ryad/4679293.html.
100. "La presse lue par l'Agitateur: La santé d'Ali Bongo, entre rumeurs de vie et de mort!" *GabonEco*, November 2, 2018, accessed December 1, 2018, http://www.gaboneco.com/la-presse-lue-par-l-agitateur-la-sante-d-ali-bongo-entre-rumeurs-de-vie-et-de.html.
101. "La Constitution modifiée pour pallier l'absence du président malade au Gabon," *VOA*, November 15, 2018, accessed December

1, 2018, https://www.voaafrique.com/a/la-constitution-modifiée-pour-pallier-l-absence-du-président-malade-au-gabon/4659921.html.
102. "La crise au Burkina Faso en trois questions," *Libération* with AFP, October 31, 2014, accessed December 1, 2018, https://www.liberation.fr/planete/2014/10/31/la-crise-au-burkina-faso-en-quatre-questions_1133176.
103. "Modification de la Constitution au Gabon: l'opposition dénonce 'un coup de force'," *TV5 Monde*, November 15, 2018, accessed December 1, 2018, https://information.tv5monde.com/afrique/modification-de-la-constitution-au-gabon-l-opposition-denonce-un-coup-de-force-271423.

CHAPTER 4

Presidential Term Limits in Uganda: Do Elections Provide an Avenue for Alternate Power Succession?

Sabiti Makara

Introduction

Uganda stands out as a country which has not known democracy for the whole of its existence since colonial rule. It has suffered dictatorial and authoritarian regimes. Since its independence from the British colonial masters in 1962, the country has had eight heads of state of which only the current one was directly elected.[1] The Ugandan state has been dominated by militant politics, absence of elections or sham elections, and lack of an opportunity for the population to witness a peaceful hand-over of power from one president to another.[2] The military has been and remains a key factor in Ugandan politics. In 1966 Milton Obote, the then Prime Minister used the army to overthrow Edward Mutesa, the first titular head of state of Uganda. Obote too was overthrown by his own army commander Idi Amin Dada in 1971. In 1979 a combined force of Uganda exiles and the Tanzanian army overthrew Idi Amin. In 1985 Tito Okello, an

S. Makara (✉)
Department of Political and Public Administration,
Makerere University, Kampala, Uganda

army commander overthrew the second Obote's government. This propelled Yoweri Museveni's rebel forces of the National Resistance Army (NRA) to capture power in January 1986. Since then, Yoweri Museveni with the aid of his political organization, the National Resistance Movement (NRM), and the backing of the army, has stayed in power for a generation. Though elections are regularly held, they have a slim chance of changing the president. The safeguard for leadership alternation, originally inserted in the constitution was removed in 2005. The purpose of this chapter is to outline and discuss the linkage between term limits and elections, and show that personal rule has gradually eroded the promise of peaceful change of top leadership in Uganda.

From independence in 1962 to 1980 there were no elections. The 1980 elections were controversial. The rigging of that election led to a civil war. Since 1986, Yoweri Museveni's tenure in power for over thirty years has been characterized by frequent elections. Under Museveni, elections have been organized every five years, and he has won them amidst widespread criticism that the institutional architecture for these elections is skewed in his favor and his ruling party. Security forces, including the army, actively participate in the organization and direction of elections, ensuring the outcome is in favor of the incumbent and the ruling party. For the first ten years in power (1986–1996) Museveni was not elected as President. Political parties were suspended from active participation in politics from 1986 to 2005. Opposition parties were weakened after being kept in limbo for twenty years. They suffered lack of finances, interparty coordination, and were constrained by the legal framework and security forces from fully mobilizing their supporters. The ruling party in the guise of "no-party system" dominated all the political space.

A Genesis to Leadership Crisis in Uganda

Few countries in the world have suffered the leadership crisis that Ugandans have seen since independence. Leadership succession has not largely been determined by the people but by the army. The worst time of excessive military power was during Amin's reign (1971–1979).[3] Under Amin's regime, all institutions of the state were taken over by the military, several people died at the hands of state officials.[4] In the aftermath of the disputed 1980 elections, the government forces countering Museveni-led rebels left thousands either dead or homeless in Luwero Triangle in central Uganda. Most of the atrocities were attributed to the ruthlessness of

Obote's government soldiers. On Museveni's ascendency to power, the Lord's Resistance Army (LRA) began a long, ruinous, and barbaric war that left most of Northern Uganda and its people devastated for twenty years (1988–2008). As much as Uganda has not had a peaceful handover of power from one president to another, peace has also eluded the country.

Constitutional Antecedents to Term Limits

The subject of term limits was not a key concern in the early political history of Uganda. The independence constitution negotiated in London (referred to as the Lancaster constitution) did not include term limits. Modeled on the British constitutional framework, Uganda's independence constitution left the leadership to be determined by elections.[5] Kanyeihamba asserts that because that constitution was not "homegrown" it had a potential for future political troubles.[6]

The independence constitution established institutions that were weak. There were various power centers. The key contending political force was the Buganda kingdom which had sought to separate from the rest of the country.[7] As a compromise, the Kabaka (king) of Buganda was installed as the first head of state without executive powers. Executive powers were to be exercised by the elected Prime Minister. The contradiction was that the Kabaka did not relinquish his responsibilities as the king of the all-powerful Buganda kingdom. He doubled as a regional king and the president of the whole country. Ironically, he did not perceive the presidency as a greater role than being a king of Buganda.[8] On the other side, the elected executive Prime Minister did not like the whole idea of reporting to another "bigger" person. Moreover, Obote, the Prime Minister and Edward Mutesa, the President and king, hailed from different social backgrounds. The king was from a higher nobility social class while the Prime Minister originated from the rural classes. Their national perspectives varied, and were bound to clash. This culminated into the 1966 crisis. The Prime Minister used central government forces to storm Lubiri, the seat of the Kabaka, and forced him into exile. This was part of the machinations to wrestle power from him and abolish kingships. The Prime Minister used the crisis to declare himself the President.[9] A hurriedly drafted constitution to create a republic was placed in the pigeon holes of the legislators in parliament. The new constitution was generally referred to as the "pigeon -hole constitution."[10] The independence constitution had created competing centers of power that were bound to clash. As if the above crisis was not enough, the all-powerful parliament almost ousted the Prime Minister at the same time, brought on board a controversial motion on floor for debate when Obote was away from Kampala. The motion was the so-called "gold allegations."[11] The parliament had received allegations that the Prime Minister and Idi Amin who was one of his trusted soldiers had stolen gold from Congo, and the proceeds were pocketed for their own benefits. This culminated in an impeachment motion on the Prime Minister. Although he managed to outwit it, its political ramifications left him politically injured. He arrested and detained Cabinet ministers (without trial), and the country was ruled under emergency rules for much of the second half of the 1960s.

While the above political quagmire prevailed, there were no elections in Uganda for 18 years (1962–1980). Elections that had been planned for 1967 were canceled due to the political crisis. The polls planned for 1971 did not materialize due to Idi Amin's military coup that removed Obote from power in January of that year. Idi Amin, the infamous dictator, did not organize any election during his stay in power (1971–1979). Confusion was also rife after the fall of Idi Amin in 1979. In a period of only two years (1979–1980), the country had unstable governments, changing three heads of state in that short period, each replacing the other by sheer manipulations.[12]

The hurriedly organized elections of 1980 have remained on Uganda's books as the most highly rigged. The ruling Military Commission under Paulo Muwanga bent on bringing Obote back and his Uganda People's Congress (UPC) party back to power, usurped the powers of the Electoral Commission to announce the results, reversing the wins of the rival Democratic Party. Indeed, the scheme succeeded, and Obote returned to power. The rigged elections sparked a rebel activity led by Yoweri Museveni, and a civil war raged (1981–1986). The war ravaged the country and brought it to its knees.[13] The civil war left an estimated 300,000 people dead, the economy crumbled; and life became short and brutal. The state collapsed and became irrelevant. Living in fear, the society disengaged from public affairs and retreated to the private realm of self-serving and survival.[14]

Museveni's Promise of a Fundamental Change

When rebel-turned president, Yoweri Museveni and his NRA/NRM captured power in 1986, he promised that his reign would not be a "change of guards" but a "fundamental change" in the politics of Uganda (Museveni's presidential inaugural speech on January 29, 1986). At the time, Museveni also wrote that the problem of Africa is not its people but leaders who seek to overstay in power.[15] Beyond thirty years since then, many Ugandans and other people interested in Ugandan politics repeatedly return to these words. Museveni's ascendency to power in 1986 was greeted by Ugandans with warmth, jubilations, and great expectations. Ugandans who had suffered abuse of their rights and lack of economic opportunity at the hands of the brutal regimes of Idi Amin and Obote were yearning for peace, stability, and prosperity.

Museveni, a Marxist revolutionary ideologically aligned with Cuba's Fidel Castro, Mozambican revolutionary Samora Marcel, political theorist Frantz Fanon, and Tanzanian socialist leader Mwalimu Julius Nyerere, was perceived by most Ugandans as a man of great promise. He talked a language not only of liberating Africans from European imperialism and exploitation, but also appeared convinced of Africa's potential to do away with dependence on the West by building local self-sustained economies.[16] The *Ten Point Programme of NRM* underscored the restoration of democracy as the number one priority for Uganda. The NRM's political vision emphasized a blending of participatory and representative democracy. Besides, it castigated the phenomenon of Africa producing goods of low economic value for export and importing the same goods from Western countries in a finished form, after processing, at a higher cost. Museveni's assertions had a convincing appeal to many who read and listened to him. However, these Marxist ideas quickly vanished once Museveni was faced with the realities of power.

Putting aside Marxist rhetoric in the name of political pragmatism, Museveni invited the World Bank to finance Uganda's decayed infrastructure. This began the introduction of structural adjustment programs (SAPs) through which the World Bank and the International Monetary Fund (IMF) have sought to reform the Uganda's economy since the 1980s. Uganda's economy has somewhat recovered, but still suffers from overdependence on the so-called donors. The country is heavily burdened with foreign debts, exports mainly unprocessed goods, imports double of what it exports, and still heavily depends on foreign donors for its budget support. Moreover, corruption in government continues to undermine effective delivery of public services.[17]

Museveni was convinced about people's power. His first task in the early years of his government was to introduce Resistance Councils and Committees (RCs).[18] RCs were quite exciting to most Ugandans. They were democratic grassroots power structures where the common man and woman freely participated in public decisions affecting their locality. These structures were an innovative departure from the oppressive system of chiefs left behind by colonialists.[19] For the first time in post-colonial Uganda, the ordinary citizen was able to question the performance of local authorities, ask questions about accountability, and to pass a vote of no confidence in an elected local leader for betraying people's mandate and trust.[20] This popular system of governance began to falter and weaken as Museveni's regime began to entrench itself politically, albeit, alienating certain political groups contrary to the stated principles.[21]

The RCs were originally conceived in the context of a "no-party" system popularly referred to as the "Movement system." The "system" was perceived to be nonsectarian, inclusive, and participatory, with elections based on "individual merit." This meant that a person standing for public election was elected on his/her own credentials without the backing of a political party because this was by then forbidden by law. The law forbade political parties from sponsoring candidates for public elections.[22] Elections of RCs ran on the model of electoral colleges where voters openly lined behind their preferred candidates. The candidate whose queue had the greatest number of voters carried the day. At the face of it, it looked democratic. The voters easily removed non-performing leaders and replaced them with new choices. It was also not costly to administer. This system, however, had many weaknesses such as intensifying domestic conflicts, communal hatred, and was easily manipulated by the local elites bribing potential voters and intimidating them. In urban areas, noncitizens voted contrary to the law which stipulated that only citizens resident in an area had a right to vote.[23] While there was a semblance of democracy at the local level through the RCs, the top level of the Movement remained largely unelected. President Museveni did not subject himself to a popular vote for ten years (1986–1996).

The first secret poll in Museveni's time was held in 1994 for election of delegates to the constituent assembly (CA) meant to debate the draft a new national constitution.[24] The first presidential elections took place only in 1996.[25] Though the turn up was high, these elections were controversial in the sense that they were held under the Movement system which was under a firm control of Museveni. Indeed, Museveni won with a landslide (76%). The voters were grateful to Museveni for bringing security and stability to the country, disciplining the army, putting the economy to some sound order, bringing women into public politics, and creating avenues for popular participation through RCs.

The Constitution-Making Process and the Question of Presidential Term Limits

Given the long history of political turmoil that beset the country for decades, a new constitution was deemed imperative to address the socioeconomic ills of the country. From 1989 to 1992, a Constitutional Commission headed by Justice Benjamin Odoki collected people's views on literally all issues that affected the governance of the country. The Commission submitted a draft report at the end of 1992. The making of a new constitution was anticipated to rekindle and rejuvenate a new social order. Instead of using the National Resistance Council (national legislature) to debate the draft constitution, a CA was elected to do so. The CA was elected in 1994, and debated the draft constitution for more than a year. Consequently, a new constitution was promulgated in October 1995.

One of the fundamental principles of the new constitution (Article 1) was that power belongs to the people, and shall be exercised through elections or referenda. The other critical article in this regard was Article 105(2) which stated thus: "A person shall not be elected under this Constitution to hold office as President for more than two terms as prescribed by this article." The spirit of the debate on this article in the CA was to reverse the past situations where leaders hung in power, and gave democracy no chance. CA delegates argued that the country had never experienced a peaceful hand-over of power from one president to another. The two-term limit on the president was also conceived in the context that other countries in Africa including the East African Community countries had term limits. CA delegates wanted to do away with the old-fashioned "big man" syndrome in post-colonial Africa where leaders stayed in power with little regard for constitutionalism, respect for human rights, respect for opposition parties, and good governance. In the past, most of the "big men" such as Kamuzu Banda of Malawi personalized power, banned opposition parties, extended patronage, cronyism, and presidential monarchy.[26] Uganda had its share of the "big man syndrome" in Amin and Obote's regimes.

Museveni and his ruling Movement endorsed the idea of presidential term limit during the CA partly because Museveni was seen an influential figure of the then famous "new breed of leaders" in Africa.[27] The new breed leadership included African leaders supposedly of new governance ethos, economic reformers who believed in people's participation in the political process and were open to new ideas, while being committed to unlocking Africa's potential and resolving the many conflicts undermining its development. These "new breed" included Yoweri Museveni of Uganda, Paul Kagame of Rwanda, Afwerki of Eritrea and Meles Zenawi (RIP) of Ethiopia.[28] Museveni had turned to the Washington consensus and embraced the World Bank and IMF sponsored neoliberal reforms, and became the blue-eyed man of the West in the Great Lakes region of Africa. This region had for long been plagued with intractable conflicts. Museveni and Uganda military forces became active in settling regional conflicts in Congo, Burundi, Somalia, and South Sudan. Apart from Congo where accusations of pillage of its resources by Ugandan actors in the 1990s were reported, Uganda has played a positive role in the settlement of most of the regional conflicts. These regional interventions elevated Museveni's political stature, not just as a regional player but also as an international actor and confidant of the Western powers.[29] This international political stature and support boosted Museveni's desire to stay in power and was instrumental in helping him achieve this goal.

REMOVAL OF TERM LIMITS

The adage that "power is sweet" cannot be far-fetched in the Ugandan context. When President Museveni was preparing his campaign for the 2001 election, his second elected term under the 1995 constitution, he promised in his election Manifesto (page 9) that he was seeking the second and last term in office to put in "place an orderly succession." Most people believed his word. However, he was later to renege on this promise.

In the aftermath of the 2001 elections, Museveni appointed a committee headed by veteran and respected politician Crispus Kiyonga to study the working of the Movement system. It collected people's views and submitted a report. At the national executive committee (NEC) of the NRM in March 2003, held at national leadership institute at Kyankwanzi, the Kiyonga committee presented its findings which affirmed that most Ugandans interviewed were of the view that the Movement system (no-party system) should continue to rule the country. To the contrary, in the course of the discussions, an idea was brought up by Museveni that political parties should be allowed to sponsor candidates hence the country should be opened up to a multiparty political dispensation. However, it was concurrently suggested that the opening up of political space for parties should go along with an amendment of the constitution to end the term limits on the president.

This surprise proposal took many at the meeting by storm. The majority at the meeting agreed with the president's proposal. However, some participants at the meeting were uncomfortable with the latter proposal and publicly dissented. These included senior cabinet ministers. The leading dissenters were Eriya Kategaya, Deputy Prime Minister and Minister of Foreign Affairs, a close friend of Museveni; Bidandi Ssali, the powerful minister of local government; and Ms. Miria Matembe, the outspoken minister of Ethics and Integrity. These cabinet members stood their ground in opposing the proposal of removing presidential term limits. However, Museveni was determined to have it his way, and these cabinet Ministers were sacked. The sacking of ministers with views contrary to Museveni's wishes, once and for all rested his long term claims that the Movement was multifaceted and multi-ideological, and that divergent views were tolerated therein. Museveni gave no reason for their sacking.

The motion for termination of presidential term limits was soon tabled in parliament. The Legal and Parliamentary Committee of parliament scrutinized this motion, and submitted its report on the amendment of Article 105 (2) on term limits in December 2004. The government advanced some reasons for amending this article. The main view advanced was that a leader's long-standing experience in democratic governance helps to build a young nation. Instead of term limits, it was argued, elections in themselves represent an important check power on the power of the president and a democratic avenue for removing bad leaders. The government added that the two-term limits weakens the president because he does not concentrate on national duties in the first term since he would be planning to contest for the second and final term. Furthermore, pro-government MPs argued that supporters of the opposition were adamant about term limits because they wanted to advance their political interests and to capture power from NRM.[30]

When the motion was tabled to parliament for plenary debate, some of the government-leaning MPs were uncomfortable with the proposal, and crossed over to the opposition side to oppose that motion. Sensing danger that the motion could be defeated, the government side devised two strategies: the first one was to bribe MPs with UGX 5 million each. The second strategy by the government side was to propose that the rules of procedure for that specific motion be changed from secret voting to open voting in parliament. On July 24, 2005, the motion was passed to delete Article 105 (2) to allow a person holding the office of the president to contest beyond two terms. This amendment made it possible for Museveni to be nominated to contest the 2006 elections. Thus, his 2001 promise that he was seeking election then to serve the last term in office and create orderly succession was debunked. However, criticism was rife that Museveni was seeking to entrench himself in office and become "president for life." Other voices argued that it was not politically prudent to amend an article of the constitution that had not been tested and to do so just for one person, President Yoweri Museveni.[31]

Internationally, the removal of term limits was a matter of serious concern. While visiting London, where journalists challenged him on removal of term limits, Museveni defended the removal saying,

> We are in serious business, dealing with the destiny of our people, and that is what will determine what we will do ...the legacy will not be undermined. On the contrary, it (removal of term limits) may actually enhance it, add more success to whatever we have done, we want a flexible constitution because we have got issues we must deal with, which may not be time bound, which may need more time.[32]

Again, while on the same visit to London, Museveni told Skynet Television in an interview that he did not intend to stay in power until 75 years of age. Responding to the Skynet TV anchor's question whether he wanted to be president for life, Museveni said,

> When there was the phenomenon of president for life, that was in 1960s and 70's when there was really no democracy, in a situation like Malawi where we had Kamuzu Banda, he would be the only candidate and the electorate would be required to vote 'Yes' or 'No'. Now with multiple candidates and multiple parties, there is no possibility of having life presidency, unless he is popular. Moreover, even if he is popular, he cannot do

so forever. He would not go beyond a certain age. Our constitution says you cannot go beyond 75.[33]

He added: "I will not make it to 75 years. I am sure because I have got a lot of other things to do."[34] Since the lifting of term limits, Museveni has stood for election three times (2006, 2011 and 2016). All indications are that, like with prior promises, he will renegate on this one and seek another term.

Soon after the 2016 elections and with Museveni's blessings, his party supporters engaged in a coordinated political campaign aimed at scraping the constitutional age limit of 75 years while imploring the big man to stand again for reelection in 2021. This well-orchestrated campaign was successful. On December 20, 2017, the Uganda Parliament passed an amendment to the constitution which, among other measures, eliminated the requirement that candidates for the presidency be under 75 years of age.[35] Museveni is now free to run again in 2021 if he so wishes. By then he would have been in power for over 40 years and he will be 77 years of age.

Along with scrapping the constitutional age requirement, the Parliament also attempted to extend the tenure of its members from five to seven years. In the aftermath of that vote, Museveni indicated that the tenure of the presidency too should be extended from five to seven years, arguing that such an extension was warranted for efficiency sake. However, an extension of the presidential term would require a popular referendum. Though extensions did not materialize, still Museveni had stated that

> For these [African countries] will all these problems…five years is just a joke… [and] leaders in Africa have much more to do and need adequate tome (between elections) to develop the continent.[36]

Although the idea of scrapping presidential term limits in 2005 did not originate from the popular masses but from the elites in the ruling party, there is some evidence that a few pockets of Museveni's rural supporters set this in motion. On May 23, 2001, at a gathering celebrating Museveni's electoral victory, Fred Tindimutunga, the chairman of Rushere (Museveni's home town) told him in the local dialect, "Haza ogarukye oyesimbe tukurongoore" (Please stand again and we will reward you with more votes). The then chairman of Mbarara district local council, Fred Kamugira, also voiced support for the idea saying, "We know that the law does not allow standing beyond two terms but can't this law be changed?" Even though Museveni did not openly comment on the matter at the celebration rally, the zeal and determination shown afterwards in getting Article 105 (2) amended is an indication he roundly approved of these maiden requests. It is noteworthy that such demands for constitutional change to allow scrapping of term limits were not spread throughout the country. Most people believed the Museveni they knew, the liberation hero, would not be power-hungry and would not break the constitution he helped to write before it was tested on this particular article on term limits. Moreover, many believed Museveni would not repeat the mistakes of the past leaders he disparaged as "swine" and "bankrupt," especially his predecessor Milton Obote who abrogated the constitution in 1966 to install himself as Uganda's president. Many believed Museveni was far above the Obotes of this world whose political ethos was defined by greed and manipulation. However, some of Museveni's critics remained skeptical of such widespread imaginations. Kiiza Besigye, Museveni's former personal physician, turned-main-political challenger at three polls said "Museveni is a victim of his own making. The biggest problem with Museveni is that he fought institutions and replaced them with himself."[37]

The removal of term limits from the constitution drew further attention from the international community. The political situation in Uganda was discussed at the Commonwealth Heads of State and Government Meeting (CHOGM) in Malta on November 25, 2005. With president Museveni in attendance, Uganda was criticized for removing term limits and the violent arrest of Museveni's main political challenger, Dr. Kiiza Besigye. At this meeting, the shadow Foreign Secretary of Britain, Liam Fox, pressed the British Prime Minister Tony Blair that it was wrong for Museveni to ignore the arrest of his main opponent by telling the meeting that it was patronizing for Western countries not to link good governance with the debt relief. Exasperated by the criticism, Museveni said, "Europeans really have bad manners ....as soon as they arrive, they lecture to you "do this do that."[38]

The three-day Malta CHOGM that was supposed to discuss fair trade was crowded by concerns on Uganda's governance challenges. At a press conference in Malta, Museveni said he had decided to run again because of the remaining strategic challenges for Uganda and Africa which were not time bound. He said Besigye's efforts to play a martyr (after his arrest) before the world media, hoping to scare the state would not deter the government from enforcing justice. He added he would not tolerate impunity.[39] After Musevenis' meeting with British Prime Minister Tony Blair in Malta, Blair issued a statement indicating that "The UK has made clear its concern about what is happening in Uganda. It is one of the basic principles of the Commonwealth that there should be respect for proper functioning of democracy, and therefore what has been happening in Uganda has caused us a great deal of concern."[40] Commenting on Dr. Besigye's arrest in a rejoinder press statement in Malta, Museveni insisted that "If anybody is accused of engaging in terrorism which is the greatest violation of human rights, you cannot call it bad governance. It is good governance." Defending his record in Malta, Museveni told the Skynet Television anchor, "An emphasis of the new democracy in Uganda is no impunity. Therefore, when we are implementing that, we would have expected acclaim."[41] He added, referring to his political organization, the NRM, "In Africa we are the pioneers, *Abatembuzi*. We are starting afresh. Some challenges can be faced in short term; others are not time – bound. If you have such projects, what is important- the rituals of one term, two terms or the programme? Therefore, we need a flexible constitution with term limits but these term limits will be politically decided not constitutionally decided."[42]

It is clear from the above statements that Museveni's determination to hold on power was unwavering. Besides, Museveni sounded like a prosecutor and a judge in the arrest and determination of his arch rival Dr. Besigye's case when he said, "it does not matter whether one is a popular politician or not, he cannot be above the law because crime knows no popularity."[43] Like most of his ideological comrades such as Robert Mugabe of Zimbabwe, Museveni could tolerate all sorts of criticism, but not political competition that threatened to unseat him from power. More than anybody else in Uganda, Besigye appeared serious on pursuing that goal, and Museveni would not tolerate it. Museveni talked of "short term" and "timeless strategies" that were not defined. By mentioning "timeless" strategies, he appeared to advance a proposition that if he were not in power no one else would do anything. Interesting as it appears, when he promised in the above quoted interview with Skynet Television that he had a lot of other things to do, hence, he would not be in power until 75 years of age, this assertion could now pass as a joke. In 2005, when Museveni fervently urged the members of parliament to pass the motion on Article 105(2), he then argued that the lifting of term limits was not meant to benefit him as a person but future leaders. Contrary to this claim, he has since stood three times and his supporters believe could still stand in 2021, well beyond 75 years of age. He also argued that it was good for the stability and development of the country.

Indeed, there has been a period of relative stability in the county, especially after the LRA rebellion, which caused mayhem in Northern Uganda for over two decades, was decisively defeated in 2008. Other observers would argue that there has been regime stability rather than social stability in the country, in the sense that Museveni, just like Putin in Russia, effectively controls all the instruments of force and the state apparatus. Because political dissent is treated contemptuously and at times ruthlessly, the country has attracted only few large scale, long term foreign private investments in industry and tourism, which would have turned the country around and possibly pushed it to a middle-income status. Because the political question of power succession remains uncertain, the investment climate remains unpredictable. Some people believe Museveni only trusts his son, and is grooming him for succession. This is something that Museveni roundly denies, referring to that suggestion as "an insult."[44] However, given Gen. Muhoozi-Kainerugaba (Museveni's son) fast rise in the ranks of the army and his strategic positioning as the commander of the Special Forces and in-charge of his father's security, he is well placed to succeed him. This speculation is given credence by the fact that Museveni has entrusted key positions not only to his son but also his wife (Minister of Education) and brother (senior security advisor), and adopted daughter (Permanent Secretary of Minister of Health). Moreover, most of Museveni's comrades in the bush war in the 1980s appear to have been politically edged out, or old age has weakened their capacities. To that extent, if Museveni wishes, his son has few obstacles ascending to the presidency. However, many would still raise a question, if that was what Museveni meant in 2001, when he talked of putting in place "an orderly succession" in the NRM.

In more than thirty years Museveni's rule, Uganda remains one of the least developed countries in the world. However, Museveni's image appears to be bigger than the country he leads. His name rings quickly to the ears of many outsiders. This could be positive. In the past, Uganda was associated with the murderous dictator Idi Amin, at least to the outside world. Museveni's supporters make a simple comparison between his regime and that of Idi Amin and partly Obote's second regime when people would simply disappear at the hands of state security officials. Today under Museveni, the people say "*Kasita twebaka kutulo*" (at least we sleep without disturbance or terror). This partly explains Museveni's rural support at elections. On the other hand, urban elite as well as the urban poor are disappointed with the lack of jobs and economic opportunities, poor health services, and poor education, corruption and failure of other social services. This then explains Museveni's dwindling electoral support in many urban areas.

Elections in the "No Term Limits" Era

Since 2005, when the constitution was amended to remove the term limits, three elections (2006, 2011, and 2016) have been held under a multiparty dispensation. The key question raised by these elections is whether or not they are transparent, fair, free, and provide a strong basis for popular accountability. And the more fundamental one is whether or not the process and the conduct of such elections can make them an effective alternative to term limits in changing the leaders.

Long-serving leaders abhor the idea of presidential term limits. They argue that term limits deny the people an opportunity to keep seasoned and tested leaders on the job. For example, during his recent reelection campaign, President Nguema of Equatorial Guinea is quoted to have said: "Many say they are tired of seeing me, it's been 36 years already. True but I've dedicated my life to this country."[45] Such leaders may bring about political stability and even, some economic prosperity, but many are reported to have fallen to temptation of corruption and fleecing resources from their countries for self-enrichment. Long time leaders contend that as long as there are democratic elections, the population should be free to choose them too. Some of the long-serving leaders have brought economic backwardness and social despair to their countries. For example, in the once prosperous country of Zimbabwe, Mugabe's long stay in power caused the people untold economic misery. Some commentators have been cynical, asserting that some autocrats have ruled for so long that they are feared even after their death.[46]

The long-serving African leaders tend to argue that term limits are an imposition of Western powers. They cite Western countries like Germany and Britain that do not have term limits. However, there are two fundamentals upon which Western leaders retain or lose power, the existence of fully democratic, transparent, free and fair elections, and the separation of political parties and leaders in power from the state. For African long-serving leaders, these are fused.

On the other side, there are scholars who argue that focused autocratic leadership could have some dividends. They point to Singapore's Lee Kuan Yew, a nondemocratic leader who ruled for a long time but succeeded in transforming Singapore from a third to a first world country.[47] These authors argue that most autocracies are bad, but some are economically successful. China, it is often argued, has lifted hundreds of millions of people out of poverty and maintained a high rate of growth for the past twenty years, bringing prosperity to its people. However, the historical evidence shows that this model has only succeeded in a few countries.

Most autocratic regimes today hold multiparty elections and yet the behavior of the parties and their supporters remain puzzling.[48] In such cases, autocracy is hidden behind elections and regimes appear legitimate. These regimes organize elections to "… reap the fruits of electoral legitimacy without running the risks [of] democratic uncertainty." Electoral autocracy manifests in several ways. The advantage of incumbency tends to fuse the functions of the ruling party, government, and state. The military, police, and security forces owe allegiance to the ruling leader, not the state. The electoral management body is solely appointed by the incumbent leader, and a large number of patrons—benefiting from the regime—campaign vigorously for the incumbent. This has come to be termed as a *selectorate* rather than an electorate.[49] Autocrats basically rely on select groups to stay in power and it is these groups who tend to determine the outcomes of the elections, not the electorate as a whole.

The functioning of autocratic regimes contradicts the fundamentals of a democratic regime. From a purely theoretical point of view, a democratic regime derives legitimacy from transparent and democratic elections. Such elections are intended to increase participation, accountability, and policy alternatives which form the basis of voters' support for particular parties and candidates.

In situations where the autocrat has a strong hold over power, voters' choices are limited or even determined by him. This has come to be termed as a "choice-less democracy."[50] Mkandawire argues that some African leaders decide that it is not up the voters to determine the leader but up to the leader to choose who vote. By staying in power regardless of the outcome of the polls, bribing the voters, disabling the campaigns of their opponents, arresting the supporters of their opponents, solely choosing the managers of the electoral body and using state resources for their election campaign, these leaders are telling voters their choices and preferences do not matter. As a cosmetic necessity, these leaders accept to introduce multipartyism but do not believe in the idea of opposition.[51] Opposition leaders are perceived as inconveniencing and sabotaging the status quo. Supporters of the opposition are perceived as undisciplined, unruly, rowdy, and unwilling to "see development and progress" ushered in by the ruling party. Internally, autocracy sustains itself by resorting to a spoils system or patronage to induce and boost support for the regime, while challenges from the outside are met with repression.

Goran Hyden has observed that in a number of African states "... the person in power is more important than the role he occupies, in short, politics in Africa is particularly difficult to constitutionalize—a tough and elusive beast to tame."[52] Adapting this view to the Ugandan context, elections for long were absent and irregular. Currently they are more regular than before, yet democracy and democratic practices attained through elections are still unpredictable and controlled by the leaders in government.

Uganda Elections in a Historical and Contemporary Perspective

While elections were scarce in the first two decades after independence, one of the most ubiquitous elements of Museveni's regime is the holding of regular elections since 1994. However, Ugandan elections cannot pretend to be an alternative to term limits. Other countries from the East African Community, namely Tanzania and Kenya, adopted term limits after sensing that elections would not bring about desired leadership change and the stability necessary for development. In Uganda, starting with the first direct presidential poll of 1996, the country's general elections have not passed without considerable controversy. In particular, the 2001 elections were marred by extensive violence. Again, during the first multiparty elections held in 2006, state agencies unleashed violence and intimidation on the main opposition leader, Dr. Kiiza Besigye of the Forum for Democratic Change (FDC). Trumped-up charges of engagement in rebellion and subversive activities were placed on his head. Other trumped-up cases included rape. To disable his campaign for election, he was arrested and detained. He was nominated to contest the elections while in jail. Violence also climaxed when security officials shot, killed, and injured some of Besigye's supporters at a rally in Bulange.[53]

Besigye had contested the election in court in 2001. After the 2006 elections he again contested them in court. In both cases, the court gave the same verdict: that though there were irregularities, they were not substantial enough to warrant nullification of Museveni's victory. In 2011, Besigye vowed not to go to courts of law. He mentioned the "court of public opinion." The second multiparty elections in 2011 elections took place after the government had rejected civil society's demand for electoral reforms, including implementation of recommendations by the Supreme Court to improve election management. The 2016 elections were also preceded by the civil society's Citizens Compact on Free and Fair Elections, which outlined 17 specific demands to improve election management, all of which were ignored by the government.

The role of political parties in shaping the political landscape of any country cannot be overemphasized. However, in struggling political systems like Uganda, dominated by one leader for 30 years, the role of opposition parties has been severely constrained. Under Museveni's regime, political party activities were suspended for 20 years, giving them no chance to mobilize their supporters.[54] As Rakner and van de Walle have posited, it appears that the preponderance of autocratic regimes has affected the emergence of viable and robust political parties in Africa, leading to the dominance of incumbent parties.[55] Since the reintroduction of multiparty politics in Uganda in 2005, the NRM has been dominant.[56] Some scholars have observed that hegemonic regime parties have the means of keeping power although the cost may be high.[57] In the 2016 Uganda elections, the institutional framework for managing elections was similar to the previous two multiparty elections. There was no reform of the Electoral Commission, no lesser violence, or intimidation of voters. Money was extensively used in the campaign.

After refusing to consider the electoral reforms proposed by civil society on the ground that of time constraint, the parliament, however, found time to accommodate new electoral laws which were proposed by Cabinet and designed to: (i) increase the number of administrative units (counties and municipalities) which under the constitution qualified to be represented as electoral areas (43 new counties), and (ii) amend the Presidential and Parliamentary Elections Bills. Passed on September 30, 2015 and assented to by the President on October 1, 2015, the new laws substantially increased the financial requirements for nomination.

Presidential candidates were required to pay UGX 20 million (up from UGX 8 million) and a candidate for MP UGX 3 million (up from UGX 200,000). Also, presidential candidates would no longer receive vehicles from the EC for their campaigns as was the case in 2011. These changes were clearly aimed at disadvantaging and discouraging aspiring presidential aspirants. The proposal to increase administrative units was a means of creating new constituencies aimed at further increasing the dominance of NRM in parliament. To compound matters, the EC applied these laws retrospectively which significantly disadvantaged the opposition presidential candidates. The ground was clearly not level because, while opposition presidential candidates were faced with a barrage of constraints specifically designed to limit their mobility and hinder their candidacy, the incumbent had been freely campaigning and was allowed to use the resources and facilities of the state to his full political advantage.

Enter the Police and the Militia in the 2016 Election Process

The preelection period witnessed the training by police of millions of a militia force code-named "crime preventers." This was a militia force because there was no law passed by parliament to authorize their recruitment, training, deployment, and payment. The Inspector General of Police (IGP), Kale Kayihura, said he aimed to train 11 million "crime preventers." The trainees were, on several occasions, visited by President Museveni who would implore them to be patriotic. Kayihura told crime preventers in Kapchorwa: "All we need to do is to change the sticks and give them (crime preventers) rifles and, by the way, I would like to tell you this, you are a reserve of the army, in case of war, you will be called upon because the police are the reserve of the army, according to the law."[58] On some occasions the crime preventers were shown on TV donning yellow T-shirts with Museveni's portrait, presenting the image of NRM cadres trained at public expense and meant to bolster support for the ruling party. On its part, the police was widely criticized and branded as a partisan organization working for NRM and Museveni. Responding to this charge at a media briefing, Kale Kayihura said, "If anybody in this government thinks that they are not working for NRM, they don't know where they are."[59] It is clear that the ground for political competition was biased in favor of the incumbent and seems, in many respects, antagonistic to his challengers. For example, when Amama Mbabazi (former Secretary-General of NRM) declared his intentions to stand as an independent candidate, at first the EC and the Attorney General gave him a nod. A week later, the EC issued a statement rescinding its earlier position, telling Mbabazi that he could not consult because the law only allowed him to do so if he was nominated by a political party. The irony is that this was not expressly provided for in the law. The EC was taking the liberty to interpret the law the way it wanted. Mbabazi attempted to address a rally in Mbale but was stopped and prevented from doing so by the police.

PERSONALIZATION OF POWER BY PRESIDENT MUSEVENI

President Museveni's portrayal of himself as an indispensable leader of Uganda and an icon of stability brought great gains for his NRM party and put other contending parties at a disadvantage. While his personal love for power is no secret, President Museveni likes to remind his audience how he is sacrificing for the country. For example, in Masaka at the Muslim *Eid Mubarak* prayers on July 17, 2015, he told that congregation that those opposed to him wanted to "steal my oil."[60] He added that those in opposition had witnessed the transformation he brought to the country and they just wanted to "reap where they did not sow". On several other occasions, Museveni asserted that he would not retire until he had seen the East African Federation become a reality. Addressing a press conference during his 2016 election campaign, he said "I am here to see whether we can help you get the East African Federation so that we have a critical mass of strength that can guarantee your future."[61] This is similar to what he had told a gathering in Jinja in 2009, where he said,

> I saw people knocking themselves over leadership when am still around and I said these people are going *kutomeza* (crash) the revolution ushered in by the NRM. So, I decided to hang around. If somebody brings *ffujo* (chaos) near me I won't rush to call for help. *Tutandikirawo* (we start immediately) and by the time *my army* comes to assist I would already be handling the enemy.[62]

Such pronouncements had the effect of assuring NRM supporters to stay with him, captured in their slogan "Museveni *paka last*." (Museveni forever!). On the other hand, they demoralized those citizens who supported the opposition and believed in the slogan *"agende"* (let him go!). Indeed, for various sections of the population—especially the youth—Museveni's 30-year rule was simply enough. In response, Museveni argued that the issue was not whether or not Museveni should go, rather the issue was the mission.[63] He frequently criticized his opponents as demagogues who had nothing to offer apart from wanting power, and predicted that in the next five years (2016–2021), the opposition would be "wiped out."[64] For some time, Musevni had been obsessed with power and did not hide his desire to stay. For example, speaking on his tour of eastern Uganda, in August 2008, President Museveni said that he was in good health and capable of ruling for many more years. He asked the people rhetorically: "Why should NRM lose elections?" In the same vein, addressing a rally on August 16, 2008 at Apuuton Primary School grounds in Katakwi, he said, "We are the ones who restored democracy in Uganda. Who else should win in this country? Do you see me as somebody who is about to collapse?"[65] At a different occasion, Museveni seemed more emphatic. He told a rally in Bushenyi District where he reportedly said in his local dialect, Runyankore, "Ninyenahiigire enyamaishwa yangye nkagi-ita, mbwenu ngu ngyende, nzehi?," which literally translates as "I hunted my animal, now they are saying that I go, go where?".[66] By this he meant to remind the Ugandan people that he went to the bushes to fight for power, and he would not let go of it.

ELECTION FINANCES AND EXPENDITURES

One of the key factors that has tremendously influenced elections in Uganda concerns electoral finances. There is no doubt that money is a necessary factor in elections but it should not be the determining factor. If money in an election is unregulated, many experts content, "… you have an election outcome determined by banknotes, not popular votes."[67] In Uganda, however, money has increasingly become a determining factor of election results. Several countries including Tanzania and Kenya have put in place specific laws to regulate election finances. These cover issues of state funding for political parties, the limits of a candidate's expenditure of personal funds, and limits on donations, etc. In 2010, Uganda's Parliament made an amendment to the Political Parties and Organizations Act (PPOA) to allow the government to finance political parties on the basis of their numerical strength in Parliament. This provision was implemented through the 2014/2015 budget, and parties received funding on this basis. However, the ruling party which had a majority of legislators took the lion's share, giving it a further advantage.

Under the provisions of the PPOA, each party is supposed to declare its sources of funds to the EC (both income and expenditure). However, most Ugandan political parties do not make such declarations, especially donations. Consequently, the lack of transparency in party finances has shrouded the financial transactions in political parties. Some opposition parties receive donations from abroad, some of which they do not declare. Equally, Museveni, the chairman of the ruling party, frequently boasts of getting support from friends locally and abroad, which is never declared to EC.

Expenditure on campaigns is high for presidential candidates. According to the Alliance for Campaign Finance Monitoring (ACFM), it is reported that between November and December 2015, candidate Museveni spent UGX 121 billion equivalent to USD 35 million, Besigye UGX 3 billion equivalent to USD 865,000, and Mbabazi UGX 1.5 billion equivalent to USD 432,000.[68] This expenditure was for only two months. Civil society activists monitoring the campaign finances argued that this kind of expenditure could undermine the integrity and fairness of the election because the ground was clearly not level. To compound matters, in November 2015, just at the beginning of the election campaigns, the government introduced a Bill in parliament to amend the Public Finance Management Act in order to allow the government to borrow from the Central Bank or to switch budgetary allocations between different government departments without prior authorization of parliament. Civil society activists believe that this bill was intended to give government the unfettered authority to raid public finances for election campaigns, without accountability.

The challenge with party election finance is that it keeps many people suspicious of its sources. For example, when the new NRM officials were designated in 2014, new state of the art 4-wheel vehicles were bought for them. The Secretary-General of NRM was asked by journalists about the source of the money, she replied that some came from the savings of the party and some was raised by the party chairman.[69] In the NRM political universe, most of the money is raised by the party chairman but the methods employed to that end are not transparent, especially since the ruling party and the state seem to be closely fused, giving room for widespread suspicion that public money pays for the ruling party's activities. This suspicion grew stronger when, in the aftermath of the elections,

State House officials requested parliament to authorize a supplementary budget of UGX 70 billion for operations at State House for 3 months to the end of the financial year. State House chief finance officers told parliament that the budget had been depleted by election expenditures.[70] The national currency, the Uganda shilling, also depreciated by 17% causing government to request parliament to authorize borrowing from the Eastern and Southern Preferential Trade Area (PTA) Bank to the tune of US$200 million.

This level of funding was unprecedented in Ugandan politics. FDC President Mugisha Muntu lamented that instead of people seeking to support their parties and candidates, they want their parties to pay them, and this is a sign of a total breakdown of the political system and its political culture.[71] This is particularly problematic with the opposition parties having no possibility of raising funds close to those of the ruling party. In this instance, the NRM was wiser than in 2011 when most of its money was stolen by some of its elites in Kampala.[72] During the campaign, Museveni also promised that his government would buy and give out 18 million hoes to all households in 2016/2017 financial year for free. However, in the middle of the campaign, the people of Terego County were the first to benefit, an act that left Kasiano Wadri (area MP) very annoyed, because it obviously broke election laws that prohibit giving out gifts to the voters during the election campaign. However, Prime Minister Ruhakana-Rugunda who oversaw the distribution of hoes said this was a government program, conceived way back before the elections.[73] Although the Supreme Court judges agreed with Rugunda's position in the case of *Amama Mbabazi v. Y.K. Museveni and 2 others*, the fact remains that the timing was wrong and probably calculated to influence the voters in favor of the incumbent. The issue of separating an incumbent president and a running presidential candidate has remained contentious and opaque in substance and meaning.

Extended Patronage Politics and Electoral Outcomes

Related to unregulated financial expenditure is the issue of patronage politics. The Ugandan state has extended patronage to various groups, which explains why the State House budget continues to grow from one year to the next. "Brown envelopes" are regularly dished out by the President to various groups and individuals, and presidential pledges increase during the campaign period. For people holding bigger offices, the president's generosity using public resources can go into millions of shillings. This extends to top religious leaders who receive 4-wheel drive cars and other largesses from the president. To expand patronage, control of the National Agricultural Advisory Services (NAADS) funds was moved from the parent Ministry of Agriculture to State House, to be commanded by Museveni's brother, Salim Saleh. The funds are used as State House finds fit. All NRM candidates for all positions are funded by NRM secretariat. But the money is raised by the president, who doubles as the chairperson of the ruling party. In such a context, it is an uphill task for the opposition to match this level of largesse.

The Management of Elections

Multiparty elections are meaningful only if the population and stakeholders generally believe the managers of electoral exercise and the rules are fair and impartial to all. Many commentators have expressed the view that the Ugandan population has little confidence in the electoral body. The trust deficit is due to its composition, the manner of its appointment, and the way it executes its mandate in conducting elections. As it has been rightly observed, "The EC still has a difficult task of proving that it is an entity independent of government. In that context, the constraints imposed on it by the manner of its appointment and operation appears to reduce its capacity to act sufficiently as a fair player in relation to all stakeholders."[74] This was made worse by the government's decision to ignore the civil society's electoral reform proposals. In this regard, the candidates, especially opposition presidential candidates, went into the 2016 elections without much trust in the EC's impartiality.

Although EC introduced biometric voter verification machines to improve voter authenticity, these failed at some polling stations. The EC failed to interact with all presidential candidates, or to address their concerns such as harassment, the pulling down of their pictures, and shutting them out of media houses. Worse still, the EC did not conduct adequate voter education. While the introduction of the biometric voter verification machines was commendable, allegations of pre-ticked ballots were fairly abundant. For example, in Sembabule, an independent candidate Joy Kabatsi—a former aide to President Museveni—alleged that there were pre-ticked ballots and ballot stuffing.[75] She reportedly handed over those pre-ticked ballots to the Police, and further reported that the pre-ticked ballots were cast for her opponent (Hanifa Kawoya) and President Museveni. "In Sembabule, she said, what I am talking about is that ballot stuffing and pre-ticked ballots was not done only for my opponent but for the President also...." She added, "My brothers died in the NRA war which was sparked by vote rigging in 1980. I now feel my brothers died in vain because this is different from what they died for, the Uganda they wanted to see... What happened in my district if similar to what happened in other districts, then our country is in trouble and in real danger".[76] Concerns of pre-ticked ballots and pool rigging appeared to be quite widespread.

The EC maintained a semblance of an organization up to the task until the Election Day fiasco. All local and international election observers noted that election management fell well below required standards. In the words of former Nigerian President Obasanjo who headed the group of Commonwealth Observers, the failure of the EC to deliver election materials on time in Kampala and Wakiso districts, a radius of 30 kilometers, was "inexcusable."[77] The Commonwealth Observer Group Interim Statement says... "The secrecy of the ballot is not adequately provided for. The results tally and reconciliation remains ambiguous. The transmission from polling station to the National Tally Centre is not adequately protected. The figures from each polling station are not being disaggregated at the National Tally Centre."[78] For example, to the surprise of everyone, the EC failed to explain its failure to deliver election materials to Namuwongo, a polling station less than a kilometer from its office until 3:00 p.m. in the afternoon, two hours to closing time. It had no excuse for ballots that were delayed until the next day. It should have interested EC to investigate areas where 100% of registered voters cast their votes and why there were so many spoilt votes (455,175 or 4.6% of the total). Thus, when CEON stated that elections did not meet the minimum standards and that the results did not reflect the will of the people, they clearly had a point.

While the EC appeared technically prepared for the election, there were many political challenges. The first challenge had to do with the lack of response to the electoral reforms presented by a group of civil society organizations under the Citizen's Compact on Free and Fair Elections. This comprehensive submission to Parliament was considered at the committee stage but nothing substantive came out of these proposals. While the parliamentary committee on legal affairs took leave to study the proposals, their report was not considered as it was argued there was insufficient time until the next election cycle begins. EC was faulted for failing in its duty to be fully responsible and transparent in the supervision, conducting, tallying, transmission, and declaration of results. Some observers queried the impartiality of EC. The European Union Election Observer Mission noted that the EC lacked independence, transparency, and the trust of stakeholders. It further observed that EC narrowly interpreted its mandate by limiting it to the organization of the technical aspects of the elections. Moreover, the EC lacked transparency in its decisions and failed to inform the voters and contestants on key elements of the electoral process in a timely and comprehensive manner.[79] To this extent, many people were not certain if the election results released on 20 February were authentic, given that they were not disaggregated as they released them.

How Security Forces Direct the Election Process

In the period before the 2016 elections, violence became widespread. The police acted with an iron-fist against those intending to challenge President Museveni. For example, when Besigye wanted to proceed to Iganga district to commission FDC offices, the police besieged his home, although he sneaked out and surprised his captors. When FDC officials decided to go to Rukungiri to launch their party campaign on October 10, 2015, the police violently arrested them at Nyakahita on Mbarara road, dragging a female FDC official across the road. Following these beating and intimidation of political opponents, and while addressing crime preventers in Mbarara on October 19, 2015, IGP Kayihura complimented the Rwizi regional Officer, Mr. Kulayigye, and Mbarara Regional Police Commander, Jaffar Magezi, as good examples to follow. On the other hand, when the police Deputy Spokesperson was asked by journalists why Museveni was freely moving around and campaigning while other candidates were being harassed by police, she answered, "President Museveni is going around the country because he is the President and Commander-in-chief."[80]

Prior to that, independent candidate Amama Mbabazi had been stopped with his daughter at Njeru on Jinja road from traveling to Mbale for his consultation with the people. He was interrogated by the police at Kiira road in Kampala for a whole day.[81] Police asserted that President Museveni had not cleared Mbabazi to go to Mbale.[82] Mbabazi's lawyers argued that it was wrong for the Police to assume that they were the interpreters of the law. Conversely, President Museveni's supporters enjoyed full police protection during their processions. In Gulu, on June 28, 2015, NRM supporters in full view of the police protested Mbabazi's decision to stand for the presidency by carrying an empty coffin marked with Mbabazi's portrait.[83] This was done regardless of the fact that in African culture, openly wishing another person death is an abomination. Addressing supporters in his home area of Kanungu on July 13, 2015, Mbabazi demanded that the government explain why it had allowed such a procession in Gulu. The police became very sensitive to any meeting held by opposition leaders. For example, after Mbabazi's consultation rally in Mbale on September 7, 2015 was well attended, the police would give different directives to limit the candidate's consultations to small townhall meetings.[84] Another Mbabazi rally arranged to take place at Soroti Grounds on September 7, 2015 was canceled by the Police without giving any reason.[85] He faced the same fate in Jinja on September 10, 2015.[86]

In terms of security, the public became sensitive about the possibility of widespread violence during the electoral process. For example, on some television channels, Maj. Kakooza Mutale of the infamous Kalangala Action Plan (a security outfit that intimidated opposition supporters in 2001 and 2006) was shown training several youth in the central region purportedly to protect Museveni's vote.

The Inspector-General of Police, Kale Kayihura emphasized that he was training 11 million "crime preventers" in the whole country as reserve force. This was during the preelection period. There were also other political groups which were reportedly training their own militia. Erias Lukwago, the mayor of Kampala, mobilized "TJ Solida" as a vigilante group to protect the interests of the opposition. Kawempe mayor, Mubarak Munyagwa, mobilized "Red Tops" and others.

There were worrying incidents which threatened to upset the electoral process. For example, Mbabazi's rally in Fort Portal on November 17, 2015 was interfered with by a helicopter carrying Lt. General Henry Tumukunde and painted in the NRM yellow color.[87] There were also cases of unknown people pulling down Mbabazi's posters in Ishaka and Bushenyi area (with police escorting them). However, the most explosive incident of violence took place in Ntungamo on December 13, 2015 when NRM T-shirt donning people occupied an area where Mbabazi was supposed to hold his rally. They were beaten by Mbabazi's supporters, and several were injured.[88] Following these clashes, Mbabazi's aide,

Christopher Aine, disappeared from his home in Kampala. His relatives alleged that he was taken away by police. Aine would reappear after the elections from Salim Saleh's home. Another notable case was when Besigye's supporters clashed with those of deputy speaker of Parliament, Jacob Oulanya, in Omoro County, Gulu district, at the same venue where the latter was supposed to address his rally. Many people were injured in the process.[89]

State institutions were clearly bent on frustrating the efforts of the opposition to compete favorably for power. Specifically, the EC repeatedly failed in its mandate to listen to opposition complaints regarding police brutality, the defacing of posters, denial of access to radio, arrest of supporters, and the closure of venues for campaigns. This time around, the EC's performance closely approximated the failures of the controversial elections of 1980. Needless to say, the actions of the police targeting the support of the opposition and treating the incumbent president who was a candidate in a special way bordered on partisanship. It remains difficult to tell why the EC refused to include the results of 1787 polling stations in the tally for presidential elections.[90] The EC has suspiciously refused to explain why it failed to conduct proper elections and to deliver election materials to areas deemed to be opposition strongholds. The lack of transparency in the electoral process was shrouded in government ordering the closure of all social media, denying Ugandans information about the voting process as soon as polling started, and thereafter. Kiiza Besigye, the main opposition candidate was arrested on the eve of the polling day. Even in the aftermath of elections, government slapped a ban on public media coverage of opposition. Some observers suggested that the 2016 electoral process was close to the controversial one of 1980 when the government took over the process of elections and rigged it. The rigging of that election sparked off a civil war. It will remain difficult for the government and EC to justify these actions, and to assert a claim that the elections were transparent, free and fair.

Conclusion

In Ugandan elections, the ground and rules of the game have never been level. Under President Museveni, Uganda has become an electoral autocracy with the cumbent convinced of his own irreplaceability and determined to cling to power by all means necessary and regardless of the outcomes for the country. No one else expressed this determination to cling to power and the prospect of a political alternance in Uganda better than Mr Kayihura, the inspector general of the police, when he adamantly insisted that they (NRM) were not ready to hand over power to the opposition to "destabilize peace which we fought for."[91]

In an autocratic regime, politics and elections are not all matters of formality. Informal politics is more important than what formal politics offers. Formal institutions are not allowed to work. Even a well-designed constitution can be torn like a mere piece of paper. Supporters of opposition parties are either bought off or intimidated by government forces. The resilient supporters of opposition are denied the opportunity to exercise their right to vote. In Uganda, the rules of democracy have been thwarted and institutions interned by powers that be. Thus, a transition to full democracy in Uganda remains elusive. Many people still yearn for a day when term limits will return to the constitution and the ground will be level for the opposition to have a chance of ascending to power.

Notes

1. The current head of state, Yoweri Museveni was first directly elected in 1996. Prior to these elections, all others presidents had either been indirectly elected by the Parliament or had taken power through military coups. Museveni took power by waging a rebellion against Uganda People's Congress government led by Milton Obote.
2. Francis Bwengye, *The Agony of Uganda: From Idi Amin to Obote* (London and New York: Regency Press, 1986); Sabiti Makara Sabiti, "Deepening Democracy Through Multipartyism: The Bumpy Road to Uganda's 2011 Elections," *Africa Spectrum* 45, no. 2 (2010); Eriya Kategaya, *Impassioned for Freedom* (Kampala: Wave Books, 2006).
3. Michael Richardson, *The Bloody Pearl* (Atlanta: Magesti Books, 1980).
4. Henry Kyemba, *State of Blood: An Inside Story of Idi Amin* (Kampala: Fountain Publishers, 1997).
5. George Kanyeihamba, *Constitutional Law and Government in Uganda* (Nairobi: East Africa Literature Bureau, 1975); Grace Ibingira, *The Forging of an African Nation: The Political and Constitutional Evolution of Uganda from Colonial Rule to Independence, 1894–1962* (New York: The Viking Press, 1973); Samwiri Karugire, *A Political History of Uganda* (London: Heinemann Educational Books, 1981).
6. Kanyeihamba, op. cit.
7. Phares Mutibwa, *Uganda Since Independence: A Story of Unfulfilled Hopes* (Trenton, NJ: Africa World Press, 1992).

8. In 1964, when a referendum was held to determine the location of the so-called "lost counties" of Buyaga and Bugangaizi that had been carved from Bunyoro to Buganda, Mutesa is said to have retorted he could not accept any result that would take that part away from his "country," when both Buganda and Bunyoro kingdoms were obviously part of Uganda.
9. Mutibwa, op. cit.
10. The term "pigeon-hole constitution" came to be synonymous with a draft republican constitution introduced by Prime Minister Milton Obote to legislators who were asked to pick copies of that draft from their pigeon holes as the debate on was introduced in parliament. Most of them were taken unaware, and had not read it.
11. Ibingira, op. cit.
12. Tony Avirgan and Martha Honey, *War in Uganda: The Legacy of Idi Amin* (Westport, CON: Lawrence Hill and Company, 1982).
13. Holger Hansen and Michael Twaddle, *Developing Uganda* (Oxford: James Currey, 1998).
14. Nelson Kasfir, *State and Class in Africa* (London: Frank Cass, 1984).
15. Yoweri Museveni, *What Is Africa's Problems?* (Kampala: NRM Publications, 1992).
16. NRM Secretariat (1987).
17. Andrew Mwenda and Roger Tangri, "Patronage Politics, Donor Reforms, and Regime Consolidation in Uganda," *African Affairs* 14, no. 416 (2005): 449–467.
18. Sabiti Makara, "The Dynamics of Political and Administrative Change in Uganda: The Role of Resistance Councils and Committees in Promoting Democracy in Uganda," Unpublished paper, Department of Political Science and Public Administration, Makerere University, Kampala, 1992; Expedit Ddungu, "Popular Forms and the Question of Democracy: The Case of Resistance Councils in Uganda," in Mahmood Mandani and Joe Oloka-Onyango (eds.), *Uganda: Studies in Living Conditions, Popular Movements, and Constitutionalism* (Vienna: JEP Book Series, 1994).
19. Republic of Uganda, *Local Government Act 1997*; Mahmood Mamdani, *Citizen and Subject* (Princeton: Princeton University Press, 1996).
20. Makara (1992), op. cit.
21. Sabiti Makara, "Political and Administrative Relations in Decentralisation," in Apolo Nsibambi (ed.), *Decentralisation and Civil Society in Uganda: The Quest for Good Governance* (Kampala: Fountain, 1998).
22. Nelson Kasfir, "'Movement' Democracy, Legitimacy and Power in Uganda," in Justus Mugaju and Joe Oloka-Onyango (eds.), *No-Party Democracy in Uganda: Myths and Realities* (Kampala: Fountain, 2000).
23. The law governing elections of RCs stipulated that only citizens residing in an area had the right to choose leaders. However, there were no registers

of voters and no citizen identity card, hence noncitizens could easily vote or be voted.
24. Sabiti Makara et al. (eds.), *Politics, Constitutionalism and Electioneering in Uganda* (Kampala: Makerere University Press, 1996).
25. Sabiti Makara et al. (eds.), *Voting for Democracy in Uganda: Issues in Recent Years* (Kampala: LDC Publishers, 2003).
26. Thandika Mkandawire, "Crisis Management and the Making of 'Choice Less Democracies' in Africa," in Richard Joseph (ed.), *The State, Conflict and Democracy in Africa* (Boulder: Lynne Rienner, 1998).
27. Joe Oloka-Onyango, "'New-Breed' Leadership, Conflict, and Reconstruction in the Great Lakes Region of Africa: A Sociopolitical Biography of Uganda's Yoweri Kaguta Museveni," *Africa Today* 50, no. 3 (2004): 29–52.
28. Ibid.
29. Uganda's deployment of its army as part of AMISOM in Somalia where the nine US soldiers had been killed helped Museveni to gain international recognition.
30. Clare Atoo et al. "Changing the Rules of the Political Game," in Julius Kiiza et al. (eds.), *Electoral Democracy in Uganda: Understanding Institutional Processes and Outcomes of the 2006 Multiparty Elections* (Kampala: Fountain, 2008).
31. Atoo et al. op. cit.; Kategaya, op. cit.
32. *The New Vision*, October 31, 2005.
33. *The New Vision*, October 27, 2005.
34. Ibid.
35. According to one survey, the overwhelming majority of the population was opposed to the removal of the age-limit clause of the constitution. See URN, 85% of Ugandans Opposed the Age Limit Amendment—Survey, *The Observer*, December 9, 2017; Hanibal Goitom, "Uganda: Bill Eliminating Presidential Age Limit and extending Parliamentary Term Passed," *The Law Library of Congress*, December 27, 2007, http://www.loc.gov/law/foreign-news/article/uganda-bill-eliminating-presidential-age-limit-and-extending-parliamentary-term-passed/.
36. Quoted in Goitom, op. cit.
37. *The Monitor*, October 29, 2005.
38. *The New Vision*, November 26, 2005.
39. Ibid.
40. Ibid.
41. Ibid.
42. *The Sunday Vision*, November 27, 2005.
43. Ibid.
44. *The New Vision*, October 24, 2014.
45. *Mail & Guardian Africa*, April 24, 2016.

46. Ghandhi Jennifer and Adam Prezeworski, "Authoritarian Institutions and the Survival of Autocrats," *Comparative Political Studies* 40, no. 11 (2007).
47. Tim Basle and Masa Kadumatsu, "What Can We Learn from Successful Autocrats," retrieved from www.voxe4.org/article/what-canwe-learn-successful-autocrats.
48. Beatriz Magaloni Beatriz, "Elections Under Autocracy and the Strategic Game of Fraud," Paper prepared for the project on "Governance Under Authoritarian Rule" presented at the Hoover Institution (2007).
49. Besley and Kudamatsu, op. cit.
50. Mkandawire, op. cit.
51. Samuel Huntington, *Political Order in Changing Societies* (New Haven: Yale University Press, 1968).
52. Goran Hyden, "The Challenges of Constitutionalising Politics in Uganda" in Holger Hansen and Michael Twaddle (eds.), *Developing Uganda* (Oxford: James Currey, 1998), 111.
53. Julius Kiiza et al., *Electoral Democracy in Uganda* (Kampala: Fountain Publishers, 2008).
54. Justus Mugaju and Joe Oloka-Onyango, *No Party Democracy in Uganda: Myth and Realities* (Kampala: Fountain Publishers, 2000); Godfrey Asiimwe, "Of Fundamental Change and No Change": Pitfalls of Constitutionalism and Political Transformation in Uganda, *Africa Development* XXXIX, no. 2 (2014).
55. Lise Rakner and Nicolas Van de Walle, "Opposition Weaknesses in Africa," *Journal of Democracy* 20, no. 3 (2009).
56. Makara Sabiti, Lise Rakner and Lars Svasand, "Turnaround: The National Resistance Movement and the Reintroduction of Multiparty System in Uganda," *International Political Science Review* 30, no. 2 (2009).
57. Mohamed Salih, *African Political Parties: Evolution, Institutionalism and Governance* (London: Pluto Press, 2003).
58. *Red Pepper*, January 16, 2016.
59. *The Daily Monitor*, July 18, 2016.
60. *Chimp Reports*, July 18, 2015.
61. *The Daily Monitor*, February 11, 2016.
62. *The New Vision*, February 28, 2009.
63. *The Daily Monitor*, February 22, 2016.
64. Ibid.
65. *The Monitor*, August 18, 2008.
66. *The Monitor*, August 8, 2008.
67. IDEA (2014), 24.
68. ACFIM (2015).
69. *The Monitor*, April 30, 2015.
70. *The Observer*, April 3, 2016.

71. *The Observer*, February 3, 2016.
72. Kristof Titecca, "The *Commercialization* of *Uganda's* 2011 *Elections* in the Urban Informal Economy: Money, Boda-Bodas and Market Vendors," in Sandrine Perrot et al. (eds.), *Elections in a Hybrid Regime* (Kampala: Fountain, 2014), 178–207.
73. *Red Pepper*, February 9, 2016.
74. Sandrine Perrot et al., op. cit., 137.
75. *Red Pepper*, February 29, 2016.
76. *The Daily Monitor*, February 23, 2016
77. *Commonwealth*, February 20, 2016.
78. Ibid.
79. EUEOM (2016).
80. *NTV NewNight*, October 10, 2015.
81. *The Observer*, September 10, 2015.
82. Ibid.
83. *Red Repper*, June 30, 2015.
84. *The Observer*, September 7, 2015.
85. *The Observer*, September 9, 2015.
86. *The Monitor*, September 10, 2015.
87. *The Observer*, November 18, 2015.
88. *The Monitor*, December 15, 2015.
89. *The Monitor*, December 23, 2015.
90. *The Monitor*, February 22, 2016.
91. *The Observer*, January 27, 2016.

PART II

Touche pas à ma Constitution[1]

---

[1] "Hands off my constitution," a rallying slogan used by many civil society organizations in the debate over presidential term limits in Francophone Africa.

CHAPTER 5

The Undoing of a Semi-authoritarian Regime: The Term Limit Debate and the Fall of Blaise Compaoré in Burkina Faso

Daniel Eizenga and Leonardo A. Villalón

Introduction: *Fin de règne* in Ouagadougou

On 30 October 2014, tens of thousands of protesters poured into the streets of Ouagadougou, stormed the National Assembly, and set it on fire to prevent the legislature from voting on a bill to revise the constitutional provision establishing presidential term limits. In a rapidly escalating and startling turn of events, the regime lost control of the uprising, and within forty-eight hours President Blaise Compaoré had resigned from office and fled the country, putting an abrupt end to his twenty-seven years of rule. The speed at which these events unfolded stunned outside observers, and indeed caught the participants themselves by surprise.[1]

D. Eizenga
National Defense University's Africa Center for Strategic Studies, Washington, DC, USA
e-mail: Daniel.j.eizenga.civ@ndu.edu

L. A. Villalón (✉)
University of Florida, Gainesville, FL, USA
e-mail: lvillalon@ufic.ufl.edu

© The Author(s) 2020
J. R. Mangala (ed.), *The Politics of Challenging Presidential Term Limits in Africa*, https://doi.org/10.1007/978-3-030-40810-7_5

To be sure, questions about the president's future had long circulated in Burkina Faso, yet for years the Compaoré regime had displayed an adept ability to out-maneuver political opponents and to impose order in the face of demonstrations and social unrest. Compaoré had in fact already successfully managed to modify presidential term limits twice, in a series of political maneuvers that had allowed him reelection to third and fourth terms. The tone and intensity of national debates about the rumored intent of the regime to once again modify the constitution to allow a fifth term, however, had gradually escalated since the beginning of his fourth term in 2010. Periodic angry protests against the manipulation of ostensibly democratic political institutions, and the frequent expressions of political grievances across all sectors of Burkinabè society, had clearly suggested that any constitutional modification would be hotly contested, and there was much debate as to whether Compaoré could even succeed in the effort.[2] But few if any imagined that the attempt to do so would bring about such a rapid downfall of the regime in Ouagadougou.

The months preceding what would become known as the *insurrection populaire* (the popular uprising) had been characterized by massive protests against a rumored intent to propose a referendum to modify Article Thirty-Seven, the provision of the constitution establishing presidential term limits. The political opposition, joined by former allies and even members of Compaoré's political party—the *Congrès pour la Démocratie et le Progrès* (CDP)—staged massive demonstrations warning against any attempts to modify the constitution. Women's movements, youth associations, popular culture celebrities, and longtime human rights activists led some of the most extensive protests and campaigns of civil disobedience that the country had ever witnessed. Faced with such wide-scale movements against a modification of term limits, the government was keen to avoid a referendum. To modify the constitution otherwise, however, required the support of a super-majority of three-quarters of the deputies in the National Assembly. Because the CDP had seventy of the 127 deputies, it would have to both ensure the full adhesion of its own—increasingly disgruntled—deputies, as well as convince or co-opt at least twenty-seven deputies from parties friendly to the "presidential majority" to join them. Having apparently concluded that it had managed to assemble the necessary votes, on **21 October 2014** the CDP attempted to by-pass public debate by sending a bill to modify the article directly to the National Assembly.[3]

News of the introduction of the bill in the Assembly immediately sparked a public outcry throughout Ouagadougou, as well as in several regional capitals. Civil society and political opposition leaders marshaled their supporters to the streets, staging rallies, protest marches, and other demonstrations against the proposed amendment. On 23 October, the government closed all schools throughout the country in an attempt to control student protests. Well-known public places in the center of the capital such as the *Rond Point des Nations Unies*, *La Maison du Peuple*, and *La Place de la Nation*, became the sites of around the clock protest against the proposed changes. Security forces routinely dispersed the crowds that attempted to prevent deputies from arriving at the National Assembly by blocking streets. Then, on the morning of 30 October, in a surprising turn of events that was to provoke much subsequent speculation and debate, the crowds broke past security forces, entering the National Assembly and preventing the vote. As order broke down, crowds looted and burned buildings and private residences associated with the regime, including the home of the president's brother, the headquarters of the CDP, and the Ministry of Communication.

The de facto popular veto of the attempted constitutional change, however, failed to satisfy popular outrage. While crowds continued to loot and burn symbols of the regime, several thousand people gathered outside the presidential palace where they were stopped by the presidential guard, the *Régiment de la Sécurité Présidentielle* (RSP). After military leaders met with the leaders of these demonstrations, Compaoré publicly announced the cancellation of the bill, dissolved the government, and promised not to run in the presidential elections scheduled for 2015. This, however, proved to be insufficient; the various organizations composing the popular movement against the modification of Article Thirty-Seven had by then raised the stakes and united around a more ambitious demand: the immediate resignation of Blaise Compaoré.

On the morning of 31 October, the leaders of this movement, including university professors, lawyers, civil society leaders, and well-known popular culture personalities, held an urgent meeting with the leaders of security forces. Emerging from the intense discussions, the military's official spokesperson announced the immediate resignation of Blaise Compaoré from the presidency. The striking political miscalculation by the Compaoré regime thus not only put an end to attempts to modify presidential term limits in Burkina Faso, but it also brought an abrupt and unceremonious end to his twenty-seven years of rule.

The year that was to follow witnessed a series of dramatic events. Immediately following Compaoré's resignation two different leaders of the military claimed the position of interim president: military chief of staff General Honoré Traoré and deputy head of the RSP Lt. Colonel Isaac Zida. Pressure from civilian leaders who had led the insurrection, however, forced the military leaders to allow for a civilian-led political transition for which a charter was adopted on 13 November 2014. The political transition included a twenty-five-member cabinet, led by interim President Michel Kafando who was himself elected by members of civil society, the political opposition, and the military. Kafondo subsequently appointed Lt. Col. Zida as his Prime Minister. The Transitional Charter also prescribed a ninety-member interim legislative body, *Le Conseil National de Transition* (CNT) which provided thirty seats for the former political opposition, twenty-five seats for the military, twenty-five seats for civil society, and ten seats for parties from the former "presidential majority," that is the partisans of Compaoré. The principal task set for the CNT was to organize and administer democratic presidential and legislative elections so as to return the country to civilian rule within a year. From the beginning, however, the political transition was fraught with tensions as former members of the CDP and its allies sought to retain some of their political power.

Tensions between the former political opposition and the CDP remained high, and the CNT voted to exclude all politicians who had supported Compaoré's attempt to modify presidential term limits from standing in the legislative or presidential elections in 2015. This further exacerbated tensions between the transitional government and the former presidential guard, the RSP, as it became clear that the CNT also intended to undercut their powers. These tensions exploded into a revolt when, on 16 September, the RSP took transitional President Michel Kafando, Prime Minister Zida, and two other ministers in the transitional government hostage at the presidential palace. The apparent coup was short-lived, however, as the national military led a dramatic counter-coup over the course of several tense days, eventually forcing the RSP to surrender, and to disarm. The transitional government was immediately reinstated, Kafando returned to power, and the RSP was subsequently disbanded.

Despite the disruption resulting from the failed coup, the transitional government in fact managed the significant step of organizing elections before the end of 2015. The joint presidential and legislative elections held on 29 November were widely acknowledged as the freest, fairest, and most competitive elections in the country's history, raising expectations for the future of democracy in Burkina Faso.[4]

Burkina's transition raises significant and important questions about democratic transitions from semi-authoritarian regimes in Africa, and in itself will merit much more study and analysis.[5] In this chapter, however, we concentrate on the events leading up to the fall of Blaise Compaoré, and offer an explanation for this failed effort at changing presidential term limits. The Burkina Faso case raises a number of perplexing questions in this regard. Why would what appeared to be a strong, stable, and dominant regime collapse so suddenly? How can we explain the size, coordination, and speed at which popular demonstrations were organized, and why were they so effective? Why, in the end, was the Compaoré regime unable to impose another constitutional change in 2014, and how do we explain this failure considering the successes of other neighboring regimes in doing so?

In what follows we argue that while these events surprised many, largely due to the sheer velocity at which they unfolded, they are in fact the outcome of long processes of institutional debates and incremental reform in Burkina Faso. Although at some level Burkina had appeared to be a politically blocked system with a firmly entrenched semi-authoritarian regime, in fact a quarter century of institutional debates about the establishment of functioning democratic institutions had raised expectations and contributed to the gradual erosion of the foundations of the Compaoré regime. The 2014 debates about term limits served as a catalyst for the mobilization of popular disenchantment against a regime that, despite appearances, could no longer withstand such pressures.

Our analysis of the collapse of Blaise Compaoré's regime demonstrates that, despite appearances and electoral performance, semi-authoritarian regimes that have played the game of attempting to manage and control processes of "democratic" reform can in fact lose control of the process and be undermined by a gradual erosion of popular and internal-party support. In turn, these regimes become susceptible to collapse when a highly politicized issue such as the modification of presidential term limits galvanizes the populace into action. In the following sections, we first review the political context of Burkina Faso and the origins of Compaoré's semi-authoritarian regime. We then analyze the nature of the regime and the sources of both its resilience and vulnerability. The following sections explore the emergence of cracks in the regime's foundation, before analyzing the process that ultimately led to its demise.

Political Origins of the Compaoré Regime

Blaise Compaoré came to power via a military coup in 1987. Military coups and popular mobilization against the government feature prominently in Burkina Faso's political history since independence from France in 1960. By the time of Compaoré's arrival in power, the country had already experienced four military coups, multiple military regimes, a failed attempt at a political transition to a civilian regime, and a leftist revolutionary regime led by Captain Thomas Sankara, with the support of his then political ally, Compaoré himself.[6] This turbulent political history was paralleled by the development of a highly politicized civil society, marked in particular by the strength of trade and student unions. The revolutionary regime of Sankara sought to capitalize and co-opt the unions' ability to mobilize people by creating a wide-scale state network of National Revolutionary Committees (CNRs).[7] The CNRs diffused the party ideology throughout the country while simultaneously engendering a high level of public participation in state affairs. The dramatic restructuring of the Burkinabè state and the political legacy of Sankara's revolutionary ideology continue to leave their mark on Burkinabè politics, and indeed across West Africa.[8] Political parties continue to use the name Sankara to associate themselves with his ideals, and the 2014 *insurrection populaire* reflects the continued strength of the culture of high mobilization and political participation that is the legacy of Sankara's regime in Burkina Faso.

Despite his wide popularity early in his term, Sankara failed in the end to institutionalize his short-lived revolutionary regime, along the way losing the support of his former political advisors, the fellow military officers who had helped bring him to power.[9] In a sequence of events that continues to provoke intense debate, Sankara and several of his aides were assassinated in 1987 by troops loyal to Blaise Compaoré.[10] After Sankara's death, Compaoré rose to the head of the *Front Populaire*, a politico-military organization established to lead the country out of the political crisis brought on by Sankara's death. Compaoré's election to the presidency of the *Front* and the appointment to first and second vice-presidents of his close allies—Jean-Baptiste Boukary Lingani and Henri Zongo, respectively—took place in the context of widespread opposition and little legitimacy, given the widespread belief that they were responsible for Sankara's death. During his first several years in power Compaoré thus faced several attempted coups, and numerous executions of alleged coup planners were carried out. Indeed, in September 1989 both Lingani and Zongo were themselves accused of plotting a coup against Compaoré and were summarily executed. In this difficult context, and having insisted from the beginning that he would "rectify" the "revolution" by putting it back on the democratic road from which Sankara had deviated, Compaoré's search for legitimacy left him with little choice but to undertake tentative processes of political reform.

The stated goal of the *Rectification* was to end the chaos that had been caused by the risky and erratic leadership of the CNRs.[11] *Rectification* thus marked a shift from the leftist political orientation of Sankara's regime to a political system that purported to embrace the liberal democratic institutions that seemed inevitable at the time. In fact, the political exigencies of the worldwide "wave" of democratization of the early 1990s provided Blaise Compaoré an opportunity to secure his tenure and to provide a veneer of legitimacy to his rule—even if in the long run it also was to sow the seeds of his eventual demise. Attempting to avoid the fate of Moussa Traoré in Mali—whose resistance to democratic reform had led to his downfall—as well as that of Ali Saïbou in Niger—whose concession to negotiating changes resulted in his marginalization—Compaoré opted for pre-emptive "democratization" as a strategy for survival. Rejecting calls for a "National Conference" to decide the country's future,[12] he instead established an inclusive commission including members of the *Front Populaire*, unions, non-governmental organizations, as well as religious and traditional leaders to write the constitution of what was to be called the Fourth Republic.[13] More than a dozen political parties accepted the proposed constitution, largely modeled on the French Fifth Republic.[14] The constitution was adopted by referendum on 11 June 1991 with ninety-three percent of the vote in favor.

While the constitution allowed for the free creation of political parties, unions, and other civil society organizations, Compaoré kept tight control over the first elections and his political party, named at the time the *Organisation pour la Démocratie Populaire – Mouvement du Travail* (ODP/MT), maintained a hegemony over the *Front Populaire*.[15] In protest, the political opposition chose to boycott the first elections, and Compaoré was thus the sole presidential candidate in the inaugural elections of 1991, which also recorded the lowest participation rate in the country's history, some eighteen percent.[16] In the 1992 legislative elections that followed the ODP/MT won a majority of the seats in the National Assembly, solidifying the political dominance of Compaoré and his political party. Burkina Faso in the early 1990s thus appeared to join the ranks of what Bratton and Van de Walle labeled Africa's "flawed transitions."[17]

In 1996 the ODP/MT formed a political alliance with several smaller parties, including the rival *Convention Nationale des Patriotes Progressistes* (CNPP), to create the CDP. The new party was subsequently to win a majority of the seats at the National Assembly in each of the following legislative elections—until 2015.[18] The legislative elections of 1997 gave the CDP more than two-thirds of the seats at the National Assembly, allowing Compaoré to use his party's legislative dominance to modify presidential term limits in order to run for a consecutive third term. However, following Compaoré's contested re-election in 1998, large-scale opposition against the increasingly authoritarian nature of the regime began to emerge for the first time. These were sparked and driven largely by what would later be termed the "Zongo Affair."[19] This political crisis, which we explore further below, and the increased opposition to Compaoré and his regime, resulted in negotiations that led to a series of political, institutional, and electoral reforms which were adopted in July 2001.

Conceding to strong opposition demands, among the reforms implemented was the reinstitution of presidential term limits; the constitution henceforth prescribed that the president could serve a maximum of two five-year terms in office. In a blow to the opposition, however, the constitutional court ruled that the modification was nonretroactive, effectively treating Compaoré's 2005 bid to the presidency as if it were his first term. This same decision thus enabled Compaoré to run for re-election to a "second" constitutionally allowed term in 2010. Despite much dissatisfaction and amid challenges to his legitimacy, Compaoré in fact ran and won in the elections of 2005 and 2010. Importantly, however, under Article Thirty-Seven of the constitution, adopted as part of the reforms of 2001, Compaoré could not seek re-election in 2015. The question of Compaoré's future was thus at the center of political debates from the moment of his reelection in 2010. And it is in this context that the question emerged of whether the constitution's term limits provision should again be modified.

In retrospect, and despite the overwhelming electoral dominance of Compaoré and his party, the 1990s adoption of democratic institutions, the political reforms of 2001, and the regime's most recent failure to modify presidential term limits suggest that Burkina Faso did in fact experience some democratic progress over the period of his rule. Yet, the entirety of this progress took place in the shadow of Compaoré's power. For this reason, Burkina Faso under Compaoré, is frequently categorized by political scientists under one of the various subtypes of authoritarianism.[20] For our purposes here, however, we find it most useful to conceptualize the regime as "semi-authoritarian," and we understand that term to signify that the regime included both authoritarian and democratic traits, which varied throughout its existence. We contend that any given classification of the regime does not, in itself, offer much insight into how or why Compaoré's bid to change presidential term limits failed.[21] Rather, we believe it is more productive to examine the development of different aspects of the regime, the political context in which the term limits debate emerged, the shifting room to maneuver and the shifting incentives for key actors as the debate intensified.

What is striking to note from a consideration of the evolution of the Compaoré's regime are the ways in which it would gradually lose control of the very political institutions that it had adopted, at times simply by default given its origins and timing. Born in a military coup from the leftist revolutionary regime of Thomas Sankara, the new regime was quickly obliged to legitimize itself in the name of "democratic" rectification. Although tightly controlled from the beginning, these origins nevertheless sowed the seeds of democratic contestation, obliged the establishment of a political system officially opened to all political parties and with constitutionally protected space for a free press and civil society. To be sure, steps were regularly taken to ensure the political dominance of Compaoré and his political party. But increasing popular discontent with the dominance of the regime also led to continued and constant negotiation and contestation, carried out within the framework of "democracy" that had been established by the transition to the Fourth Republic. Gradually, and in incremental steps, these confrontations between government and opposition changed the political game in Burkina Faso, politicizing and reinforcing the importance of democratic political institutions and the principles they uphold through practices such as the limitation of presidential terms. The insurrection which would prove to be the regime's undoing grew out of this context and was mobilized by two decades of discussions of democracy.

We now turn to the various strategies employed by the Compaoré regime to better understand the nature of this political evolution and to explain the ultimate inability of Compaoré to change presidential term limits.

THE NATURE OF SEMI-AUTHORITARIANISM UNDER COMPAORÉ

In many ways, the Compaoré regime resembled many other semi-authoritarian regimes throughout Africa. Political dominance, based on a vast patrimonial network, allowed the CDP to dominate the legislature in successive elections, and the strong reliance on the executive throughout the political system entrenched Compaoré as a seemingly invincible political ruler.[22] Compaoré also used a strategy of co-optation by allying with the strongest political parties in the National Assembly in order to keep the opposition fragmented. Indeed, it was the frequent success of this strategy of crafting political alliances within the National Assembly that led the regime to believe that it would be able to modify presidential term limits in 2014.

While the regime was long successful in managing the political sphere via such techniques, its authoritarian face fueled popular disenchantment, which was to grow following each incidence of violent repression or abuse of power. From the onset of Compaoré's rule he faced significant popular resentment because of the regime's violent origins. The "original sin" of Sankara's death left a stain that continued to haunt Compaoré,[23] and popular discontent was further fed with each violent abuse of power.

At select junctures, Compaoré attempted to counter popular mobilization against his regime by conceding a variety of political reforms. To alleviate pressures for further democratic reform, he also periodically relied on a strategy of adopting a series of political compromises that could be manipulated to his benefit, by imploring religious, traditional, and opposition leaders to embrace political "forgiveness" for the sake of national unity and in the name of a culture of reconciliation. Compaoré implemented this strategy with some success during the "*Réctification*," as well as later during the "Zongo Affair." Cyclically, however, reactions to violent repression would again challenge Compaoré's political dominance and again force the regime to make political compromises with the political opposition.[24] These incremental compromises gradually strengthened notions of democracy and slowly undermined his regime, ultimately allowing political opposition and civil society sufficient political sway with the citizenry to fracture and weaken the regime's hold on power. The politics of oscillation between compromise and repression are crucial to the nature of Compaoré's semi-authoritarian regime, and their history is essential to an understanding of its longer-term trajectory.

Already in 1990, when a student union leader named Dabo Boukary died while in police custody, a wide array of student unions came together to protest the repressive nature of the regime. A second wave of protests and a broader movement against the repression of the Compaoré regime joined ongoing student activism following the deaths in 1998 of investigative journalist Norbert Zongo and three of his colleagues.[25] These politically motivated killings sparked a socially diverse movement against the regime under the umbrella organization of *Collectif d'Organisations Démocratiques de Masse et de Partis Politiques* (CODMPP) which included the student unions, university professors, opposition parties, media actors, labor unions, and women's associations.[26] The CODMPP spearheaded a country-wide anti-regime movement called *"Trop c'est trop"* ("Enough is enough"), and placed an enormous amount of pressure on the Compaoré regime to dramatically reform the political system. The movement sustained constant critiques of key leaders in the Compaoré regime, publicly calling on President Compaoré to account for the death of Zongo and his colleagues.[27] Strikingly, the regime was unable to suppress such critiques, and the continuous denunciations of abuses by Compaoré's regime and the calls for justice and accountability persisted.

In 1999, in response to the wide-scale protests and demonstration led by the *"Trop C'est Trop"* campaign, Compaoré appointed a special commission known as the *Collège des Sages*, composed of religious, traditional, and former political leaders. The commission generated a report to the government with a series of recommendations for institutional reform intended to help reestablish stability in the country.[28] Among the various recommendations in the report were reforms to the electoral code, the constitution—notably the reinstatement of presidential term limits—and the administration of elections. In 2001, the government in fact adopted many of these reforms, most significantly by changing presidential term limits to a maximum of two five-year consecutive terms, and the adoption of proportional representation for legislative elections. Initially, these reforms were met with some satisfaction, and they did indeed lessen popular pressure on the regime and restored some social calm to the country.

The actual political consequences of the reforms, however, were mixed. On one hand, the reforms to the electoral code and the administration of elections dramatically improved the level of competition in legislative elections. The 2002 legislative elections under proportional representation thus yielded the strongest results that the political opposition has ever received, winning roughly forty-nine percent of the seats in the National Assembly.[29] On the other hand, the impact of the modification to presidential term limits—ostensibly made to promote the possibility of political turnover at the level of the executive—was effectively muted when the Constitutional Council ruled that the new limitations could not be applied to Compaoré's previous terms. His candidacy in the 2005 presidential elections would thus be considered his first term, under the new presidential term limits.

This political victory for Compaoré and his regime appears to have disillusioned civil society movements, which had up to then seen the reforms as a hard-fought victory for democracy. In a study conducted following the 2005 presidential election, Mazzocchetti[30] found that student mobilization no longer centered on grievances against the authoritarian nature of the regime, but rather had shifted to a focus on the economic interests of the students. Indeed, she found that students were so disillusioned with the results of the *"Trop C'est Trop"* campaign that rather than attempting to challenge the regime, student leaders had begun to rely on protests and mobilization as a means of demonstrating the value of their allegiance to Compaoré's patrimonial regime.[31] Compaoré had not only won the opportunity to remain in power for another two terms, but in the wake of this success his party reasserted its dominance over the political system and weakened the power of political and civil society actors for democratic contestation.

In hindsight, Compaoré's electoral victory in 2005 appears to have been the peak of his regime's tenure in power. The regime had weathered the political crisis of the Norbert Zongo affair and the subsequent mass demonstrations led by a strong and politicized civil society. Despite electoral losses at the National Assembly, the Constitutional Court's decision not to apply the new presidential term limits retroactively all but guaranteed the continuation of Compaoré's presidential leadership for the next decade. Yet, despite these political victories for the regime, the reinstatement of presidential term limits and the massive protests which had brought them into being meant that the regime would need to take institutional rules more seriously in the future, and they demonstrated the importance with which the CDP and Compaoré would need to consider his eventual succession.

The very nature of semi-authoritarian regimes, like the one established under Compaoré, is characterized by ambiguity about the possibilities for political change. The events that pressured the regime to reform certain aspects of the electoral code and constitution demonstrated that, although difficult, aspects of the political system in Burkina Faso were debatable and open to political change. Therefore, while Compaoré's political victories helped secure his continued political domination for a time, they also displayed an inherent weakness. By crafting a political system based formally on democratic institutions, Compaoré's regime was unable to completely eliminate the voice of the people and, in fact, reform of that system could augment the ability of the people to be represented in the political system. The political reforms forced upon the regime by the popular mobilizations of the *"Trop C'est Trop"* movement strengthened mechanisms of vertical accountability even if they did not amount to the full democratization of the regime.[32] The regime appeared durable, but in reality, its stability depended on the acquiescence of the political opposition and civil society to the political game. It is within this context, as the end of Compaoré's second constitutional term approached in 2015, that the looming succession crisis emerged, and Compaoré's regime began to unravel.

Cracks in the Edifice: The Fragmentation of the CDP and the Erosion of Compaoré's Power

Following Compaoré's re-election in 2005 and the subsequent announcement that he would once again plan to run in 2010, factions of the CDP began to raise questions about the lack of democratic procedures in the party. These concerns would eventually erode the support from many of Compaoré's closest allies in the party, gradually weakening the seemingly invincible CDP political machine. The opposition and civil society followed these developments closely, taking advantage of the moment to mount increased criticism against the regime. Even before his re-election in 2010, CDP party members started laying the groundwork for their own 2015 presidential campaigns, evoking presidential term limits as a central pillar of the democratic system. These small internal cracks in the party edifice were to grow, eventually providing an opening for much broader, external mobilizations to limit the regime's hold on power. While the actual sequence of events which deposed Compaoré from power took only a matter of days, the erosion of Compaoré's political support and the increased popular mobilization behind civil society and the political opposition against the removal of presidential term limits in fact commenced already following Compaoré's election in 2005.

By 2007, two years after his reelection and after twenty years of Blaise Compaoré as president, internal divisions within the CDP began to emerge, raising serious questions for the future of the party and for Compaoré's rule. Initial tensions within the CDP revolved around the representation of the original ODT/MT members of the CDP and the CNPP—the political party that had merged with the ODT/MT in 1996 to form the CDP. Leaders of the CNPP faction accused the CDP leadership of marginalizing their contingent of the party in the 2007 legislative elections, in which none of the former CNPP members won seats in the National Assembly. Breaking party solidarity, the leadership of the CNPP made their grievances public, denouncing the CDP's authoritarian style of leadership. In the context of growing internal tensions, leading members of the CNPP were suspended from the party in 2009, and subsequently resigned from the party. Among those leaving the party were Marc Oubriki Yao, a former ambassador to Ghana, vice president of the National Assembly, and second vice president of the CDP. This schism culminated in the creation of a new opposition party, the *Convention Nationale du Progrès du Burkina* (CNPB), ahead of the 2010 presidential elections. The founding congress of the new party drew some 400 delegates, including former supporters of the CDP, and thus signaled the significance of the rift within the leadership of the CDP.

Other changes in the political leadership of the CDP also pointed to rising internal divisions and to the erosion of the party's base. In 2008 Salif Diallo, the first vice president of the CDP, minister of state for agriculture and fisheries, and a longtime political advisor to Compaoré, was dismissed from his ministerial post. This followed an open political rivalry with the then-Prime Minister Tertius Zongo, and an alleged conflict between Diallo about the increased responsibilities of François Compaoré—the president's brother—in the CDP. Diallo was later appointed ambassador to Austria, essentially condemning the former political baron to exile. In the following year, Diallo gave an interview to an important local newspaper "*L'Observateur Paalga*" in which he indirectly questioned President Compaoré's leadership. Diallo called for significant democratic reforms to Burkina's political system, including a move from the presidential system to a parliamentary one.[33] This attack on Compaoré incited outrage within the CDP, and Diallo was quickly suspended from all of his leadership positions. The suspension was removed in 2010 after Diallo submitted a letter of self-criticism to the executive committee, but the damage had been done. Diallo's actions mark the beginning of a gradual fraying of cohesion within the CDP's leadership.

Aware of the brooding internal debates in the CDP, the political opposition and civil society organizations seized the opportunity to reignite their fight against the authoritarian nature of Compaoré's regime. On the tenth anniversary of Norbert Zongo's murder, the CODMPP revived its campaign for a review of the Zongo case and the suspected involvement of government officials by submitting a petition with 100,000 signatures. In 2009, as the 2010 presidential elections approached, prominent figures including professor of political science Augustin Loada, human rights lawyer Prosper Farama, and former government minister and deputy director of the United Nations Development Program Zéphirin Diabré, established the *Forum des citoyens de l'alternance*, to militate for political turnover ("*alternance*"). The forum brought together some 250 participants to work against the prolongation of Blaise Compaoré in power. It also marked the beginning of Diabré's political ambitions and his clear break with the CDP. Indeed, some speculated that Diabré might contest the 2010 presidential elections.

In this context, nearly a year ahead of the 2010 presidential elections, the debate over presidential term limits resurfaced and garnered support from various influential actors. In a public statement, the Burkinabè Bishops preempted some of the discussion by advocating for the preservation of Article Thirty-Seven. Similarly, an opinion poll published in June 2009 by the *Centre pour la Gouvernance Démocratique* (CGD) reported that fifty-three percent of the Burkinabè population supported the maintenance of presidential terms. Leading members of the CDP quickly responded. On 30 November 2009, Mahama Sawadogo, president of the CDP parliamentary group, published an editorial in the state-run newspaper *Sidwaya*, in which he argued that the limitation to two terms strips the people of their democratic right to voice their approval or disapproval of the president's administration. While there was no significant contestation of Compaoré's candidacy (and anticipated re-election) in 2010, the renewed debate over presidential terms was clearly launched in anticipation of the 2015 poll.[34]

In August 2010, a few months ahead of the November presidential elections, the CDP made its position on the matter of presidential term limits abundantly clear when the party's steering committee announced that the constitution needed to be amended. The main argument advanced by the CDP was that term limitations were inherently undemocratic since they deprived the people of the possibility to re-elect a leader should they want to do so. Unsurprisingly, this elicited a strong response from the political opposition and anti-regime segments of civil society. Organizations such as the human rights organization, *Mouvement Burkinabè des Droits de l'Homme et du Peuple* (MBDHP), the CGD, and trade unions, continued their public opposition to any change to the term limits. Meanwhile, the formal opposition leader and president of the *Union pour la Renaissance/Parti Sankariste* party, Bénéwendé Sankara, called for demonstrations of civil disobedience. The Catholic Bishops Conference of Burkina Faso, which had supported Compaoré in his 2005 bid for re-election, publicly declared themselves against any proposed amendment to the constitution. A newly created movement, the *Coalition Contre la Révision de l'Article Thirty-Seven*, organized a public petition against changing the constitution, and gathered some 30,000 signatures. These various events underscored the growing internal tension within the CDP, the continued opposition to term limit reforms from both political and civil society organizations and, importantly, signaled a loss of support for the regime from the religious community. Apparently tone deaf to popular sentiment, however, these factors did not affect the CDP's resolve, and it continued to signal its intent to seek a modification of term limits ahead of the 2015 elections.

Following Compaoré's re-election in late 2010, the rising popular discontent with the regime resulted in dramatic large-scale mobilizations from trade, public worker, student, and teachers' unions. Strikes and other demonstrations were held throughout 2011, focusing on improving work conditions, lowering prices, and improving educational facilities and support. More importantly, they displayed the growing discontent of the populace with the practices of the regime and the unions' ability to mobilize their members into action against the regime. More surprising than the unions' demonstrations was the reaction of disgruntled soldiers.

The same fundamental causes—economic grievances, political impunity, and the almost exclusive political dominance of the CDP—sparked resentment and discontent within the military, an institution that had long been a pillar of Compaoré's power. The death of a student, Justin Zongo, in police custody sparked widespread popular protests and a new wave of public dissatisfaction with the regime.[35] When the police officers implicated in Zongo's death were taken into custody, brewing discontent and perceptions of mistreatment by the regime within the security forces resulted in significant insecurity. Mutinies spread throughout the country during the month of March 2011, characterized by soldiers looting and acting with impunity in Ouagadougou and several of the country's regional capitals. Despite the government's convening of meetings of the leaders of security forces to attempt to bring things under control, the military uprising continued to escalate.[36] In April members of the RSP, the presidential guard, rioted and fired weaponry in the streets of Ouagadougou, leading Compaoré to be evacuated from the capital to his hometown of Zinaré. While economic grievances might explain the actions of other segments of the security forces, the RSP was and continued to be one of the best-funded branches of the military. Their revolt thus seemed to signal significant internal problems and a rising disenchantment with the Compaoré regime.

Within two days of the first RSP revolts, Compaoré dissolved the government and named a new one, which promptly made a series of concessions in an attempt to put an end to the rioting of both the military and the various unions. However, with no clear concessions to the military other than the overhaul of the leadership and promises to disburse the salaries that were in arrears, the mutinous soldiers continued their anti-regime campaign. More military riots and civilian strikes broke out throughout the month of May, spreading to additional military bases. On 31 May the military riots led to violent events in Bobo Dioulasso, the country's second largest city. These events sparked an immediate reaction from Compaoré, and special forces—including segments of the RSP, Parachutist, and the *Gendarmerie Mobile*—were dispatched to end the riots by force. As a consequence of the widespread nature of the revolts the government dismissed all regional governors. The response to the RSP mutinies also included the dismissal of several close political allies of Compaoré from their leadership roles in the military. While the decision to use force to put an end to the mutinies was effective, the events underlined the extent to which military support for Compaoré and his regime was waning.

In light of the declining support, Compaoré and the CDP again launched an ambitious reform program in an attempt to bolster their position ahead of legislative elections scheduled for 2012. The implementation of these reforms was spearheaded by the *Conseil Consultatif sur les Réformes Politiques* (CCRP) headed by one of Compaoré's closest allies, Bongnessan Yé, Minister of State for Institutional Reforms. In principle, the CCRP was a consensual and inclusive institution, however, the political opposition considered the institution to be illegal and boycotted the entirety of the reform process. The CCRP submitted a report outlining a variety of institutional reforms, but remained silent on the issues of Article Thirty-Seven and presidential terms. The government then convened a series of regional conferences and a national conference to "openly debate" the proposed reforms. The CODMPP, which comprised the strongest opposition parties and civil society organizations, boycotted the conferences, thus effectively removing their voices from the process. More than 1500 delegates took part in the national conference held in Ouagadougou and most of the proposed reforms were approved, most significantly the creation of a second chamber in the legislature, the Senate.

The National Assembly promptly adopted the reforms proposed by the CCRP, modifying over sixty articles of the constitution, most of them linked to the creation of the Senate so as to introduce a bicameral legislature. The new Senate was slated to be established the following year and was designed to provide representation to sub-national administrative units, religious and traditional leaders, employers and trade unions, as well as the diaspora. However, a number of ambiguities remained around the Senate's implementation, including the exact number of senators, its precise powers beyond serving as a consultative institution, and the ability of the president to appoint members to this new institution. These ambiguities fueled political conflict, and the Senate became another focal point of political debate as a new political opposition mobilized to contest Compaoré.

In 2010 Zéphirin Diabré, one of the leaders of the *Coalition Contre la Révision de l'Article Trente-Sept*, created a new political party the *Union pour le Progrès et le Changement* (UPC). Although Diabré did not contest the presidential elections of 2010, his party set up a national network with their eyes fixed on the upcoming legislative elections. These elections were to solidify Diabré and the UPC as important actors within the political opposition; the party won nineteen seats in the National Assembly, second to the CDP's seventy, and tied with the CDP-ally the *Alliance pour la Démocratie et la Fédération/Rassemblement Démocratique Africain* (ADF/RDA). Consequently, Diabré became the officially recognized leader of the political opposition. While the CDP maintained a very dominant absolute majority, the UPC's nineteen seats represented the largest number of seats a single opposition party had ever won in the National Assembly, signaling the possibility of an important political opening in favor of the opposition.

The UPC joined with other opposition parties and civil society organizations, such as the *Coalition Contre le Vie Chère* (CCVC), which had participated actively in the civilian strikes of 2011, in a critical campaign against the creation of the Senate. CCVC capitalized on public disenchantment with the economic situation of country, enabling the campaign to mobilize tens of thousands of demonstrators in marches across Ouagadougou. Much of the debate against the Senate denounced the institution as an unnecessary budgetary expense. Others, notably Compaoré's political opponents, argued that the Senate might be manipulated by Compaoré to modify Article Thirty-Seven, thus allowing the president to run for re-election in 2015. The tense political context of popular mobilization again fed the birth of new civil society organizations such as *Le Balai Citoyen* (The Citizen's Broom). Launched by well-known and wildly popular young local musicians, Smockey and Sams K Le Jah, the movement protested the autocratic practices of the regime.

Despite the rising tide of protests, some CDP politicians continued to argue that presidential term limits restricted the people's choice, and were thus inherently undemocratic. In light of the massive popular mobilizations against the Senate, however, former supporters of the CDP began to distance themselves from that project. The law stipulated that unions, employers, traditional chiefs, religious groups, and the diaspora would receive representation in the Senate, yet it found little support among these groups. Trade unions, largely considered allies of the civil society movements joined in the boycott called by the political opposition. The Catholic bishops openly criticized the institution and signaled their unwillingness to take part in any government institutions. At the Episcopal Conference of Burkina Faso and Niger, the archbishop of Bobo Dioulasso went so far as to say that the creation of the Senate was a danger to social peace. Both traditional chiefs and evangelical leaders withheld their support, with both groups stating that they favored social peace over institutional reforms. Compaoré reacted to the lack of support by creating an Evaluation Committee to propose recommendations on how to increase support for the Senate. The committee neglected to consult with the principal critics of the institution, a fact which the political opposition publicly deplored. By the end of October 2013, the *Médiateur du Faso* (National Ombudsman), a government-appointed official, publicly sided with the notion that the Senate should not be created in the present social context. Ultimately, the Senate was never established.

This failure to force the creation of a Senate clearly signaled the waning support for Compaoré among sectors of society on which he had previously relied, such as traditional and religious leaders. It also underlined the changing social context faced by the Compaoré regime. The protests against the Senate led by civil society organizations primed the population for action against the modification of presidential term limits. They also served to increase the amount of coordination among organizations with similar goals, reinforcing their ability to coalesce around a common cause. Finally, the fact that the Senate was never established despite being approved by the National Assembly demonstrated that a stronger and more unified political opposition had emerged from the 2012 legislative elections. If the political opposition did not have the votes to beat the CDP in the legislature, the ability to mobilize massive demonstrations against the regime's attempts to further entrench its political dominance offered the opposition an alternative tool to prevent the CDP's political project from coming to fruition. Recognizing the weakening state of the political party and the increased political support for the political opposition, CDP members were then to break from the party when it became clear that Compaoré would indeed attempt to run for re-election in 2015.

One of the first members of the CDP to resign from the party was Saran Sérémé. She was sidelined by the CDP prior to the legislative elections of 2012 and as a result did not win a seat in the National Assembly. Sérémé filed a grievance with the *Commission Electorale Nationale Independante* (CENI), claiming that her position on the ballot had been illegally changed. When that grievance was denied, she resigned from the party. Sérémé would then go on to lead one of the largest women's movements against the Compaoré regime. The most significant blow to the CDP's strength, however, occurred in the beginning of 2014 when seventy-five members of the party collectively resigned.

The resignation letter listed a variety of grievances, but chief among them were the authoritarian leadership of the party and the desire of the president to modify presidential term limits and remain in power. Among those who resigned were three very influential members who had recently began to distance themselves from the party in the wake of the Senate debacle. Roch Marc Christian Kaboré, former president of the National Assembly as well as former president of the CDP, led the group which resigned. He was joined by Salif Diallo, the former minister who had been exiled to his diplomatic post in Austria, and by Simon Compaoré (no relation to the president) who had been mayor of Ouagadougou for seventeen years until he gave up his post at the end of 2013.

Each of these former figureheads of the CDP had seen their influence in the party weakened when the *Fédération Associative pour la Paix et le Progrès avec Blaise Compaoré* (FEDAP/BC), an organization with close ties to the president's brother, became one of the strongest organizations to mobilize voters to the polls during the 2010 presidential elections. In a reshuffling of both the CDP leadership and the FEDAP/BC leadership all three of the former party heavyweights were excluded from leadership positions. Additionally, those who were appointed to leadership positions suggested that Compaoré was attempting to enhance his personal ties with business leaders close to his brother François and perhaps even set François up for a bid at the presidency. The move by Kaboré, Diallo, and Simon Compaoré to break with the CDP indicated the growing divisions within the party, especially among the leadership.

Two weeks after their resignation from the party, these three major political figures and their supporters joined Diabré, president of the UPC and formal leader of the opposition, in a demonstration in Ouagadougou. The demonstration drew tens of thousands of protesters, with the principal demand being to maintain Article Thirty-Seven. Other demonstrations organized by the political opposition took place in the cities of Bobo-Dioulasso, Koudougou, Fada N'Gourma, Dédougou, Kaya, and other regional capitals. Following this country-wide campaign against the modification of term limits, those who had resigned from the CDP created a new political party the *Mouvement du Peuple pour le Progrès* (MPP). At its founding congress, the party comprised 117 members, all of whom had previously belonged to the CDP. The MPP joined the political opposition which, along with civil society organizations against the modification of presidential terms, would launch the largest campaign against the regime that Burkina Faso has ever witnessed.

In the following months the political opposition, led by the UPC and MPP, held a series for protests, conventions, marches, and rallies. The opposition also often joined with civil society organizations like the *Balai Citoyen* to coordinate among their supporters. The message was simple: these organizations, parties, and their supporters opposed any attempt by the government to modify Article Thirty-Seven, even by popular referendum. The fear of a referendum was based on the fact that the CDP had a large amount of support throughout the countryside and had in place the patronage networks to get out the vote that might allow the party then to secure a victory in a referendum. Nevertheless, preparing for this possibility, some media outlets allied with the anti-modification civil society organizations reached out to rural populations and published news articles against the referendum and the modification of term limits in local languages throughout the country.

The CDP nevertheless continued to call for the modification of Article Thirty-Seven. They held counter-demonstrations in the same venues as the opposition. An alliance of political parties called the *Front Républicain* was created to campaign actively in favor a referendum on the term limits and pro-Blaise civil society organizations like FEDAP/BC marshaled supporters in stadiums where they would hear from popular music icons (local and international) as well as the president of the CDP, Assimi Kouanda. The real extent of popular support was unclear; many private local media outlets reported that "supporters" were being paid and transported to these events in an effort to give the impression of widespread support for a referendum and for modification of the term limits.

At the 2014 US Africa Summit in Washington, DC Compaoré sparked outrage and condemnation from the opposition in Ouagadougou. Taking a stance against US President Obama, Compaoré was quoted as saying that in Africa there "will not be strong institutions unless there are strong men" to lead them.[37] The statement seemed to have only increased support for the anti-referendum camp. Indeed, following this statement, the largest demonstration to date took place when a reported 100,000 filled the streets of Ouagadougou on 23 August, for an eight-kilometer protest march. After this protest the US Ambassador to Burkina Faso, Tulinabo Mushingi also joined the fray, expressing the concern of the United States over the increasing political tensions and stressed that upholding institutional rules and respecting the constitution were key to reinforcing democracy. Mushingi went on to point out that the country had never experienced a peaceful transition, suggesting that the current political tensions elicited a fear of an uncertain future. These high-profile comments from the US Ambassador, as well as similar concerns for social peace expressed by religious and traditional leaders, provoked another round of attempted mediation between the political opposition and the presidential majority. Within this context a relative calm spread briefly over Ouagadougou. Suspicions soon rose, however, that these mediated negotiations were only a ploy to calm the situation so as to provide time for the CDP to work on lining up the support of the necessary three-quarter of the deputies, so as to be able to pass a bill modifying presidential term limits without recourse to a popular referendum.

Dénouement: The End of Twenty-Seven Years in Power

In the face of clear and strong public sentiment, Blaise Compaoré and the CDP nevertheless attempted to pursue their goal of lifting presidential term limits by other means, side-stepping the population and avoiding a popular referendum. The decision immediately produced public outrage, and in the days before the vote on the bill was scheduled, the population took to the streets in mass protests. Although security forces initially secured the National Assembly, in a still-debated and surprising turn of events on 30 October, as the deputies were scheduled to take the vote on the bill, the forces stationed outside of the National Assembly stood down to the masses and allowed them to pass. Protesters stormed the National Assembly, lighting it on fire and preventing the vote.

Demonstrations continued throughout the capital on the following day, with much looting and burning of public buildings and of the private residences of officials associated with the regime. As the climate of insurrection and anger escalated, the demands also grew: from the initial goal of simply blocking the vote to remove Article Thirty-Seven of the constitution, the street now raised the stakes, demanding no less than the immediate resignation of the president. Compaoré scrambled to control the situation, announcing major concessions including a promise not to seek reelection in 2015. But his efforts proved to be too little, too late. After a dramatic meeting between the leaders of the security forces, civil society organizations and the political opposition, a spokesperson for the military emerged to announce that Compaoré had resigned. Thus, this seemingly invincible regime, one of the most stable in Sahelian Africa and led by a president who had proven to date to be remarkably adept at oscillating between repression and comprise to stay in power, came to an abrupt end.

How to explain not only this important failure to amend the constitution to remove presidential term limits, but indeed that the effort to do so would prove to be the regime's undoing? Certainly, several factors contributed to the demise of the Compaoré regime. To begin with, one must underline the inability to erase the legitimacy gap inherent in the regime's origins in the assassination of Thomas Sankara. In a political culture with an extremely low tolerance for violence and especially murder, Compaoré's association with this death plagued him from the start, and this was to be further fueled by other incidences of violence, notably the death of Norbert Zongo. Many of the civil society organizations that played a crucial role in the demonstrations against the modification of the term limits in fact had their origins in the Zongo Affair. Increased political grievances coupled with the authoritarian and repressive history of the regime's origins meant that gradually Compaoré and the CDP lost support and popular legitimacy, even if the political system was crafted in such a way that electoral results did not demonstrate this fact.

The loss of public support and increased political discontent had consequences within the ruling party as well. As the future of the regime gradually seemed in doubt, political grievances emerged among the diverse coalition of actors that had been brought together under the party's umbrella. The resulting restructuring of the CDP to bring the familial and business interests closer to the president was to cost Compaoré the support of other important members of the party. This dynamic reached its peak with the resignation of seventy-five members and the creation of the new MPP opposition party. This incident itself grew out of the growing political crisis that had followed the presidential elections of 2005, when the CNPP broke away from the party, Salif Diallo became ambassador to Austria, and Zéphirin Diabré left the private sector to create a new political party aligned with the opposition. All of these events suggest that a long-term dynamic was at work from the moment of Compaoré's re-election in 2005, as the specter of a succession crisis loomed for 2015, when term limits would require a change.

As his control over political dynamics slipped, Compaoré found himself losing influential support from a variety of other important sectors: traditional chiefs and religious leaders, the media and, importantly, both the military and outside powers. While these actors had often served the regime well in terms of lending support and helping to control and calm social movements, they gradually distanced themselves from the regime. The Catholic bishops proved to be the most stalwart in their opposition to the modification of term limits, and they also served an important role in the failure to establish the Senate. Similarly, the evangelical churches stood against the reform, as well as important traditional chiefs. Private media also played a role, in some cases directly, by participating in the leadership of organizations like the *Balai Citoyen*, and by taking the message to the rural areas in local languages.[38]

Of crucial importance, in the context of diminishing legitimacy and increased contestation, the regime proved unable to keep control over an increasingly restive military. The 2011 military mutinies were the first very clear manifestation of the regime's inability to address the growing political and economic grievances of the armed forces. While the fact that a coup was averted at the time suggests that at least some factions were still loyal to Compaoré, the extent of the protests and the government's eventual need to make concessions underlined the waning support for the regime within this crucial state institution. By 2014, rumors around Ouagadougou suggested that important segments of the military had actually come to side with the movements against the modification of presidential term limits. Military men, it was said, had circulated crucial information about their positions prior to the storming of the National Assembly, and had tellingly stood aside at the crucial moment when the crowd took control.

While we can identify these as the main factors specific to Burkina's political evolution that contributed to the failure of the effort at modifying term limits, all of these factors must be understood in terms of a much more profound and important dynamic. The "democratization" announced by the regime in the early 1990s, in the African context of the Third Wave and as a survival tactic for a regime with no initial legitimacy, created a framework and set in motion a dynamic that was in the longer run to undermine the regime itself. Even if frequently challenged and undermined, the framework of "democracy" could never be fully abandoned, and it was this very framework that gave rise to debates about constitutional provisions and other political institutions. In Burkina as in much of the region and elsewhere in Africa, we are still seeing the implications of the efforts to build durable political institutions in the name of the democratic transitions that were announced a quarter century ago—even when they seemed fundamentally "flawed" at the time. While in very different ways and dynamics, we have seen other presidents in the region fail in their efforts to remain in power into a third term—in Niger in 2010 or in Senegal in 2012, for example.

The political struggles to control and define democratic institutions can produce a gradual erosion of the support that semi-authoritarian regimes tend to enjoy immediately following their creation. This is especially the case for what some have called "hegemonic party regimes"[39] in which one party dominates all aspects of the political system, as with the CDP. In such cases the looming problems associated with succession may produce debates over presidential term limits, but they also divide the party as would-be successors, and often former political allies, are sidelined to protect support for the incumbent president. This brings about internal political dissent and creates incentives for actors to search for external political support, all at the expense of the regime and its ability to control the reform process. Immediately following Compaoré's re-election in 2005, the CDP began strategizing for the inevitable problem of the 2015 elections. This contributed to the internal deterioration of the party's cohesion as prominent members of the party were marginalized. These very same members later emerged as leaders of one of the most important political parties in the movements against the modification of presidential term limits.

Burkina Faso thus suggests the possibilities for democratic progress to occur within semi-authoritarian regimes. Even when a dominant party has perfected the apparatus that makes it seemingly invincible at the polls, the gradual development of political and civil society organizations that can brandish the rhetoric of democracy to contest and open a space for independent action creates new possibilities and encourages the development of norms of behavior associated with, and desirable for, democratic institutions. And somewhat paradoxically, then, these regimes produce—or at least allow for the production of—the very elements that create their undoing in the longer run.

Acknowledgements This paper is based on extensive research in Burkina Faso, carried out under the auspices of the Sahel Research Group at the University of Florida, and made possible by a Minerva Initiative grant for a research project on "Political Reform, Socio-Religious Change, and Stability in the African Sahel." We gratefully acknowledge the support of the Minerva program, which has made possible extensive fieldwork in Burkina Faso and neighboring countries. The views expressed in this chapter are those of the authors and are not an official policy or position of the National Defense University, the Department of Defense or the U.S. Government.

NOTES

1. Professor Augustin Loada, a key actor in the uprising and who was to serve as a minister in the transitional government to follow, was among many who expressed this sentiment in an interview we conducted with him in March 2015.
2. Lila Chouli, "The Popular Uprising in Burkina Faso and the Transition," *Review of African Political Economy* 42, no. 144 (2015): 325–333.

3. In accordance with the constitution, amendments that receive three-quarters of the vote in the National Assembly become law without being voted on by the public. If the proposed amendment receives a simple majority of the vote in the National Assembly (but less than seventy-five percent) it then precedes to a national referendum where it must obtain a majority of the popular vote to become law. The decision to take the bill to the National Assembly in October 2014 suggested that the government was assured that it had secured the support of the required three-quarters of deputies and could thus avoid a referendum.
4. Independent observers, both locally and internationally, described the elections this way and congratulated the CENI and civil society's efforts to ensure that the elections took place with as few irregularities as possible. See Eloïse Bertrand, "How Burkina Faso Ensured Its Freest and Fairest Elections Ever," *African Arguments*, December 2, 2015. http://africanarguments.org/2015/12/02/how-burkina-faso-ensured-its-freest-and-fairest-ever-elections/; Daniel Eizenga, "Burkina Faso Elections Mark Turning Point in Country's Recent Political Turmoil," *Washington Post's Monkey Cage*, December 6, 2015. https://www.washingtonpost.com/news/monkey-cage/wp/2015/12/06/burkina-faso-elections-mark-a-turning-point-in-a-country-in-political-turmoil/; National Democratic Institute, "High Expectations for Democracy in Burkina Faso After 2015 Elections," December 11, 2015, https://www.ndi.org/burkina-faso-elections-2015.
5. For an in depth comparative analysis of regime trajectories in Burkina Faso, Chad and Senegal that gives special attention to the 2015 political transition in Burkina Faso, see Daniel Eizenga, "Managing Political Liberalization After Multiparty Elections: Regime Trajectories in Burkina Faso, Chad and Senegal," PhD dissertation, University of Florida, 2018.
6. Maurice Yaméogo, the first President of Burkina Faso, was ousted from power by the military following massive protests led by labor unions. Lt. Col. Aboubakar Lamizana subsequently became president of a military regime. Lamizana initiated a transition process aimed at returning the country to civilian rule in 1978, but in 1980, before the transition was completed, he was deposed by a military coup. Col. Saye Zerbo then became president before he was himself removed from power by another military coup in 1982. The military then appointed Maj. Jean Baptiste Ouégraogo president. He was overthrown in 1983 by the revolutionary regime of Captain Thomas Sankara. Blaise Compaoré was to become president after a contingent of the military loyal to Compaoré assassinated Sankara in 1987.
7. Charles Kabeya Muase. *Syndicalisme et Démocratie en Afrique Noire: L'Experience du Burkina Faso* (Paris: INADÉS Éditions and Karthala, 1989),

213–214. Muase offers an in-depth account of the development of unions in Burkina Faso from before independence through Sankara's regime.
8. Thomas Sankara and Michel Prairie, *Thomas Sankara Speaks: The Burkina Faso Revolution, 1983–87* (Pathfinder, 2007).
9. Pierre Englebert, *Burkina Faso: Unsteady Statehood in West Africa* (Boulder, CO: Westview Press, 1996).
10. Among those who were killed alongside Sanakra were journalist Paulin Bamouni, university professor Sibiri Alain Zagré, *Sergeants-Chefs* Emmanuel Bationo and Amadé Sawadogo, as well as employees of the presidency Frédéric Liemdé and Bonaventure Compaoré.
11. Bruno Jaffré, *Les Années Sankara, de la Révolution à la Rectification* (Paris: l'Harmattan, 1989).
12. In the early nineties, a number of francophone African countries held "national conferences," or similarly structured deliberative bodies, to elaborate new constitutions based largely on the liberal democratic model of the West. These included: Benin 1990, Gabon 1990, Congo-Brazzaville 1991, Niger 1991, Mali 1991, Togo 1991, Congo-Kinshasa (then Zaire) 1992, Chad 1993. For comparative discussions of this phenomenon, see F. Eboussi Boulaga. *Les Conférences Nationales en Afrique Noire: Une affaire à suivre* (Paris: Karthala, 1993). Pearl Robinson, "The National Conference Phenomenon in Francophone Africa," *Comparative Studies in Society and History* 36, no. 3 (1994): 575–610. On the political transitions in Mali and Niger, which weighed heavily on Compaoré's decisions, see Leonardo A. Villalón and Abdourahmane Idrissa, "Repetitive Breakdowns and a Decade of Experimentation: Institutional Choices and Unstable Democracy in Niger," in Leonardo A. Villalón and Peter vonDoepp (eds.), *The Fate of Africa's Democratic Experiments: Elites and Institutions in Comparative Perspective* (Bloomington: Indiana University Press, 2005), 27–48; Leonardo A. Villalón and Abdourahmane Idrissa, "The Tribulations of a Successful Transition: Institutional Dynamics and Elite Rivalry in Mali," in Villalón and vonDoepp (eds.) (2005), 49–74.
13. To better understand the political context of the time, see interviews with Blaise Compaoré: "Èlections d'abord, reconciliation après," *Jeune Afrique*, 23 to 29 October, 1991 and "Tout est discutable sauf une conférence nationale," *La Croix*, 4 December 1991.
14. This closely parallels the experience of many other Francophone countries. See André Cabanis and Louis Martin, *Les Constitutions d'Afrique francophone: Evolutions Récentes* (Paris: Karthala, 1999).
15. Vincent Ouattara, *L'Ère Compaoré: Politique, Crimes et Gestion du Pouvoir* (Paris: Éditions Publibook, 2013).
16. René Otayek, "Voter Ça Veut Dire Quoi? Sur les Elections Législatives du 24 Mai 1992," in René Otayek, Michel Sawadogo, and Jean-Pierre Guingané, *Le Burkina Entre Révolution et Démocratie (1983–1993): Ordre*

Politique et Changement Social en Afrique subsaharienne (Paris: Karthala, 1996).
17. Michael Bratton and Nicolas Van de Walle, "Neopatrimonial Regimes and Political Transitions in Africa," *World Politics* 46, no. 4 (1994): 453–489.
18. For more on the electoral performance of Compaoré's party and the electoral arena under Compaoré's rule, see Daniel Eizenga, "Political Uncertainty in Burkina Faso," in Claire Metelits and Stephanie Matti (eds.), *Ruling on the Margins: Democratic Performance in Small African Countries* (Lanham, MD: Lexington Books, 2015). For more on the elections of 2015, see Eizenga, "Burkina Faso Elections Mark Turning Point," op. cit.
19. The "Zongo Affair" refers to the murder of investigative journalist Norbert Zongo and three of his colleagues. Zongo had been investigating the death of David Ouédraogo in which members of Compaoré's family and presidential guard had been implicated. Further discussion of the "Zongo Affair" can be found in Sten Hagberg, "'Enough Is Enough': An Ethnography of the Struggle against Impunity in Burkina Faso," *The Journal of Modern African Studies* 40, no. 2 (2002): 217–246; Augustin Loada, "Réflections sur la Société Civile en Afrique: Le Burkina de l'après Zongo," *Politique Africaine* 76 (1999): 136–151.
20. Burkina Faso is classified as a military oligarchy in 1989 by Bratton and Van de Walle, "Neo-Patrimonial Regimes," op. cit.; as a semi-authoritarian regime following the 2001 reforms by Carlos Santiso and Augustin Loada, "Explaining the Unexpected: Electoral Reform and Democratic Governance in Burkina Faso," *Journal of Modern African Studies* 41, no. 3 (2003), 395–419; and as a competitive authoritarian regime in the period leading up to its collapse in 2014 by Eizenga, "Political Uncertainty," op. cit. From 1991 to its demise it also fits the definition of electoral authoritarianism proposed by Andreas Schedler, *The Politics of Uncertainty: Sustaining and Subverting Electoral Authoritarianism* (Oxford, UK: Oxford University Press, 2013).
21. Indeed, recent research on such regimes in Africa demonstrates that regimes which are composed of both democratic and authoritarian traits evolve in a variety of different trajectories affording sometimes increased, and at other times decreased, opportunities for democratic contestation (see Metelits and Matti, *Ruling on the Margins*, op. cit.). Of particular relevance to this chapter, then, is the nature of the regime as one incorporating both authoritarian and democratic traits, and the subsequent possibility for politics to evolve in an increasingly uncertain fashion.
22. Eizenga, "Political Uncertainty," op. cit.
23. This was to continue even after Compaoré fled to Côte d'Ivoire after his fall in 2014. Indeed, one of the main projects launched by the transitional government that replaced the Compaoré regime was to reopen the investigation into Sankara's death.

24. Ernest Harsch, *Burkina Faso: A History of Power, Protest, and Revolution* (London: Zed Books, 2017).
25. Christopher Wise, "Chronicle of a Student Strike in Africa: The Case of Burkina Faso, 1996–1997," *African Studies Review* 41, no. 2 (1998): 19–36.
26. Sayouba Ouédraogo, "Collectif des Organisations Démocratiques de Masse et de Partis Politiques contre l'Impunité au Burkina Faso," *Les Cahiers du CRISES*, no. MS0601 (2006).
27. Hagberg, "Enough Is Enough," op. cit.
28. The text of this report is available, among other places, on the site of the Norbert Zongo press center in Ouagadougou: http://www.cnpresszongo.org/spip.php?article18.
29. Santiso and Loada, "Explaining the Unexpected," op. cit.
30. Jacinthe Mazzocchetti, "Quand les poussins se réunissent, ils font peur à l'épervier," *Politique Africaine* 1 (2006): 83–101.
31. Mazzocchetti, 2006.
32. Santiso and Loada, "Explaining the Unexpected," op. cit.
33. In the Francophone African context, the relative merits of these alternatives are frequently debated. In fact, the difference between what is meant by these two systems is only about the relative power between the president and the prime minister in what is usually called a French-style semi-presidential system. Neither an American style presidential system nor a British style parliamentary one is envisaged in this debate.
34. Alexander Stroh, "Burkina Faso," in Andreas Mehler, Henning Melber, and Klaas van Walraven (eds.), *Africa Yearbook Volume 5: Politics, Economy and Society South of the Sahara in 2008*, vol. 5 (Brill, 2009).
35. Lila Chouli, "People's Revolts in Burkina Faso," in Firoze Manji and Sokari Ekine (eds.), *African Awakening: The Emerging Revolutions* (Cape Town, South Africa: Pambazuka Press, 2012), 131–146.
36. Maggie Dwyer, "Situating Soldier' Demands: Mutinies and Protests in Burkina Faso," *Third World Quarterly* 38 no. 1 (2017), 219–234.
37. US President Barack Obama had famously declared in Ghana, during his first Africa tour, that "what Africa needs is strong institutions, not strong men."
38. The role of the media was elaborated in an interview we conducted with Touwendenda Zongo, Editor-in-Chief of the independent Burkinabè newspaper, *Mutations*, September 2, 2015.
39. Scott Mainwaring and Timothy Scully, *Building Democratic Institutions: Party Systems in Latin America* (Stanford: Stanford University Press, 1995). Beatriz Magaloni, *Voting for Autocracy: Hegemonic Party Survival and Its Demise in Mexico* (Cambridge: Cambridge University Press, 2006).

CHAPTER 6

Failed Elongation of Presidential Term Limits in Nigeria Under Olusegun Obasanjo

Hassan A. Saliu and Abdulrasheed A. Muhammad

Introduction

The Presidential system has to do with the notion of a regime type which provides for the powers of the executive to be exercised independently of the elected assembly. This conception is significant and more relevant in the sense that it recognizes the prime role that the constitution plays in determining the nature and structure of the government. The constitution not only provides for the powers of the President but also determines how such powers are to be exercised, how long they are to be exercised as well as the entry and exit points of such powers. While this represents the minimum standard in most democracies and in America where the Presidential system originated,[1] there have been attempts by some leaders especially in Africa, to circumvent the limits imposed by the constitution with varying degrees of success. This is not to suggest that such practice is limited to Africa alone. Indeed, comparative experience shows that the practice is one that has a solid foundation in history.[2] Equally, scholars in their studies have engaged the need for and against term limits noting its direct link to preservation of the rule of law.[3] Explaining the prevalence

---

H. A. Saliu (✉) · A. A. Muhammad
Department of Political Science, University of Ilorin, Ilorin, Nigeria

© The Author(s) 2020
J. R. Mangala (ed.), *The Politics of Challenging Presidential Term Limits in Africa*, https://doi.org/10.1007/978-3-030-40810-7_6

of this trend in the African context, Olurode[4] came up with four possible explanations. According to him, it could be borne out of a genuine concern for good governance and accountability; the traditional orientation of African leaders whereby leaders once appointed are expected to rule for life; the phenomenon of military intervention in politics that has weakened an orderly transfer of power and elevated the use of force in political succession and; the failure of African leaders at institution building in place of leadership that is centered on a personality cult. He went further to note that African leaders, being naive tend to see themselves as *Baba* (father) of their nations and thereby indispensable. Consequently, there is the temptation to want to perpetuate in office.

Aside the possible genuine concern for good governance and accountability which, in any case has been punctured by realities on the continent, one common thread in all attempts by Presidents in Africa to extend their term limits beyond the constitutional provision is the pecuniary advantage accruable to such leaders or what Hassan Saliu has described as "political opportunism."[5] Indeed, the increasing cost of governance amidst abject poverty and development crisis in many African countries attests to the fact that rather than the desire for good governance and accountability, personal interests of Presidents in Africa often inform their desire for elongation of their terms in office. But irrespective of the taxonomy of explanations, it should be pointed out that while the attempt at term elongation has succeeded on some occasions, it has recorded abysmal failure in others such as in Nigeria during President Obasanjo Administration (1999–2003). In fact, the attempt did not only fail, it generated convulsive reactions from within and outside the country. The big question therefore is why do leaders seek extension of terms in office? Why are there different outcomes in different contexts? Could this be due to factors that are peculiar to each country? Is it due to the influence of actors and actions in the attempt or a combination of all these? Better still, what are the subsisting perspectives on the Presidential term limits in Nigeria? It is against this background that this paper seeks to examine the politics of Presidential term limits in Nigeria under President Olusegun Obasanjo with the intent of unraveling the roles and influence of various actors in determining the outcome of the attempt.

The Presidential System, Constitution, and Term Limits

The Presidential system is one of the geniuses of constitutional government and one of America's contributions to the world's political organization.[6] This is because of the common belief that the system has its origin in the American political system. Riggs[7] identified four main conceptions of the Presidential which includes the simplistic notion of a regime type whose head is called President; a regime in which the head is popular; a regime in which the President plays a strong leadership role and fourth; a regime type in which the constitution provides for the power of the Head (President) to be exercised independently of the elected Assembly (Congress).[8] Implicit in this last definition is a functional and constitutional separation of jurisdictions between the executive and the legislative arms. While not implying a water-tight compartmentalization of governmental powers, the Presidential System allows the dispersion of governmental powers among the branches of government in the state and at the same time it allows for mutual dependence by the arms of the government. This perception constitutes the dominant trend in the attempt at understanding the nature of Presidential systems across countries.

In relation to other forms of governance especially the parliamentary system, considerable debate exists in the literature but central to this is "the capacity of the two systems to promote democratic intensity and ensure substantive forms of accountability."[9] In Nigeria, the formal adoption of the Presidential System dated back to its Second Republic ushered in 1979 and lasted till 1983 when it was terminated by a military coup. The adoption of the system was based on the preferences of the then military government that constituted the Constitution Drafting Committee (CDC) of 1976. The CDC and the Constituent Assembly (CA) that was convened in 1977 to review decisions of the CDC aligned with the intentions of the then military government to discourage institutionalized opposition to the government in power which had characterized the erstwhile parliamentary system that the country had operated under the First Republic (1960–1966). Instead, the military government was poised to develop a consensus politics and government based on a community of all interests rather than the interests of sections of the country. It thus eventually adopted the Presidential System which satisfies this desire for the country.

sIt needs to be emphasized, that the adoption of the Presidential System for the Second Republic as against the parliamentary system of the First Republic was expected to help avoid the failures and disjoint created by the latter, part of which led to the collapse of the First Republic. Underscoring this fact, A. A. Akinsanya[10] writes that the 1964–1965 constitutional crises had demonstrated how a bifurcated executive, ab initio, designed to foster national unity could result in conflict of interests and authority. This is because; the President and the Prime Minister were constantly at loggerheads in terms of power relations between them. The adoption of the Presidential System therefore was to ensure a more effective administration as well as remove a major source of discord and instability in the governance of the country. Thus, the crafters of the 1979 constitution proposed an executive Presidential System in which powers of the three arms of the government are to be entrusted into the hands of separate institutions. That is, the Legislature, the Executive, and the Judiciary. But accompanying this is the limitation on the tenure of the President, Vice President, State Governors, and their Deputies. Indeed, the 1979 constitution that provided the Judicial norms for the Second Republic placed a limitation on the terms of these political office holders not to exceed 2 terms of four years each. This provision was again repeated in subsequent constitutions including the 1999 constitution of the Federal Republic of Nigeria. For instance, while section 130 subsections 1 and 2 of the 1999 constitution says that "there shall be for the Federation a President" who "shall be the Head of State, the Chief Executive of the Federation and Commander-in-Chief of the Armed Forces of the Federation,"[11] section 136 subsection 2.1 pointedly notes that the President shall vacate his office at the expiration of a period of four years thereby limiting the term of the President. However, section 137 subsection 1b extends the limit to a maximum of two terms of four years each as it states that "a person shall not be qualified for election to the office of President if he has been elected to such office at any two previous elections."[12] The implication of this is that the maximum number of years that a President can spend in office according to the constitution is two terms amounting to eight years altogether and he cannot seek re-election to the same office in future. The same thing applies to the State Governors and their Deputies. It also follows that anything contrary to this in the form of an extension to the period is illegal and unknown to the constitution. This practice which is in line with the tradition of the Presidential system has been consistently maintained since 1999 till date including under the current Fourth Republic.

An Overview of Democracy in Nigeria Under Obasanjo

Democracy, especially its liberal variant is a unique process of arriving at collective and binding decisions through institutions that recognize and guarantee the achievement of social, political, and economic aspirations of the society. It is a system that is "premised on the informed and active participation of the citizens"[13] in choosing their government; freedom, equality, and justice in state–society relations as well as promoting the expression and accommodation of plurality of opinions. What cannot be denied in relation to democratic rule is playing by the norm and observance of the rule of law.

Nigeria came about as a product of imperial expansionist activities. Colonialism and colonial policies produced attendant implications for political processes in post-independence Nigeria as it resulted in complexities that led to the collapse of both the First and the Second Republics and the consequent prolonged years of military rule that spanned two epochs (1966–1979 and 1983–1999). The implications of this trend on the body politic were a militarized mentality among Nigerians, underdevelopment of democratic institutions and inability of civil political leaders to learn from their mistakes. The intense wave of democratization beginning from the 1980s and sweeping across continents coupled with resilience on the part of Nigerians arising from their negative experiences under the military rule led to the strong desire for democratic rule that was eventually enthroned in 1999. Suffice to say, therefore, that the swearing in of President Olusegun Obasanjo in May 1999 signaled the formal re-enthronement of democratic rule. This feat was consummated with a formal inauguration of the National Assembly (NASS) on June 6, 1999. Noteworthy also is that accompanying the swearing in of President Obasanjo was the coming into effect of the Nigerian Constitution of 1999 which, among other things, set limit on the tenure of political officeholders. It must, however, be stated that although the executive and the legislature constituted the hub of public policy making and delivery in a democracy such as Nigeria, both arms from inception have had a frosty relationship. This frosty relationship manifested in hosts of antagonistic behaviors over national budgetary matters especially between 1999 and 2007, surreptitious interference by the executive in the affairs of the NASS as well as mutual distrust between the two arms on several issues. Scholars have pointed to the personality and character of President Obasanjo as factors to note in the frosty relation.[14] Although the President had often been described in glowing terms in some quarters,[15] there was a consensus that he was quick-tempered and not willing to listen to other views apart from his own. Moreover, the fact that he often considered the legislature to be an "irritant" points to his aversion to the legislative arm.[16] On the one hand, he considered most legislators to be too young (most still in secondary school) while he was military Head of State between 1976 and 1979. Who were they, therefore, to oversight his activities, the President often wondered. On the other hand, he seemed to be influenced by his military background of not subjecting his decisions to another body for scrutiny. Why would the legislators, therefore, want to scrutinize his actions? Indeed at a point, the President directed some of his ministers to ignore summons by the NASS because he considered the summons as interference, illegal, and an avenue for corruption and extortion of the ministers.[17] This antagonistic context between the President and the NASS had implications for their relations especially on issues requiring mutual concurrence such as constitutional amendment.

Upon coming to power and notwithstanding the above, the challenges facing the new democracy were not lost to the new President as he promised to harness the nation's human and material resources toward ensuring progress, justice, harmony, unity, and confidence among Nigerians for the country to occupy its prime place in the comity of nations.[18] Consequently, the Obasanjo administration embarked on a series of reforms in the social, political, and economic environments.

At the domestic level, high points of the reforms included institutionalizing and strengthening the fight against corruption through the establishment of the Independent Corrupt Practices and other Related Offences Commission (ICPC) in the year 2000 and in 2003, he established the Economic and Financial Crimes Commission (EFCC). Both agencies have remained foremost institutional mechanisms for combating corruption in the country even though their performance levels have been an issue of continuous debate among scholars and policy makers.[19] Other aspects of the reforms included rightsizing and downsizing of the civil service, health sector reform, education reforms, pension reforms, and convening of the political reform conference, among others. Indeed, it was the era of reforms which, scholars have concluded, came with varying degrees of success.[20]

In the political environment, the government's effort at reform was initially at lower ebb until the 2005 National Political Reform Conference (NPRC) came on stream. This is because; there was much initial focus on reforming the country's socioeconomic terrain than the political sector. But by 2005, the Obasanjo government responded to the imminent threat posed by unceasing agitations for a review of the 1999 Constitution. Indeed, agitations for a review of the 1999 constitution of Nigeria dated back to the early years of Nigeria's Fourth Republic in 1999 and were championed by some citizens and civil society groups. Among the many issues requiring reforms were nature of Nigerian federalism which is more Unitary than federal going by over-bloating of the exclusive legislative list containing issues which are better dealt with by states and local governments; fiscal federalism which is, at present, largely in favor of the federal government; issues of indigene-ship and citizenship; the language of the constitution which is not gender friendly and; non-consultative and non-inclusiveness of the constitution.[21] Also in his address at the inauguration of the NPRC, President Obasanjo noted the various issues that necessitated a review of the Constitution to include:

> the challenge of constitutionalism and constitutional reform; the opportunity to bring all stakeholders together to discuss the preferred political path for the nation; the challenge of building new, accountable, responsive and focused leadership; and how to build, operate and sustain real political parties. Other issues are those of nationality, identity, freedoms and liberties, social justice, rights and obligations; electoral reforms that ensure credibility and respectability of elections; relations between tiers of government; performance of government and how to ensure truly democratic governance for all. In all of these, the central challenge is still how to strengthen the social contract between the custodians of state power and the governed.[22]

Thus, the 2005 NPRC represented the factory of ideas for the proposed 2005 review of the constitution.[23] Despite the refusal by the NASS to recognize the NPRC evidenced in its refusal to appropriate funds for it, the conference still went on till July 2005 when it adjourned sine die after submitting its report to the executive. Following the refusal of the NASS to appropriate money for the conduct of the NPRC, the President went ahead to source for the required money from some executive establishments notably the Central Bank of Nigeria (CBN).[24] But as it later turned out, the NPRC was to serve as a platform for launching the extension of term limits agenda for the Obasanjo government.

At the level of interstate relations, the government of President Obasanjo was bent on convincing the international community of the commitment of the administration to the reform programs which would expectedly serve as springboard for the emergence of a new Nigeria—a democratic Nigeria. Thus, he embarked on series of foreign trips to seek support for his administration at the end of which the country would have been able to restore and consolidate diplomatic relations that have gone sour under the military; attract foreign direct investment as a way of rescuing the ailing economy and; achieve a favorable image in the comity of nations. Given this scenario, it would be less surprising to think that the international community would not be so much interested in what was going on within the Nigerian nation.

Dimensions of the Debate: Actors, Actions, and Strategies

It is important to state from the onset that the attempt to extend the term limits of President Obasanjo was one that engulfed actors that cut across the entire spectrum of the Nigerian society and even beyond the country's borders. In other words, it involved actions and reactions at domestic and international levels. At the domestic level, the actors included the President's aides including the then Vice President, members of the executive council such as ministers and advisers, members of the President's political party, elected members of the NASS, Civil Society Organizations (CSOs), and some political figures, among others. At the supranational level, some members of the diplomatic corps, International governmental and non-governmental organizations as well as other members of the international community were not left out of the debate. For example, while the debate raged on, John Kuffuor (former Ghanaian President) advised President Obasanjo to respect the spirit and letter of the constitution by adhering to the constitutionally imposed term limits.[25] Broadly, this array of actors can be classified into either antagonists or protagonists. While the antagonists were vehemently opposed to tenure elongation, the protagonists were favorably disposed to the cause. A common thread that however ran through the two was the unrestrained deployment of all arsenals to ensure that each achieved its objectives.

For the protagonists including the President himself, it could be argued that there was an attempt to key-in into genuine aspirations of the people for a constitution review as a strategy toward achieving tenure elongation. Consequently, while there were genuine aspirations from individuals and Civil Society groups for a review of the 1999 Constitution as already highlighted in this work, the government was quick to align with this expectation but infested it with its own agenda. This resulted in a confounding dilemma for the CSOs that had a high expectation on the Constitution review exercise. Articulating the civil society perspective and confounded expectations[26] over the issue of third term *vis-a-vis* the need for constitutional reforms which it has consistently championed since 1999, Jibril Ibrahim, a CSO activist noted that:

> It was now obvious that President Olusegun Obasonjo had embarked on a sinister agenda to change the constitution so that he could have a third term in office against the spirit and letter of our grand norm.... Some of us who had been in the forefront of the campaign for constitutional reform now find ourselves in the dilemma of challenging the process, because it has been reduced into an antidemocratic agenda for the country ...[27]

As noted earlier in this work, the NPRC was planned to be a platform for launching the tenure elongation bid. A manifestation of this came with claims by a section of the Nigerian press of the circulation of a strange document to conferees at the NPRC by the former adviser to President Obasanjo, Professor Jerry Gana. Although the contents of the document were largely unknown, it was believed to be tailored toward achieving favorable disposition of members to the President's intention. Consequently, many Nigerians became alerted and more expectant of when such an issue would come to the limelight.

Beyond the issue of Mr. President trying to key-in into genuine aspirations of the people for a constitutional reform, there was also what Anifowose[28] described as "controversial sign post." This concerns determining the actual intention of Mr. President on tenure elongation bid. Although the President did not make any categorical statement on either in support or otherwise for an extension of his term limits, actions of his aides without rebuff from him pointed to what his mindset was. For example, there was an open support for tenure elongation by the then

Peoples' Democratic Party (PDP) National Chairman, Dr. Ahmadu Ali and other party stalwarts especially given their unwelcome reactions to opponents of tenure elongation; purported attempt by the executive arm to bribe members of the NASS to allow amendments to the 1999 Constitution including the extension of the President's term limits, among others. Indeed, based on this, the general feeling of the Nigerian public was that the President was actually interested in having his tenure extended beyond the constitutional term limits even though President Obasanjo made it categorically clear while submitting the report of the NPRC to the NASS that he had no intention of staying beyond Constitutional approved limits in office.

It is important to state that even recently, the debate on the veracity of the President's claim was reopened when he (President Obasanjo) re-echoed the statement during an interview he had with Channels TV. According to him, the botched tenure elongation amendment clause was actually initiated by the NASS. He noted further that neither his National Assembly Liaison Officer, Senator Florence Ita-Giwa nor the public office holders who were close to him at the time, could come out to tell Nigerians that they received instructions from him to work for a third tenure.[29] However, this recent statement provoked sharp reactions from the then members of the NASS who argued that the then President, Obasanjo, was the brain behind the plot. For instance, former Senate President, Ken Nnamani, argued that Obasanjo informed him about the agenda shortly after he became Senate President but initially did not take him seriously until the events began to unfold. He also recalled how huge sums of money (Fifty Million Naira for each lawmaker) were doled out, ostensibly from the CBN to influence Senators to support the idea of a third term for the President.[30]

The former Vice President, Atiku Abubakar, also argued that the President even sought international support but was rebuked. He alluded to the personal memoir of US former Secretary of State, Condoleezza Rice, where discussions between Presidents Obasanjo and Bush over the tenure elongation bid was documented. These assertions by Nmamni and Atiku Abubakar were corroborated by a former Minister in President Obasanjo's administration who also provided insight into how the third term plot was hatched. According to the ex-minister, three groups were behind the plot. They were the Business Group; Senators led by a former Deputy President of the Senate, Alhaji Ibrahim Mantu and; loyalist governors including the late President Umaru Yar' Adua, James Ibori, Saminu Turaki, and others.[31] He, however, admitted that the ex-President was not the actual initiator of the bill. Senator Lawman has however disclaimed this perspective. He believed that there was no way the ex-President could have presented the bill himself because it was a legislative affair. He maintained that President Obasanjo was clearly in support of it as there were lobbyists from the Presidency working toward the realization of the agenda.[32]

While the veracity of the claims over the tenure elongation bid has continued till date, it is important to stress that the issue completely eclipsed other issues contained in the 2005 Constitution amendment proposal. Equally, the then President Obasanjo may have actually played safe by not openly committing himself before Nigerians that he wanted a third term but had in place machineries working in his favor.

Another strategy employed by the protagonists of term extension was to advertise the performance credentials of President Olusegun Obasanjo as what qualified him for a tenure extension. The strategy was aimed, essentially, at appealing to the consciousness of Nigerians with a view to securing their acquiescence. According to them, President Obasanjo recorded profound achievements in both the domestic and International realm and therefore needed more term to consolidate on these gains. In other words, the focus of the argument of the protagonists was on the need for continuity of leadership in order to consolidate the achievements of the government. Among other things, protagonists noted the efforts at combating corruption and in ensuring due process in governance; infrastructural development; fiscal discipline; banking and other sectoral reforms; stability in macroeconomic variables; realization of high growth rates; and high inflow of foreign direct investment. The protagonists argued further that the favorable debt relief which the country secured from the Paris and the London Clubs was legendary and that should qualify the President for continuity in office beyond the constitutional term limits. In point of fact, Nigeria's external debt at the inception of the democratic administration in 1999 stood at over 30 billion dollars with over one billion dollars expended annually on servicing it. This is presented graphically in Tables 6.1 and 6.2.

Earlier, during the first anniversary of his administration, President Obasanjo had noted that Nigeria carried a heavy burden of international debt that seemed quite likely to ensure that most of its earnings would be committed merely to paying mostly doubtful debts, leaving the country with little to address the legitimate needs of the people.[33] Therefore, the debt issue as he subsequently emphasized, was one that must be dealt with

Table 6.1 Nigeria's Debt Profile, 1985–2004 in Dollars

Year	A: Official Paris Club	A: Official Multilateral	A: Official Others (Non Paris Club)	A: Official Sub total	B: Private Promissory notes	B: Private Banks (London Club)	B: Private Sub total	Grand total (A + B)
1985	7833.00	1317.00	1939.00	11,089.00	4255.00	3560.00	7815.00	18,904.00
1986	10,228.00	1887.00	2873.00	14,988.00	4498.00	6088.00	10,586.00	25,574.00
1987	12,589.00	2985.00	2032.00	17,606.00	4850.00	5860.00	10,710.00	23,316.00
1988	14,400.00	2838.00	2685.00	19,923.00	4810.00	5960.00	10,770.00	30,693.00
1989	15,871.00	3171.00	2311.00	21,353.00	4553.00	5680.00	10,233.00	31,586.00
1990	17,171.00	3842.00	1675.00	22,688.00	4550.00	5861.00	10,411.00	33,099.00
1991	17,793.00	4016.00	1454.00	23,263.00	4479.00	5988.00	10,467.00	33,730.00
1992	16,454.70	4518.00	1226.10	22,198.80	3246.00	2120.00	5366.00	27,564.80
1993	18,160.50	3694.70	1647.30	23,502.50	3159.90	2055.80	5215.70	28,718.20
1994	18,334.32	4402.27	1456.31	24,192.90	3178.17	2057.79	5235.96	29,428.86
1995	21,669.60	4411.00	1311.20	27,391.80	3148.00	2045.00	5193.00	32,584.80
1996	19,091.00	4665.00	121.00	23,877.00	2140.00	2043.00	4183.00	28,060.00
1997	18,980.39	4372.68	79.19	23,432.26	1612.54	2043.00	3655.54	27,087.80
1998	20,829.93	4237.00	65.77	25,132.70	1597.84	2043.00	3640.84	28,773.54
1999	20,507.33	3933.23	69.34	24,509.90	1486.10	2043.21	3529.31	28,039.21
2000	21,180.00	3460.00	143.77	24,783.77	1446.70	2043.21	3489.91	28,273.68
2001	22,092.93	2797.87	121.21	25,012.01	1291.78	2043.21	3334.99	28,347.00
2002	25,380.75	2960.59	55.55	28,396.89	1153.18	1441.79	2594.97	30,991.87
2003	27,469.92	3042.08	51.63	30,563.63	911.39	1441.79	2353.18	32,916.81
2004	30,847.81	2824.32	47.50	33,719.63	783.23	1441.79	2225.03	35,944.66

Source: Debt Management Office, DMO, "Nigeria's External Debt Outstanding (1985–2004)." Available online at: http://www.dmo.gov.ng/oci/edebtstock/docs/External%20Debt%20Outstanding%20(1983-2004).pdf (Accessed December 14, 2009)

Table 6.2 Nigeria's External Debt Service Payment, 1985–2004 in Dollars

Year	A: Official				B: Private			Grand total (A + B)
	Paris Club	Multilateral	Others (Non Paris Club)	Sub total	Promissory notes	Banks (London Club)	Sub total	
1985	410.90	98.20	10.10	519.20	0.00	981.50	981.50	1500.70
1986	182.60	231.60	7.50	421.70	0.00	856.90	856.90	1278.60
1987	186.90	244.30	0.50	431.70	0.00	308.30	308.30	740.00
1988	531.80	460.70	4.70	997.20	0.00	584.70	584.70	1581.90
1989	246.60	514.70	128.80	890.10	248.30	1029.90	1278.20	2168.30
1990	1672.90	640.10	453.30	2766.30	340.90	465.20	806.10	3572.40
1991	1506.70	733.40	502.20	2742.30	376.60	316.10	692.70	3435.00
1992	536.00	810.00	141.90	1487.90	267.30	637.40	904.70	2392.60
1993	234.60	643.20	442.80	1320.60	256.10	195.80	451.90	1772.50
1994	59.20	758.90	626.60	1444.70	254.80	143.50	398.30	1843.00
1995	271.80	826.90	109.00	1207.70	251.90	161.00	412.90	1620.60
1996	359.70	814.40	336.40	1510.50	238.40	127.70	366.10	1876.60
1997	306.10	800.20	127.70	1234.00	226.80	35.80	262.60	1496.60
1998	228.54	680.23	19.77	928.54	216.29	127.71	344.00	1272.54
1999	644.49	659.17	34.80	1338.46	258.70	127.74	386.44	1724.90
2000	812.67	623.23	1.52	1437.42	149.52	129.07	278.59	1716.01
2001	1273.62	491.48	33.81	1798.91	195.18	134.08	329.26	2128.17
2002	161.55	472.12	75.86	709.54	192.12	266.75	458.87	1168.40
2003	1020.18	509.23	13.26	1542.66	176.42	90.21	266.62	1809.28

(continued)

Table 6.2 (continued)

Year	Creditor category							Grand total (A + B)
	A: Official				B: Private		
	Paris Club	Multilateral	Others (Non Paris Club)	Sub total	Promissory notes	Banks (London Club)	Sub total	
2004	994.44	487.28	11.64	1493.37	171.23	90.15	261.39	1754.75
Total	11,641.29	11,499.34	3082.17	26,222.79	3820.56	6809.51	10,630.06	36,852.86

Source Debt Management Office, DMO, "Nigeria's External Debt Service Payments (1985–2004)." Available online at: http://www.dmo.gov.ng/oci/edebtservice/docs/External%20Debt%20Service%20Payments%20(1985 2004).pdf (Accessed December 14, 2009)

even at times of near economic collapse because of the belief that there is great inequity and injustice in the debt issue which required global attention.[34] Consequently, through negotiations, the country was able to achieve some relief in 2005 with the cancelation of half of the amount while the balance was to be paid within a period of six months.[35] Related to this was that the administration of President Olusegun Obasanjo was able to beef up the country's external reserves to well over 30 billion dollars and had excess crude oil reserves of over 16 billion dollars, with a target of about 50 billion Dollar external reserves before 2007.[36]

At the international level, protagonists noted the changed status of Nigeria from that of being a pariah state under the military to one of indispensability in the comity of nations. This was to the extent that any major international event especially concerning countries in the southern hemisphere was always having Nigeria as a major consideration and player.[37] Specifically, protagonists noted the readmission of Nigeria into organizations such as the Commonwealth, which had hitherto suspended the country from its activities; lifting of sanctions on Nigeria hitherto imposed by several European countries and; restoration of the bilateral air agreement between Nigeria and the United States of America (USA), among others.[38] Added to this was the prominence enjoyed by Mr. President within the comity of nations. Thus, they concluded that for these achievements to be sustained there was the need to extend the constitutionally imposed term limits.

On the part of the antagonists, efforts were concentrated on stressing the amoral aspect of such ambition and disputing and disparaging the figures and records of achievements advertised by the protagonists. For instance, they argued that it is only moral and right for the President to obey the spirit and letter of the Constitution including spending not more than the constitution's limit of two terms in office. For instance, an Afro barometer survey revealed that there was strong support among the Nigerian public for term limits and constitutional government.[39] The survey went further to note that in a national, representative survey of Nigerians, an overwhelming majority of 84% agreed that Nigeria's President should "obey the Constitution, including serving no more than two terms in office," while about 17% of the citizens believed that the President "should be able to serve as many terms in office as he wishes."[40] The implication of this is that there was a strong resentment on the part of most Nigerians for an extension of term limits beyond constitutional provisions. Similarly, the extension of term limits was perceived by opponents to be a breach of an unwritten agreement between political actors that after President Obasanjo's tenure of eight years, power would shift back to the north. Thus, the northern region was expecting President Obasanjo to quit power in 2007, while a northerner assumes leadership of the country.[41] This expectation was re-echoed in an interview granted by the former Zamfara state governor, Alhaji Sani Yerima, to a Newspaper when he was asked where power would go in 2007. According to him: It was automatically supposed to go to the north... South had taken eight years, and the North should have its own eight years.[42] Perhaps, it may be reasoned that it was for this reason that many northerners were opposed to an extension as it constituted a threat to the political future of the north.

Also, antagonists of the extension of term limits contradicted the achievements of Mr. President which his supporters had used to justify the need for extension. For example, they argued that although the administration of Olusegun Obasanjo may have recorded some successes in economic management, there was high doubt whether the figures paraded were real or an approximation of the reality of the Nigerian situation. They argued that "a critical examination of the trend of economic variables was indicative of a misplaced perception of economic performance" under the Obasanjo-led administration.[43] This according to them was because, inflation rates, poverty, unemployment, etc., remained on the rise all of which pointed to the fact that the reforms in the economy were not successfully delivered. For instance, while the exchange rate of the Naira to a US dollar was a little over 21 Naira in 1999, it rose to over 130 Naira to a dollar by 2005. On the issue of debt relief, the view of the opposition was that it was confounding for a debtor country to have coughed out 18 million dollars within a year to pay some questionable debts to the Paris Club. They reasoned that Nigeria may soon find herself in another debt crisis arising from contradictions contained in the debt forgiveness effort of the Paris Club.[44] Above all, such an amount should have been channeled toward some revenue yielding ventures for the country which in turn would have led to an increase in Gross Domestic Product (GDP) and more income for the country. They therefore concluded that Nigeria may have been reaped off.[45] Arising from the unfavorable economic terrain at home, antagonists of tenure extension argued that the country was facing serious challenges at home and abroad ranging from prostitution, child trafficking, and business scams to insecurity especially in the Niger Delta region. These imperatives had made a change of leadership necessary in order to test new hands in economic development initiatives. More so, it is really absurd to think that there is only one competent hand in a population of about 150 million that can fix Nigeria's problems.

But as the debate raged and many actors found themselves on either side of the divide, there existed a not too conspicuous group notably among members of the (NASS) who were neither antagonists nor protagonists of the term extension campaign. To this group, the term extension campaign was only diversionary as they believed that President Olusegun Obasanjo would stick to his oath of office of defending the constitution including spending the maximum of two terms of eight years in office. To them, therefore, President Obasanjo was merely using the campaign to divert the attention of the opposition, while scheming to plant his choice in office as successor in 2007.[46] Perhaps indicative of this attempt was the timing of the term extension bid which came up barely two years to the end of his second tenure (when the politics of succession would have commenced) and the President's already known stance of aversion to his Deputy as his successor. Although this group, as noted earlier, was not too conspicuous but the fact that some lawmakers abstained during debates and voting on the issue at the NASS suggested the existence of such perspective.

Outcomes and Reactions

From the preceding analysis, it is clear that both protagonists and antagonists deployed various strategies to ensure the triumph of their idea. But it must be pointed out that in modern societies, such disaggregate of interest is left for the law to resolve. Although the judiciary played little or no role in the debate, the legislature as the highest lawmaking body certainly had a constitutional role to play in resolving such conflict of interests. This becomes more compelling given the fact the Nigerian constitution places a specific role on the shoulders of the legislature when it comes to amending the constitution of the country that was expected to serve as harbinger for term extension. Thus, by its constitutional role, the legislature was central to determining the outcome of the term extension bid which in any case was not successful. Two factors explain the failure of the attempt. The first which can be located within the actions of the legislative arm has to do with issues of moral justification and conformity with due process, while the second has to do with sociocultural make-up of Nigeria and its politics.

As already made clear, the attempt to extend the tenure of the President, his Deputy, State Governors, and their Deputies beyond the constitutional limit of two terms was built into the necessity of amending the 1999 Nigerian Constitution. The initiative to amend the Constitution, on the part of the executive arm, started with the convocation of an NPRC. In August 2005, the then President, Olusegun Obasanjo, submitted the report of the NPRC to the NASS with the expectation that it would serve as input into the work of the legislature in the process of amending the 1999 Constitution. In his speech while submitting the report, the President noted that although the conference had come and gone, it had generated and unleashed new discourses that would only deepen political awareness, strengthen political engagements, and enrich the country's political lexicon.[47] Since the legislature then already had a committee working on possible review of the Constitution, the report of the NPRC was taken as another reference source for the NASS' Joint Committee on the Review of the 1999 Constitution (JCRC). Some issues arose in the course of the committee's work which was, partly informed by the legislature's decision. First, the work of the committee including the clause pertaining to term limits was shrouded in secrecy to the extent that some members even denied knowledge of some provisions in the committee's report thereby rendering the report lacking in credibility and legitimacy. For instance, they alleged that the hearings on the constitution amendment were only held in the six geopolitical zones and not in the states which section 2(2) of the 1999 Constitution recognized as the federating units; such hearings were conducted and concluded in 2 days which apparently were not enough for any meaningful engagement of the issues involved as Nigerians were denied access to effectively participate in the hearings. Security personnel also prevented members of the public from freely entering the premises selected for the hearings and in some cases, presenters were prevented from completing their presentations because they spoke against elongation of term.[48] Consequently, some lawmakers petitioned the Senate President and Speaker of the House of Representatives (HoR) over what they described as illegalities in the method adopted by the JCRC.[49]

Second, there was controversy over insertion of the clause allowing term elongation in the recommendations of the committee given the fact that the report of the NPRC did not contain such.[50] For instance, Hon. Aminu Waziri Tambuwal asserted that as a Member of the National Assembly Joint Committee on the Review of the Constitution of the Federal Republic of Nigeria 1999, he participated actively in the deliberations of the Joint Committee but was not aware of any record of the adoption of an amendment to Section 182 (1) *(b)* of the Constitution under "Disqualifications" to read that "he has been elected into such office at any three previous elections in accordance with this Constitution." He argued that this amendment was not contained in the Report of the Joint Committee laid before the House on April 12, 2006, but was mysteriously inserted in House Bill 248 by some members of the JCRC.[51] These surreptitious attempts only increased volatility of opposition to term extension which by then had been taken as synonymous with general constitution amendment. While the debate over term extension and Constitution amendment continued in the public arena, the attempt was finally killed by the Senate on May 16, 2002, when it discontinued debate on it.

In his remarks to the Senate before the commencement of the debate on the 16th, the then Senate President, Ken Nnamani, charged Senators to rise above partisan and alleged pecuniary considerations in making their decision noting as well that "now that we are at the threshold of concluding this historic debate on the proposed amendment to the constitution, I urge every Senator to rise up to the challenge of patriotism."[52] The HoR followed suit on May 17, 2006. Thus, it could be asserted that failure of the legislature to acquiesce to the executive's preference was a major factor in the failure of the term extension bid.

Apart from the legislature's pugnacious stance on executive's preference, ethno-regional consideration for power shift to the north could be seen as other factors in the opposition to the term extension bid. Any careful observer of Nigerian politics would easily recall that struggle for ascendancy between the north and the south which predates Nigeria's independence in 1960 has always been informed by self-interest of the two regions. Mutual suspicion and the desire of one group to dominate the other have been the hallmarks of intergroup relations in the country.[53] On the issue of term extension, therefore, this trend was glaringly played out. While opposition to the term elongation cut across different facets of the Nigerian society, the strongest opposition, according to a survey by Afro barometer, was found in the north while a higher degree of acceptance was found in the south.[54] Another indication of the ethno-regional sentiments influencing behaviors on the term extension and constitution amendment could be noticed in reactions of participants at the Fourth Northern Senator's Forum in Kaduna in 2006. At the occasion, placard-carrying demonstrators taunted the then deputy Senate President, Alhaji Ibrahim Nasiru Mantu, who was also the Chairman of the National Assembly, JCRC, Senate leader, Dr. Sarki Dalhatu Tafida and Senator Umar Hambagba (all northerners) as working against the interest of the North to produce the President in 2007, adding that they were opportunists who wanted to trade off the North for personal gains.[55]

Similarly, former Governor of Zamfara state who later became a Senator was unequivocal in his advocacy. According to him, power is automatically supposed to go to the north because the south had taken eight years and the north should have eight years.[56] This was against the background that the then incumbent President Olusegun Obasanjo and beneficiary of the proposed term extension, is from the South. Moreover, the vociferous opposition of Alhaji Atiku Abubakar, the then incumbent Vice President, a northerner and Presidential hopeful in the 2007 election to tenure elongation spoke eloquently to the ethno-regional dimension of the opposition.

Although the President, Olusegun Obasanjo, consistently denied being interested in extending his term in office, the body language of his aides without rebuff from him, gave a strong indication about his mindset. But the stack reality of the failure of the term extension bid brought about the continuation and perhaps intensification of intimidation, hostility, and persecution of opponents of the term elongation bid which had started when the bid was on. Capturing this trend, Jonathan Majok[57] enthused that: What we had under the increasingly desperate third term subtle campaign was: your support or your reputation. This was in apparent reference to political office holders that showed signs of aversion to the term elongation agenda. The implication of this is that some supporters of the term elongation bid were coerced into giving their support for it. And even after the bid had failed, they stood the risk of humiliation perhaps owning to excesses which they may have committed in office and which were traded off with support for term extension. Also, former Senate President, Adolphous Wabara reported that he was persecuted for failing to align with the term extension bid.[58] According to him, President Obasanjo had approached him as early as 2003 to hint him on his desire to have his term extended beyond 2007 to which he was averse. The plan, however, came to limelight in 2005. But the cost of his aversion was denial of a national award and his implication in the 2005 bribe-for-budget scandal.[59] Similarly, some members of the NASS, who apparently were opposed to tenure extension (for example, Ghali Umar Na'aba, former speaker of the HoR) could not secure their party's (PDP) ticket and therefore had their hope of returning to the NASS dashed. This was made possible because of the President's stronghold on the party and by extension, lack of internal democracy within the parties. By the PDP constitution, the President is the party leader at the National level while the Governors lead the party at the state's level. This places them in a vantage position to determine who is to be nominated for what. Therefore, denial of a return ticket was a punitive measure to party members who opposed the extension of term limits.

Apart from the above, it is generally believed that President Obasanjo, using the party, PDP, picked Alhaji Umaru Yar'Adua and Dr. Goodluck Jonathan to succeed him in 2007 because they were weak and so would be servile to him after he must have left office as aftermath of his inability to have an extension of his term. The President was quoted as saying that the period between 2007 and 2011 was just a transition period. Nothing was going to change as he would only be in Ota, running the government from there.[60] Indications to the veracity of this claim emerged recently when spokesman for the Jonathan campaign organization claimed that after Jonathan came to power, Obasanjo not only tried to control and tele-guide him, but he also asked him to do a number of things that were simply wrong and unacceptable.[61] This was a reflection of the extent of disappointment produced by the failure of the term elongation bid. The actions and reactions from the term elongation bid, no doubt, hold serious implications for democratic consolidation in Nigeria.

Implications for Democratic Consolidation

Democratic consolidation implies strengthening the process, stability, depth, and practice of democracy. Consensus exists to the fact that democratic consolidation is about ensuring the stability of democratic process both in its institutional and behavioral contexts as well as avoiding tendencies that will not only stunt the growth but also leads to decline in the quality of democracy.[62] The significance of this perspective is that it reveals both the attitudinal and institutional components of democratic consolidation. To this extent, the crisis generated by the term extension imbroglio has great effects on the consolidation of democracy in Nigeria. First, it led to serious antagonism between the executive and legislative institutions thereby exposing both arms to contempt from the public. Antagonistic relations between the two arms of the government over extension of term limits first began with refusal of the legislature to allocate money for the conduct of the NPRC (harbinger of term elongation) and that led the executive to source finance for it from some executive agencies notably the CBN. The outcome of the exercise which was not in favor of the executive further pitched the two arms against each other as evidenced in the intensification of hostility between the two arms. Related to this was that the legislative arm became debased with emergence of intra-institutional antagonisms among members. The emergence of antagonistic groups at the NASS such as the Unity Forum, a group of pro-tenure extension legislators and the 2007 movement, members of which were basically anti tenure extension reflected the incoherence of the legislative arm.[63] This is largely antithetical to institution building which democratic consolidation requires as there are more diversionary issues to contend with. Related to this were the high turnovers of legislators which were permitted by the President or Governors' stronghold on the party. The argument is that the necessary germination is not permitted by the high number of them that are not returned at the end of first or second terms. As a result, the legislature was always starting afresh at the beginning of every democratic administration. For example, in 2007, barely 20% of the 2003 Senators returned to the Senate while in the HoR, roughly 71% did not return.[64] The implication of this is that the institution lacks the benefit of experienced lawmakers for legislative duties. It also reflects a fall out of the legislature's aversion to tenure elongation against the background that the President was the leader of the party and he determines who stands for what election.

The exercise equally stultified the genuine aspirations of the people in a democracy. As noted in this chapter, there have been genuine concerns among Nigerian since 199 for a review of the 1999 Nigeria Constitution. For many Nigerians, the setting up of the NPRC was a welcome development as it would provide opportunity for channeling their preferences into the arena of policy making. More so, the setting up of the JCRC by the NASS was an indication that the executive and legislature were on the same page as far as Constitution review was concerned. However, the turn-out of events created a confounding situation for most Nigerians who had expected peoples' oriented Constitution at the end of the exercise. Indeed, the issue of tenure extension distorted and overshadowed other governance issues in the constitution amendment debate to the extent that the whole amendment process had to be sacrificed for term extension not to succeed. This may not be surprising given the fact that the whole amendment including provision on term extension, was meant to enjoy block passage such that the passage of one implies the passage of the others. Therefore, if discarding the entire amendments meant discarding term elongation, so be it.

Third, the term elongation attempt led to disharmony within the polity. This was because; it pitched the executive against the legislature; polarized the NASS; and also pitched citizens against one another. In fact, it led to the resurgence of ethnic politics in Nigeria as the north–south divide in Nigerian politics came forcefully to the fore again. Fourth, it brought out the resilience and desire of Nigerians to sustain democratic rule. Democracy is sustained through active participation of the people in deciding matters that concern their lives and democratic consolidation is assured when there is an attitudinal commitment on the part of the citizens toward its sustenance. This was aptly demonstrated during debates on the term elongation. It became a public issue that every Nigerian was ready to volunteer an opinion. The presence at the NASS of eminent Nigerians, including former State Governors, Ministers and former Lawmakers, as observers of proceedings during debates on the Constitution amendment underscored the significance of the exercise and how important it was to Nigeria's democratic development.[65]

From the economic angle, the term elongation attempt represented a serious drain on the country's economy. This is because, huge sums were spent on prosecuting the NPRC and financing the JCRC yet, no meaningful reform or amendment was achieved. Equally, sums of money were surreptitiously spent to influence the trends of debate in the NASS. For instance, former Senate President, Ken Nnamani, recalled how sums of money—about N50 million for each lawmaker was given out from the CBN on behalf of the President to influence Senators to support the term elongation bid.[66] Related to this is that the attempt rubbished the corruption crusade of Mr. President. During his inauguration in 1999, he had promised Nigerians to tackle corruption headlong and true to this fact; the ICPC and EFCC were established in 2001 and 2003, respectively, as institutional mechanisms to tackle corruption in the country. These attempts coupled with the whistle blowing in 2005 by Mr. President on the bribe-for-budget scandal involving some executive agencies and members of the NASS bestowed on him, a personality with zero tolerance for corruption. However, his use and reliance on monetary inducements to ensure easy passage of the term extension exposed him as a self-serving personality and that has tended to validate the thought in some quarters that he was not sincere with the corruption crusade.

Also, the attempt laid the foundation for a bad precedent for future Presidents in the country. It could be reasoned that the not too long attempt by the Jonathan administration (2009–2015) to seek an amendment to Presidential term limit in Nigeria reflects this tendency.[67] Related to this is that Nigeria could be plunged into a crisis of succession at the point of exit of beneficiary of term extension, especially considering the sociopolitical make-up of the country which often produces crisis at the slightest prompt of political competition. This is because the tendency is for many power potentates to have emerged and seeking to capture political power. In such an atmosphere of intense competition, the democratic project is likely to become threatened leading to democratic reversal. Also stemming from this, Nigeria may likely lose its rising image in the comity of nations. There is no doubt that the enthronement of democracy in the country in 1999 led to the rising profile of Nigeria in the international system. This was evident in Nigeria's prominence in several international engagements such as hosting of Commonwealth Heads of Government (CHOGM) meeting, Chairmanship of African Union (AU) and a host of others. The attempt by President Obasanjo to extend his term limit, therefore, created an impression of insincerity on the part of his government and thus sowed the seed for suspecting every move of the country's leaders.

Conclusion

The study has examined Presidential term limits in Nigeria under President Olusegun Obasanjo. It found out that the issue of term limit or its extension is not peculiar to Nigeria alone as comparative experiences show that both developed and developing democracies have passed through the controversy at some points of their history. While some have been successful, some others have failed. In Nigeria, the attempt under President Obasanjo failed due to the legislative arm's aversion to the idea. This is not to suggest that the NASS in Nigeria has been a nationalistic institution working based on what is best for the nation. But given the background of the existence of frosty relations between the executive and the legislature since 1999, it was not surprising that such a request by the executive would necessarily meet with stiff resistance from the legislature.

Also, the sociopolitical make-up of the country and the nature of its politics is a factor in the failure of the extension of tenure attempt. It was believed by some from the northern part of the country that the period from 1999 to 2007 featured a southerner as President; therefore, it was the turn of the north to produce the President. Equally, it was realized from the analysis in this paper that the issue of extension of term limit was elitist. This is because, the extent to which Nigerians exercise influence on the political process cannot be easily ascertained or at best, remains at a very low ebb. This tendency mirrors the situation in some other parts of Africa where the practice of democracy has not led to an increased standard of living for the people. Unfortunately, however, the imbroglio over tenure extension marred genuine clamor by sections of the populace for a review of the 1999 Constitution of Nigeria. This is because the Constitution amendment became entangled and overshadowed by the issue of term elongation. As a consequence, the country became polarized along several lines while democratic consolidation became threatened. Thus, Nigeria's democracy had faced an imminent reversal before the attempt at tenure was eventually defeated at floor of the parliament in mid-2006. While the episode had come and gone, it speaks to the extent of the readiness of Nigerian leaders to obey the country's constitution.

Notes

1. Some had argued that before the ratification of the 22nd Amendment which limited the terms for Presidents in the United States to two, Franklin Delano Roosevelt was elected to four terms in the White House in 1932, 1936, 1940, and 1944. It is thus contended that the 22nd amendment merely put on paper the unwritten tradition held by Presidents in the United States of retiring after two terms. See, "Why Presidents Can Serve Only Two Terms," available online at: http://uspolitics.about.com/od/history/a/Why-Presidents-Can-Serve-Only-Two-Terms.htm, accessed April 17, 2015.
2. See Hassan Saliu and Abdulrasheed A. Muhammad, "Perspectives on the Tenure Extension Bid in Nigeria's Fourth Republic," in A. D. Aina (ed.), *Corruption and the Challenge of Human Development* (Ilishan-Remo: School of Management and Social Sciences, Babcock University Press,

2007), 534–535; see also, "History and Debate of Term Limits," available online at: http://www.debate.org/term-limits/, accessed April 16, 2016.
3. Alexander Tabarrok, "A Survey, Critique, and New Defense of Term Limits," *Cato Journal* 14, no. 2 (Fall 1994): 335–339; Tom Ginsburg, James Melton, and Zachary Elkins, "On the Evasion of Executive Term Limits," *William and Mary Law Review* 52:1807 (2011): 1818–1826; Also, "History and Debate of Term Limits," op. cit.
4. Lai Olurode, "Introduction: The Crises of Political Succession," in Lai Olurode (ed.), *A Third Term Agenda: To Be or Not to Be?* (Lagos: Faculty of Social Sciences, University of Lagos, 2006), 6.
5. Hassan Saliu, "Democracy and Political Opportunism in Nigeria," *Ife Social Science Review* 19, no. 1 (2001): 72.
6. Oladipo O. Okege, "The Politics of Separation of Powers: An Assessment of the Workings of Presidential System of Government," *International Journal of Social and Policy Issues* 1, no. 1 (2002): 138.
7. F. W. Riggs, "The Survival of Presidentialism in America: Para Constitutional Crises," *International Political Science Review* 9, no. 4 (1988): 248.
8. Ibid.
9. S. Shastri, "Parliamentarism vs Presidentialism: Problems and Prospects in Indian Context," in D. D. Khanna and G. W. Kueck (eds.), *Principles, Powers and Politics* (Delhi: McMillan Press, 1999), 291–316. For more of these debates see, H. E. Bagce, "The Role of Political Institutions in Tackling Political Fragmentation and Polarization: Presidentialism versus Parliamentarism," *C. U. Iktisadi ve Idari Bilimler Dergisi*, Cilt 3, Sayi 1, 2002, available online at: http://iibfdergi.cumhuriyet.edu.tr/archive/, accessed December 14, 2009; A. Stepan and C. Skach, "Constitutional Frameworks and Democratic Consolidation: Parliamentarism Versus Presidentialism," *World Politics* 46, no. 1 (1993): 3–4; M. M. Lyne, "From Conflict to Cooperation: The Voters Dilemma and Executive–Legislative Relations in Latin America." Paper for the 2002 Meeting of Midwest Political Science Association, Chicago, April 22–28.
10. A. A. Akinsanya, "Four Years of Presidential Democracy in Nigeria," in A. A. Akinsanya and J. G. Idang (eds.), *Nigerian Government and Politics, 1979–1983* (Calabar: Wusen Publishers, 2002), 122.
11. Federal Government of Nigeria, *Constitution of the Federal Republic of Nigeria, 1999* (Abuja: Government Printers, 1999).
12. Ibid.
13. P. Mba, "Opposition Parties and Democratic Consolidation in Nigeria: The Case of ANPP and ACN," in I. S. Ogundiya (ed.), *Political Parties and Democratic Consolidation in Nigeria* (Ibadan: Codat Publications, 2011), 122–143.

14. See, A. A. Muhammad, "An Assessment of the Legislatures View About Executive-Legislature Relations in Nigeria, 1999–2007," Unpublished PhD Thesis, Ahmadu Bello University, Zaria, Nigeria, (2015): 208–211.
15. S. T. Olali, "Olusegun Obasanjo: The Personality and Philosophy of a President," in T. Wuam, S. T. Olali, and J. Obilikwu (eds.), *Obasanjo Second Era; 1999–2007* (Makurdi: Aboki Publishers, 2011), 35; J. Ibrahim, "Legislation and the Electoral Process: The Third Term Agenda and the Future of Nigerian Democracy," Paper for the Centre for Democracy and Development (CDD) Nigeria Roundtable, London, April 26, 2006.
16. Muhammad, Unpublished PhD Thesis, 195.
17. J. S. Zwingina, "An Appraisal of the Oversight Functions of the Parliament," in L. Hamalai (ed.), *Report of the 2008 Senate Retreat Abuja: Policy Analysis and Research Project* (Abuja, 2008), 86.
18. O. Obasanjo, "Text of Inaugural Speech at Swearing in Ceremony on May 29, 1999," available online at: www.ngex.com/nigeria/govt/President/obasanjospeeches.htm, accessed December 14, 2009.
19. A. A. Muhammad, "EFCC and the Fight Against Corruption: A Review of the President Obasanjo Years," in Terhembe Wuam, S. T. Olali, and J. Obilikwu (eds.), *Obasanjo Second Era, 1999–2007* (Makurdi: Aboki Publishers, 2011), 107–143.
20. H. A. Saliu, E. Amali, and R. Olawepo (eds.), *Nigeria's Reform Programmes: Issues and Challenges* (Ibadan: Vantage Publishers, 2007); W. O. Alli (ed.), *Political Reform Conference, Federalism and the National Question in Nigeria* (The Nigerian Political Science Association, 2005).
21. Muhammad, Unpublished PhD Thesis, 143.
22. O. Obasanjo, "Dialogue Not to Dismember Nigeria." Speech at the Opening Ceremony of the National Political Reform Conference in Abuja on February 21, 2005.
23. Muhammad, Unpublished PhD Thesis, 145.
24. This point was tacitly admitted by Mr. President during his speech to the nation on preparations for the conference when he noted that the National Assembly's response has encouraged the executive to look inwards and to become creative at sourcing funds for the conference with assurances that the conference will have enough resources to complete the assignment in the time allocated to it. See O. Obasanjo, "Why We Should Not Discuss in Fear," Being Text of a Broadcast by President Olusegun Obasanjo on Preparations for the National Political Reform Conference, February 15, 2005; Muhammad, Unpublished PhD Thesis, 146.
25. *Thisday Newspaper*, November 14, 2005, 1.
26. Saliu and Muhammad, "Perspectives," op. cit., 541.
27. Jibril Ibrahim, "Legislation and the Electoral Process: The Third Term Agenda and the Future of Nigerian Democracy," Paper for the Centre for

Democracy and Development (CDD) Nigeria Rountable, London, April 26, 2006.
28. Remi Anifowoshe, "Controversial Signposts of the Alleged Third Term Agenda," in Lai Olurode (ed.), *A Third Term Agenda: To Be or Not to Be?* Lagos, Nigeria: Faculty of Social Sciences, University of Lagos, 56.
29. *The Punch Newspaper*, April 7, 2012, 1.
30. *The Punch Newspaper*, April 8, 2012, 1; Daily Post Newspaper online, April 8, 2012.
31. *The Nation Newspaper*, April 8, 2012, 8.
32. *The Punch Newspaper*, April 8, 2012, 1.
33. O. Obasanjo, Address to the Nation by His Excellency, President Olusegun Obasanjo on the Occasion of the First Anniversary of his Democratically Elected Government, Abuja, May 29, 2000.
34. O. Obasanjo, "We Will Heal Nigeria," Being President Olusegun Obasanjo's Inaugural Speech at Eagle Square, Abuja, May 29, 2003, available online at: www.dawodu.com/obas13.htm, accessed December 13, 2011.
35. Saliu and Muhammad, "Perspectives," 537.
36. See *Tell Magazine*, April 3, 2006, 21.
37. Saliu and Muhammad, "Perspectives," 537.
38. Muhammad, Unpublished PhD Thesis, 104.
39. Afrobarometer, "Term Limits, the Presidency, and the Electoral System: What Do Nigerians Want?" Afrobarometer Briefing Paper No. 35, April, 2006, 1.
40. Ibid.
41. Saliu and Muhammad, "Perspectives," 539.
42. Sani Yerima, Interview with *Saturday Sun Newspaper*, Lagos, April 8, 2006, 2.
43. Isaac Nwaogwugwu, "Third Term Agenda and Its Purported Economic Performance Justification," in Lai Olurode (ed.), *A Third Term Agenda: To Be or Not to Be?* (Lagos: Faculty of Social Sciences, University of Lagos, 2006), 67.
44. see Tell, May 8, 2006, 61.
45. Saliu and Muhammad, "Perspectives," 538.
46. see, Tell, March 13, 2006, 25–26.
47. O. Obasanjo, "Report of the National Political Reform Conference and Recent Debt Relief Granted to Nigeria." Briefing by His Excellency, President Olusegun Obasanjo, to the National Assembly on the Report of the National Political Reform conference and Recent Debt Relief Granted to Nigeria Abuja, July 26, 2005.
48. T. Harriman, "Is There a Future for Democracy in Nigeria?" Text of Public Lecture Delivered by Honourable Temi Harriman, Member for Warri Federal Constituency, House of Representatives of Nigeria, at the Department of International Development, Oxford University, on Monday, June 5, 2006.

49. House Votes and Proceedings, May 2, 2006.
50. An examination of the report of the NPRC revealed that the conference recommended retention of existing two terms provision in the 1999 constitution (recommendation on tenure) but in the proposed amendment by the JCRC submitted to the NASS, the provision has been altered to read three terms. See, National Political Reform Conference Report, available online at: www.dawodu.com/nprc1.pdf, accessed September 30, 2011.
51. House Votes and Proceedings, op. cit.
52. Senate Votes and Proceedings, May 16, 2006.
53. Muhammad, Unpublished PhD Thesis, 215.
54. Afrobarometer, 1.
55. Muhammad, Unpublished PhD Thesis, 215.
56. Yerima, "Interview," 2.
57. Jonathan Manok, "Third Term Ambition: Fear or Patriotism?" available online at: http://www.gamji.com/article5000/NEWS5582.htm, accessed August 3, 2015.
58. Adolphous Wabara, "I Was Offered N250 Million for Obasajo's Third Term," Interview with *The Punch Newspaper*, November 7, 2014. The Punch Newspaper online, available at: http://www.punchng.com/politics/i-was-offered-n250m-for-obasanjos-third-term-wabara/, accessed August 3, 2015.
59. Ibid.
60. See, Obasanjo, "Told Us, 'No Third Term, No Nigeria'," https://www.naij.com/22440.html, accessed August 3, 2015; Nasir Ahmad El Rufa'I, *The Accidental Public Servant* (Ibadan: Safari Books Limited, 2013).
61. See, http://pointblanknews.com/pbn/exclusive/obasanjo-wants-third-term-govt-jonathan/, accessed August 3, 2015.
62. F. Onuoha, "Religious Violence in a Decade of Democratic Rule in Nigeria: Implications for Democratic Consolidation," A Paper Presented at the Conference on Ten Years of Nigeria's Democracy, Organized by the African Centre for Peace Research, Empowerment and Documentation (ACPRED), Ilorin, April, 2010.
63. *Tell Magazine*, March 13, 2006, 25–26.
64. C. N. D. Anyanwu, The Lawmakers: Sixth Assembly, Federal Republic of Nigeria (Abuja: Startcraft International Limited, 2007), 8.
65. Senate Votes and Proceedings, May 16, 2006.
66. See, *The Punch Newspaper*, April 8, 2012, 3; Daily Post online, April 8, 2012.
67. The Jonathan administration (2010–2015) sought to amend the tenure of the President to one single term of six years. This attempt was also rejected by the NASS.

BIBLIOGRAPHY

Afrobarometer. "Term Limits, the Presidency, and the Electoral System: What Do Nigerians Want?" Afrobarometer Briefing Paper No. 35, April 2006.

Akinsanya, Adeoye A. "Four Years of Presidential Democracy in Nigeria," in Adeoye A. Akinsanya and J. G. Idang (eds.), *Nigerian Government and Politics, 1979–1983*. Calabar: Wusen Publishers, 2002, 122–135.

Alli, Warisi O. (ed.). *Political Reform Conference, Federalism and the National Question in Nigeria*. Lagos: The Nigerian Political Science Association, 2005.

Anifowoshe, Remi. "Controversial Signposts of the Alleged Third Term Agenda," in Lai Olurode (ed.), *A Third Term Agenda: To Be or Not to Be?* Lagos: Faculty of Social Sciences, University of Lagos, 84–90.

Anyanwu, C. N. D. *The Lawmakers: Sixth Assembly, Federal Republic of Nigeria*. Abuja: Startcraft International Limited, 2007.

Bagce, H. E. "The Role of Political Institutions in Tackling Political Fragmentation and Polarization: Presidentialism Versus Parliamentarism." *C. U. Iktisadi ve Idari Bilimler Dergisi*, Cilt 3, Sayi 1, 2002. Available online at: http://iibfdergi.cumhuriyet.edu.tr/archive/. Accessed December 14, 2009.

Being text of a Broadcast by President Olusegun Obasanjo on Preparations for the National Political Reform Conference, February 15, 2005.

Daily Post online, April 8, 2012.

Debt Management Office, DMO. "Nigeria's External Debt Outstanding (1985–2004)." Available online at: http://www.dmo.gov.ng/oci/edebtstock/docs/External%20Debt%20Outstanding%20(1983-2004).pdf. Accessed December 14, 2009.

Debt Management Office, DMO. "Nigeria's External Debt Service Payments (1985–2004)." Available online at: http://www.dmo.gov.ng/oci/edebtservice/docs/External%20Debt%20Service%20Payments%20(1985-2004).pdf. Accessed December 14, 2009.

El Rufa'I, Nasir Ahmad. *The Accidental Public Servant*. Ibadan: Safari Books Limited, 2013.

Federal Government of Nigeria. *Constitution of the Federal Republic of Nigeria, 1999*. Abuja: Government Printers, 1999.

Ginsburg, Tom, James Melton, and Zachary Elkins. "On the Evasion of Executive Term Limits." *William and Mary Law Review* 52:1807 (2011): 1818–1826.

Harriman, T. "Is There a Future for Democracy in Nigeria?" Text of Public Lecture Delivered by Honourable Temi Harriman, member for Warri Federal Constituency, House of Representatives of Nigeria, at the Department of International Development, Oxford University, on Monday, June 5, 2006.

"History and Debate of Term Limits." Available at: http://www.debate.org/term-limits/. Accessed April 16, 2016.

House Votes and Proceedings, May 2, 2006.

http://pointblanknews.com/pbn/exclusive/obasanjo-wants-third-term-govt-jonathan/. Accessed August 3, 2015.

Ibrahim, Jibril. "Legislation and the Electoral Process: The Third Term Agenda and the Future of Nigerian Democracy." Paper for the Centre for Democracy and Development (CDD) Nigeria Roundtable, London, April 26, 2006.

Lyne, M. M. "From Conflict to Cooperation: The Voters Dilemma and Executive—Legislative Relations in Latin America." Paper for the 2002 Meeting of Midwest Political Science Association, Chicago, April 22–28, 2002.

Manok, Jonathan. "Third Term Ambition: Fear or Patriotism?" Available online at: http://www.gamji.com/article5000/NEWS5582.htm. Accessed August 3, 2015.

Mba, P. "Opposition Parties and Democratic Consolidation in Nigeria: The Case of ANPP and ACN," in I. S. Ogundiya (ed.), *Political Parties and Democratic Consolidation in Nigeria*. Ibadan: Codat Publications, 2011, 122–143.

Muhammad, Abdulrasheed A. "An Assessment of the Views of the Legislature about Executive-Legislature Relations in Nigeria, 1999–2007." Unpublished PhD Thesis, Ahmadu Bello University, Zaria, Nigeria, 2015.

Muhammad, Abdulrasheed A. "EFCC and the Fight Against Corruption: A Review of the President Obasanjo Years," in Terhembe Wuam, S. T. Olali, and J. Obilikwu (eds.), *Obasanjo Second Era, 1999–2007*. Makurdi: Aboki Publishers, 2011, 107–143.

Murse, Tom. "Why Presidents Can Serve Only Two Terms." Available online at: http://uspolitics.about.com/od/history/a/Why-Presidents-Can-Serve-Only-Two-Terms.htm. Accessed April 17, 2015.

National Political Reform Conference Report. Available online at: www.dawodu.com/nprcl.pdf. Accessed September 30, 2011.

Nwaogwugwu, Isaac. "Third Term Agenda and Its Purported Economic Performance Justification," in Lai Olurode (ed.), *A Third Term Agenda: To Be or Not to Be?* Lagos: Faculty of Social Sciences, University of Lagos, 2006, 63–69.

Obasanjo, Olusegun. "Address to the Nation by His Excellency, President Olusegun Obasanjo on the Occasion of the First Anniversary of His Democratically Elected Government." Abuja, May 29, 2000.

Obasanjo, Olusegun. "Dialogue Not to Dismember Nigeria." Speech at the Opening Ceremony of the National Political Reform Conference in Abuja on February 21, 2005.

Obasanjo, Olusegun. "Report of the National Political Reform Conference and Recent Debt Relief Granted to Nigeria." Briefing by His Excellency, President Olusegun Obasanjo, to the National Assembly on the Report of the National Political Reform Conference and Recent Debt Relief Granted to Nigeria Abuja, July 26, 2005.

Obasanjo, Olusegun. "Text of Innagural Speech at Swearing in Ceremony on May 29, 1999." Available online at: www.ngex.com/nigeria/govt/President/obasanjospeeches.htm. Accessed December 14, 2009.

Obasanjo, Olusegun. "We Will Heal Nigeria' Being President Olusegun Obasanjo's Inaugural Speech at Eagle Square, Abuja," May 29, 2003. Available online at: www.dawodu.com/obas13.htm. Accessed December 13, 2011.

Obasanjo, Olusegun. "Why We Should Not Discuss in Fear." Being Text of a Broadcast by President Olusegun Obasanjo on Preparations for the National Political Reform Conference, February 15,2005.

Obasanjo Told Us. "No Third Term, No Nigeria." https://www.naij.com/22440.html. Accessed August 3, 2015.

Okege, Oladipo O. "The Politics of Separation of Powers: An Assessment of the Workings of Presidential System of Government." *International Journal of Social and Policy Issues* 1, no. 1 (2002): 138–146.

Olali, S. T. "Olusegun Obasanjo: The Personality and Philosophy of a President," in T. Wuam, S. T. Olali, and J. Obilikwu (eds.), *Obasanjo Second Era; 1999–2007.* Makurdi: Aboki Publishers, 2011, 34–59.

Olurode, Lai. "Introduction: The Crises of Political Succession," in Lai Olurode (ed.), *A Third Term Agenda: To Be or Not to Be?* Lagos: Faculty of Social Sciences, University of Lagos, 2006, 1–8.

Onuoha, Freedom. "Religious Violence in a Decade of Democratic Rule in Nigeria: Implications for Democratic Consolidation." A Paper Presented at the Conference on Ten Years of Nigeria's Democracy, Organized by the African Centre for Peace Research, Empowerment and Documentation (ACPRED), ILORIN, April.

Riggs, F. W., "The Survival of Presidentialism in America: Para Constitutional Crises." *International Political Science Review* 9, no. 4 (1988): 247–278.

Saliu, Hassan. "Democracy and Political Opportunism in Nigeria." *Ife Social Science Review* 19, no. 1 (2001): 72–81.

Saliu, Hassan, and Abdulrasheed A. Muhammad. "Perspectives on the Tenure Extension Bid in Nigeria's Fourth Republic," in Diji Aina (ed.), *Corruption and the Challenge of Human Development.* Ilishan-Remo: School of Management and Social Sciences, Babcock University Press, 2007, 531–544.

Saliu, Hassan, Emeli Amali, and Raphael Olawepo (eds.). *Nigeria's Reform Programme: Issues and Challenges.* Ibadan: Vintage Publishers, 2007.

Senate Votes and Proceedings, May 16, 2006.

Shastri, S. "Parliamentarism vs Presidentialism: Problems and Prospects in Indian Context," in D. D. Khanna and G. W. Kueck (eds.), *Principles, Powers and Politics.* Delhi: McMillan Press, 1999, 291–316.

Stepan, A., and C. Skach. "Constitutional Frameworks and Democratic Consolidation: Parliamentarism Versus Presidentialism." *World Politics* 46, no. 1 (1993): 1–22.

Tabarrok, Alexander. "A Survey, Critique, and New Defense of Term Limits." *Cato Journal* 14, no. 2 (Fall 1994): 335–339.
Tell Magazine, March 13, 2006.
Tell Magazine, April 3, 2006.
Tell Magazine, May 8, 2006.
The Nation Newspaper, April 8, 2012.
The Punch Newspaper, April 7, 2012.
The Punch Newspaper, April 8, 2012.
Wabara, Adolphous. "I Was Offered N250 Million for Obasajo's Third Term." Interview with *The Punch Newspaper*, November 7, 2014. The Punch online. Available at: http://www.punchng.com/politics/i-was-offered-n250m-for-obasanjos-third-term-wabara/. Accessed August 3, 2015.
Yerima, Sanni. "Interview" with *Saturday Sun*, Lagos, April 8, 2006.
Zwingina, J. S. "An Appraisal of the Oversight Functions of the Parliament," in L. Hamalai (ed.), *Report of the 2008 Senate Retreat Abuja: Policy Analysis and Research Project*. Abuja, 2008, 84–88.

CHAPTER 7

Frederick Chiluba's Third Presidential Term Bid in Zambia

Cephas Lumina

Introduction

Formerly known as Northern Rhodesia, the Republic of Zambia attained independence from British colonial rule on October 24, 1964. The country's Independence Constitution of 1964 provided for a multiparty political system and an executive president. Kenneth Kaunda, leader of the United National Independence Party (UNIP)[1] and the country's prime minister since January 1964, became its first president.

As a new nation, Zambia found itself at the front line of the liberation struggle in southern Africa,[2] the intensity of which resulted in an influx of thousands of refugees into the country. Because of its support for the liberation movements in Angola, Rhodesia (now Zimbabwe), South Africa, and South West Africa (now Namibia),[3] Zambia was exposed to numerous retaliatory military attacks by the colonial/white minority regimes then in control in these countries which resulted in loss of lives and property, in an attempt to discourage it from supporting the liberation movements.[4] These hostile attacks, together with the large number of refugees, some of whom were suspected of being enemy agents sent to

---

C. Lumina (✉)
University of Lusaka, Lusaka, Zambia

© The Author(s) 2020
J. R. Mangala (ed.), *The Politics of Challenging Presidential Term Limits in Africa*, https://doi.org/10.1007/978-3-030-40810-7_7

destabilize the country, posed a security challenge for the newly independent state. As a result, the government maintained the state of emergency declared by the outgoing colonial Governor in July 1964.[5]

The country was also embroiled in internal political turmoil, eventuating in a split within the ruling party, UNIP.[6] In 1971, the Vice-President, Simon Kapwepwe, resigned from the government to form a new opposition party, the United Progressive Party (UPP). In February 1972, Kaunda banned the UPP and detained its leaders using the emergency law.[7] A new constitution adopted in December effectively introduced a one-party state through the designation of UNIP as the sole legal party and proscription of all other political parties.[8]

Despite the ban on opposition parties, challenges to the one-party system continued, albeit unsuccessfully.[9] In mid-1990, the opposition to the single-party system coalesced into an alliance of intellectuals, business people, and trade unions under the Movement for Multi-Party Democracy (MMD) with the singular aim of ousting UNIP and ensuring political change in Zambia.[10] In September, in response to increasing domestic pressure for the reintroduction of a multiparty system, President Kaunda appointed a Constitutional Review Commission (the Mvunga Commission[11]) to canvass views from the public on constitutional reforms.[12] The MMD, which had by then transformed itself into a political party[13] and the country's main opposition party, contested the process which it viewed as being dominated by UNIP.[14]

In October 1990, the Mvunga Commission submitted its recommendations, a number of which were rejected both by the government[15] and the MMD. The Commission's recommendations accepted by the government formed the basis of a draft constitution it sought to submit to Parliament for approval. The MMD rejected the draft and an impasse ensued until July 1991, when at an interparty dialogue convened by University of Zambia students, the national council of churches proposed the formation of a committee of ten delegates, five each from UNIP and the MMD, to negotiate changes to the draft. The final draft produced by the committee was then submitted to the National Assembly. On August 2, 1991, the National Assembly approved the new constitution, which repealed the 1973 Constitution and provided for multiparty democracy, as well as a two-term presidential limit.[16] The new constitution received presidential assent on August 29, 1991 and entered into force the following day. Prior to this, Parliament had, in December 1990, passed an amendment to the 1973 Constitution allowing the formation of other political parties.[17]

In the multiparty elections held on October 31, 1991—the country's first for 19 years—the MMD, emerged victorious, securing 125 of the 150 seats in the National Assembly, while the ruling UNIP won the remaining twenty-five seats. Frederick Chiluba, the leader of the MMD, defeated Kaunda, Zambia's president since independence, receiving 75.7% of votes cast, against Kaunda's 24.21% in the presidential election. On November 2, 1991, Chiluba was sworn in as the country's second president.

After the democratic transition from the one-party system to political pluralism, which saw Kaunda gracefully concede defeat and hand over power to Chiluba, Zambia was hailed as a model of democracy in Africa.[18] Ten years later, however, Chiluba's attempt to amend the Republican Constitution to allow him to extend his tenure as President cast a pall on the country's democratic aspirations.

This chapter discusses Chiluba's failed bid for an unconstitutional third term as president of Zambia. It is organized as follows. A brief discussion of the background to and constitutional provisions on presidential term limits in Zambia follows this introduction. Section "Chiluba's Third-Term Bid: A Snapshot of the Historical and Political Context" of the chapter provides a brief historical and political context of Chiluba's attempt to seek an extension of his stay in power beyond the constitutionally prescribed two terms. Section "Opposition to Chiluba's Third-Term Bid" discusses the opposition to Chiluba's third-term bid and his capitulation. Section "The Role of External Actors" focuses on the role of external actors in the anti-third term campaign. The last section of the chapter is the conclusion.

PRESIDENTIAL TERM LIMITS IN ZAMBIA

As stated above, presidential term limits were introduced in Zambia through the 1991 Constitution. Although, like the 1991 Constitution, the Independence Constitution of 1964 provided for a multiparty political system with an executive president, it imposed no term limits on the presidency. And since independence, Zambia had only had one president. The inclusion of term limits was thus driven, in part, by a desire to prevent authoritarianism.[19]

Article 35(1) of the 1991 Constitution provided that, "[s]ubject to clause (2) and (4) every President shall hold office for a period of five years." Clause 2 provided that no person who held or had held office as president for two terms of five years each was eligible for election to that office. Clause 3 made it clear that the period of two terms of five years each was to be calculated from the commencement of the Constitution (that is, from August 30, 1991).[20]

It is notable, however, that the 1991 Constitution was the result of a political compromise between UNIP and MMD with no input from the public. Because there had been insufficient time to undertake a comprehensive constitutional review, the constitution was essentially an instrument designed to facilitate the transition to a multiparty system.[21] Thus, as part of its election campaign, the MMD pledged, once elected, to undertake constitutional reforms that would enhance democracy in the country.[22] Against this backdrop, in November 1993, Chiluba appointed a Constitutional Review Commission (the Mwanakatwe Commission) to recommend a constitutional system that would ensure that the country was governed in a manner that would not only foster democracy, but would also "guard against the emergence of a dictatorship."[23] The Commission gathered views from the public through public sittings throughout the country. In June 1995, the Commission submitted its recommendations to the government. However, the government rejected the majority of the Commission's recommendations[24] and, in February 1996, prepared a bill to amend the constitution, based on the recommendations which it found acceptable.

In the National Assembly, the bill was strongly opposed by UNIP, the main opposition party, and other political parties, who walked out of the debate in protest against proposed amendments which set new restrictions on qualifications for the presidency (including a requirement that both parents of a candidate be Zambian by birth or descent[25]) and which barred traditional rulers (chiefs) from participating in politics unless they relinquished their chieftaincy.[26] These amendments were widely perceived to have been designed to prevent former President Kaunda,[27] whose parents originated from Nyasaland (now Malawi), and his party deputy, Senior Chief Inyambo Yeta (a traditional chief), from contesting the 1996 elections and effectively disqualified both.

In the face of widespread criticism, in May 1996, the MMD-dominated National Assembly passed the bill by a vote of 119 to none. The President assented to the bill on May 28 and it was enacted as the Constitution of Zambia (Amendment) Act No. 18 of 1996, which, in effect, repealed the whole of the 1991 Constitution, with the exception of Part III on the "Protection of Fundamental Rights and Freedoms of the Individual."

As a result of the controversial constitutional amendments, UNIP boycotted the country's second multiparty elections held on November 18 that year, which saw Chiluba reelected for a second term as republican president.[28] His party, the MMD, won 131 of 150 seats in the National Assembly.

Nevertheless, the amended constitution retained the limits to a president's tenure: the president could serve only two five-year terms. Section 35 of the Constitution as amended provided:

1. Subject to clause (2) and (4) every President shall hold office for a period of five years.
2. Notwithstanding anything to the contrary contained in this Constitution or any other law a person who has twice been elected as President shall not be eligible for re-election to that office.

It should be noted that the May 1996 amendment removed the explicit reference to the date of commencement of presidential terms contained in Article 35(3) of the 1991 Constitution. It was this lacuna that Chiluba's supporters would later seek to exploit in what can be considered a misguided attempt to make their case for his third-term bid.

Chiluba's Third-Term Bid: A Snapshot of the Historical and Political Context

During the campaign for the restoration of a plural political system in Zambia, Chiluba and the MMD strongly advocated for presidential term limits.[29] Moreover, throughout his presidency, Chiluba maintained that he not would seek to extend his constitutionally prescribed two-term tenure.[30] In 1998, Chiluba reiterated his commitment to leave office after the expiry of his mandated term.[31] He is reported to have said: "When my term of office comes to an end, do not even think of retaining me because *umuntu nga akota namano yala chepa*"—Bemba for "when a person gets old, he or she runs out of ideas."[32] However, barely two years later and a year before his second term of office drew to a close, it was evident that Chiluba intended to amend both the republican and his party's constitutions to enable him run for a third term.[33] In this regard, it has been asserted that events leading up to his attempt to seek an unconstitutional extension to his term suggest that his bid had been craftily devised.[34]

In January 2000, Chiluba announced the establishment of the office of District Administrator the functions of which were to "[m]anage government affairs at district level" and to "supervise all government departments, work on the *political and social mobilization of the people*, look at chiefs' affairs and know what (was) happening for democracy to thrive"[35] (emphasis). The District Administrators would also be "in charge of law and order by ensuring that there was harmony between law enforcement agencies and civil society."

The District Administrators would be appointed by and report directly to the President.[36] This move was widely considered as a ploy by Chiluba to canvass support for constitutional changes that would allow him to extend his tenure beyond the constitutionally mandated two terms. It is notable that the District Administrators were appointed from the ranks of MMD party cadres.

Not long after their appointment, the District Administrators and other MMD cadres began a campaign pushing for Chiluba to re-contest the presidential election to be held immediately after the end of his second term in 2001.[37] They argued that in terms of the 1996 Constitution, Chiluba had completed only one term in office. This claim clearly lacked merit. In this regard, it is important to recall that the constitutional reforms introduced by the government in 1996 limited the presidency to two terms of five years each. Article 35(2) of the 1991 Constitution, as amended, stated that no person who had twice been elected as president was eligible for reelection to that office. Chiluba had first been elected for a five-year term as president in 1991 and reelected for a second five-year term in 1996 which was to end in November 2001. Thus, by the time of the elections in November 2001, Chiluba would have already served two terms and would thus be ineligible for reelection. Additionally, the MMD constitution limited the party presidency to two terms. Since Chiluba had completed his two terms of office as head of the party he was ineligible to re-contest that position. Therefore, his bid for reelection to the republican presidency for a third term required changes to both the republican and MMD constitutions.

The third-term campaign launched by the District Administrators was characterized by intimidation and violence against those that were opposed, including cabinet ministers. In 2001, a group of District Administrators and pro-Chiluba MMD cadres calling themselves the "Ku Klax

Klan" began to encourage violence against those opposed to the third term.[38]

Although Chiluba remained silent on the issue, the fact that he had appointed the District Administrators and that they answered directly to him strongly suggests that he had given tacit endorsement to the pro–third term campaign.[39]

There were further indications of Chiluba's ambition for an extended stay in office. First, in July 2000, Benjamin Mwila, a senior member of the MMD and Chiluba's uncle, was expelled from the party after formally declaring his intention to contest the presidency of the party. Another ten leading members of the MMD were also expelled for supporting Mwila's candidature. Mwila's expulsion raised questions about Chiluba's intentions regarding the presidential elections due to be held in or before November 2001.[40]

Secondly, in February 2001, Vernon Mwaanga, the Secretary-General of the MMD, said that Chiluba wanted an open discussion on the third term. In a subsequent speech to church leaders, Chiluba claimed that preventing debate on the issue would be "undemocratic."[41]

In an attempt to shore up support for his bid, Chiluba extensively used a patrimonial "Presidential Discretionary Fund" (known as "the Slush Fund"), a special account approved by Parliament to be used at the President's pleasure, to buy political loyalty.[42] Although it is difficult to state with a degree of certainty how much money was spent since there was no public accounting of how the slush fund was spent,[43] it has been asserted that "large" amounts of money were spent to bribe people into supporting Chiluba's ambitions.[44] It can also be argued that the emergence of questionable churches and nongovernmental organizations in support of Chiluba's third-term ambition was a manifestation of such "rent-seeking" politics.

During January and February 2001, provincial conferences of the MMD discussed the third-term bid. The bid was endorsed by four of the country's nine provinces. It is important to underscore that these discussions often took place in an environment of intimidation and violence against those perceived to be against the bid.[45] Thus, for example, in April 2001, eight MMD Members of Parliament were suspended for opposing a resolution passed by the party's northern provincial conference to approve plans to allow Chiluba to hold the party presidency beyond the stipulated two terms, while the party's Southern Province chairperson, who had also campaigned against the proposed amendment of the party's constitution to allow for a third term, was suspended for bringing the name of the party into "contempt, ridicule or disrepute" and for "disobedience and insubordination."[46] During the party's Western Province conference, some District Administrators were alleged to have brandished firearms while other party cadres brandished knives and machetes in full view of the police.[47]

Toward the end of March, the National Executive Committee of the MMD scheduled an extraordinary convention for April 27–30, 2001 to allow party members to vote on whether to amend the party's constitution to allow for a third term for the party president. This decision was opposed by some MMD parliamentarians. On April 19, 2001, three MMD Members of Parliament—Griever Sikasote, Paul Bupe, and Francis Kamanga—applied to the High Court for an injunction restraining the party from proceeding with the convention on the grounds that the National Executive Committee had not complied with the party's constitution which stipulated that an extraordinary convention could only be called if so requested by at least a third of the party's provincial executive committees and only on ninety days' notice.[48] The High Court granted an interim injunction, but a few days later discharged it, thereby paving the way for the MMD national convention to proceed as planned.[49]

On April 30, 2001, the extraordinary convention of the MMD amended the party constitution to allow Chiluba to contest the party presidency and reelected him as the party's president. This cleared the way for Chiluba to become the MMD's candidate in the republican presidential elections scheduled for later in the year. It should be noted, however, that the convention was characterized by insults, intimidation, and violence against party delegates who were opposed to the third term. These included a number of members of the party's National Executive Committee who were blocked by pro-Chiluba cadres from participating in the convention.[50] Police confiscated a number of guns from some of the delegates.[51]

The convention marked the division of the party into two main factions: those supporting Chiluba's third-term aspirations and those against. In response, the pro-Chiluba faction in the party set in motion plans to expel twenty-two senior party members who were openly opposed to the third-term bid. On the same day, the affected party members, led by the republican Vice-President, Christon Tembo, and the MMD vice-president, Godfrey Miyanda, applied for and were granted an interim injunction by High Court judge Tamula Kakusa, restraining the National

Executive Committee of the MMD from expelling them "for holding views opposed to the amendment of both the party constitution and the Republican Constitution" to allow the incumbent party president (Chiluba) to run for a third term.[52]

In clear defiance of the High Court order, however, the MMD's National Executive Committee expelled the twenty-two members (all serving parliamentarians) on May 2, 2001 for bringing "the name of the party into disrepute."[53] On the same day, Chiluba dismissed everyone in his cabinet who had signed the petition against his reelection bid (see below), including Vice-President Tembo, and appointed a new team of ministers that he considered loyal to him.[54]

On May 23, 2001, the MMD attempted to overturn the interim injunction earlier granted by the High Court so that the parliamentary seats of the expelled MMD party members could be declared vacant but was unsuccessful. Before High Court judge Kakusa, the MMD contended that: (1) the writ of summons issued by the court had not been personally served upon the defendant, Michael Sata, who was the MMD national secretary at the time the court application was initiated but had since vacated that position; (2) it had not been served upon the MMD; and (3) the writ itself was defective.[55] All of these arguments were dismissed by the court, which referred to the argument alleging lack of service of court process as "a feeble afterthought which cannot be entertained."[56] The court also underscored that "the defendant cannot defeat the course of justice on account of a lacuna in the office of the National Secretary." It extended the injunction.

To compound matters, the Speaker of the National Assembly, Amusaa Mwanamwambwa, also refused to declare the seats of the expelled parliamentarians vacant.[57] It was a telling blow to Chiluba who had hoped that the expulsion of the twenty-two party members would reduce the number of parliamentary votes against his proposed constitutional amendments.[58]

Opposition to Chiluba's Third-Term Bid

The response to Chiluba's quest for an unconstitutional third term was strong: church leaders, the legal fraternity, civil society, opposition political parties, dissidents within the MMD, traditional leaders, students, the independent media, and ordinary citizens came together in a broad-based movement to oppose constitutional reforms that would allow Chiluba to extend his term beyond the constitutionally established two terms.[59] The

Zambia Congress of Trade Unions, once led by Chiluba during the one-party state (1973–1991), was also strongly opposed, with its General Secretary, Derrick Chaala, stating: "History has taught us that the continued stay of presidents in office has built them into dictators and that dictators often survive by resorting to large scale abuse."[60]

In response to the public statements by the District Administrators demanding changes to the MMD and republican constitutions to allow for a third term, in January 2001, the Law Association of Zambia (LAZ), the statutory body of legal practitioners, convened an emergency meeting of its Council which agreed that the LAZ had a duty to block Chiluba's attempt to manipulate the constitution.[61] In doing so, the LAZ invoked Section 4(b) of the LAZ Act[62] which provided that one of the objectives of the LAZ was to provide a forum through which all lawyers "can participate together fully and effectively in the *development of society and its institutions*" (emphasis). On January 19, 2001, the Chairman of LAZ, Christopher Mundia, held a press briefing during which he stated that the Constitution was "clear on the fact that the current president does not qualify for re-election."[63]

In a statement issued on January 25, 2001, church leaders from the three main church bodies: the Christian Council of Zambia (CCZ), the Evangelical Fellowship of Zambia (EFZ), and the Zambia Episcopal Conference (ZEC), expressed their staunch opposition to a third term for Chiluba, labeling it "unconstitutional" and "undemocratic."[64] Calling upon Chiluba to make clear his commitment to uphold the constitutional provision limiting the presidency, the church leaders underlined their firm belief that:

> Constitutional provisions must never be manipulated for the advantage of individuals or else the rule of law suffers. At this very moment when several of our neighboring African states are in the midst of terrible conflicts, Zambia must be a bright beacon of hope in the region by upholding the clear intent of constitutional provisions adopted in 1991 and repeated in 1996.[65]

They counseled Chiluba "to exercise statesmanship by unambiguously pledging to follow the ... constitution ... and thereby lead the people into a democratic electoral process that guarantee(d) peaceful, free and fair elections for a new President in 2001."[66]

On February 21, 2001, the main church bodies, the LAZ and civil society groups convened a public meeting at the Oasis Restaurant in Lusaka to mobilize public opinion against alteration of the Constitution to allow Chiluba re-contest the republican presidency after the end of his second and final term.[67] This resulted in the establishment of an alliance known as the Oasis Forum. The meeting adopted a strongly worded statement, known as the Oasis Declaration, which proclaimed:

> The Law Association of Zambia in conjunction with the Church, that is to say, the Zambia Episcopal Conference (ZEC), the Christian Council of Zambia (CCZ), the Evangelical Fellowship of Zambia (EFZ) and the Non-Governmental Organizations Coordinating Committee (NGOCC) and the People gathered here, having deemed it necessary, expedient, imperative and desirable to promote and conduct a debate in relation to the intimation by the ruling party, the MMD to amend the Republican Constitution to provide a third term of office in order to facilitate the eligibility of the incumbent President FTJ Chiluba in the forthcoming Presidential and Parliamentary Elections … [And whereas] … the Constitution of Zambia as amended in 1996 declares that "Notwithstanding anything to the contrary contained in this Constitution or any other Law, no person who has been twice elected as President shall be eligible for re-election to that office." Now this Forum declares as follows: … that the Forum calls upon the incumbent Republican President to exercise statesmanship by unambiguously pledging to uphold, protect and defend the Constitution of Zambia and not contest the 2001 Presidential Elections."[68]

The Forum further called upon "the women, men and the youth of this country to close ranks and resist ever again from being used and abused in any political process for selfish ends that may threaten our nation's peace and security." It also called upon the country's traditional leaders as "custodians of our national heritage to continue upholding our cultural values and not to be used as instruments for manipulation."

There was an extraordinary public response to this call. In the months that followed, many Zambians donned green "No Third Term" ribbons that were distributed by the NGOCC. Every Friday at 17:00 hours, the streets in Lusaka and the Copperbelt Province resounded with the honking of car horns as motorists expressed their solidarity with the "No Third Term Campaign." In addition, the Forum organized mass meetings in every provincial capital.[69] It soon became evident that most Zambians were against amendment of the Constitution to allow Chiluba another term in office. According to Gould, the Oasis Forum "catalyzed, organized, and gave focus to a nationwide social movement that challenged the abuse of executive discretion."[70]

Within Chiluba's own party, there was mounting tension between those in support of and those opposed to a third term. Toward the end of March 2001, fourteen members of the party's National Executive Committee issued a joint statement in opposition to the third term.[71] On April 10, 2001, at a prayer meeting for Members of Parliament held at the Cathedral of the Holy Cross in Lusaka, the three main church organizations in the country, some nongovernmental organizations and representatives of political parties issued a declaration stating that they were "categorically ... opposed to any attempts to confer a third term of office" on Chiluba. The fifty-nine signatories, who were all Members of Parliament and included the republican Vice-President, Tembo, and forty-two other members of the MMD, undertook to "use the mandate given to (them) by the people to do all things possible within the law to ensure that the Constitution of Zambia is upheld for the benefit of future generations."[72]

The "Cathedral Declaration" increased the pressure on Chiluba and seriously undermined his chances of amending the Republican Constitution to allow for a third term in office. At the time, the National Assembly consisted of 150 elected and eight nominated members. Amendments to the Constitution required at least 106 votes in favor. Thus, the fifty-nine parliamentarians who signed the Cathedral Declaration could block any proposed change to the Constitution irrespective of the decision of the MMD's extraordinary convention.

On April 21, 2001, the church, LAZ, and other civil society groups organized a public rally in Lusaka against the third term. The rally was attended by about 15,000 people, all the major opposition parties including UNIP, the United Party for National Development, the Zambia Alliance for Progress and the Zambian Republican Party, as well as senior MMD officials including Vice-President Tembo and foreign diplomats.[73] Police attempts to stop the rally going ahead were overturned by the High Court which ordered that police should ensure that the organizers of the rally were protected against intimidation and violence from supporters of the third term. At the rally, Tembo called upon Chiluba to "save (the) country" by ensuring that the constitution was respected. He underlined that:

There is no need for us to amend the constitution because politics like football has rules that ought to be respected by all the players. You don't go into a football match and start changing rules.[74]

On May 3, 2001, more than sixty-five Members of Parliament (mostly from the MMD and including all of those who had been expelled from the party by the pro-Chiluba faction) moved a motion in the National Assembly to have Chiluba impeached for alleged gross misconduct. The number of those in support of the motion was sufficient to compel the Speaker of the National Assembly to convene the Assembly to hear charges of gross misconduct against Chiluba. The impeachment motion outlined several offenses of "gross violation" of the Constitution against Chiluba. The motion alleged that:

> The president has grossly misconducted himself by failing to perform with dignity and leadership the functions of president in that he has initiated and orchestrated the third term debate through bribes applied to the MMD (Movement for Multiparty Democracy) members as well as other citizens for selfish rather than national interest.[75]

Under sustained domestic and international pressure, and confronted with the prospect of an embarrassing defeat in a parliament dominated by his own party, Chiluba capitulated and declared that he would not be seeking a third term in office. On May 5, 2001, he announced: "I will leave office at the end of my term. Let's take national interests into consideration. This is in the best interest of the nation."[76]

On August 23, the MMD's National Executive Committee announced that Levy Mwanawasa, the former republican vice-president during Chiluba's first term, would be its presidential candidate for the 2001 elections.[77] On May 30, the Speaker of the National Assembly postponed the debate on the impeachment motion, ostensibly to allow time for the judicial determination of a dispute over the expulsion of the twenty-two parliamentarians from the MMD since their case in the High Court was related to the impeachment motion.[78] This decision was met with some dismay by many observers including the LAZ, which argued that the Speaker had erred by refusing to convene the National Assembly within twenty-one days of receiving the motion as required by law.[79] The postponement of the debate on the impeachment motion allowed Chiluba to serve out the remainder of his term.

The Role of External Actors

In addition to broad-based opposition to the third-term bid within the country, there was significant international diplomatic pressure upon Chiluba,[80] as well as other forms of support for the anti-third term movement. For example, within the southern African region, the African National Congress of South Africa, which had resented Chiluba's treatment of Kaunda, was firmly opposed to his bid for a third term as president.[81] In particular, South African President Thabo Mbeki made it clear that he expected Chiluba to respect the constitution.[82] Botswana's President, Festus Mogae, expressed similar sentiments.[83]

The country's international development partners also provided substantial funding support to the anti-third term movement.[84] For example, the Royal Danish Embassy in Zambia donated $120,000 toward the anti-third term campaign led by the Oasis Forum.[85]

Conclusion and Lessons

The failure of Chiluba's attempt to extend his tenure beyond the constitutionally prescribed limit of two terms was the result of the concerted efforts of a broad spectrum of interest groups both internally and externally.[86] Within the country, a range of groups—including lawyers, women's organizations, church leaders, students, trade unions, and civil society groups—as well as individual Members of Parliament (both from the MMD and opposition parties) came together to oppose the third term.

Gould aptly sums up the factors that led to the failure of Chiluba's third-term bid:

> Like Kaunda's upset in 1991, Chiluba's demise was, in the end, the result of complex political tactics and processes, in which the legal rules, moral principles and popular sentiments meshed with the narrow aims of individual political actors.[87]

The successful anti-third term campaign in Zambia offers a number of important lessons. These have been well-articulated by Chella and Kabanda.[88] First, although the various stakeholders may have different agendas, it is important that they form strategic alliances to rally around an issue of shared interest. Thus, for example, in Zambia opposition political parties and dissidents within the MMD collaborated closely with a vibrant and informed civil society to vigorously oppose the third-term bid.

Second, a drive to oppose an attempt to alter a constitution so as to allow for a term of office beyond what is stipulated by the constitution requires well-defined leadership. In the Zambian context, this was provided by the Oasis Forum. According to Chella and Kabanda, the church provided moral weight and "credibility to the process" while "its structures made country outreach easier"; the LAZ provided legal expertise; and the women's civic groups facilitated women's activism.[89]

Third, it is imperative to mobilize the masses. A significant factor in the success of the anti-third term campaign in Zambia was the effective mobilization of people across the country by the Oasis Forum. In particular, the countrywide outreach enhanced the integrity of the campaign.

Fourth, there is a need for the strategic participation of the independent media. In the Zambian context, the independent media—particularly *The Post* newspaper—played a critical role in mobilizing public support for the anti-third term campaign through its coverage of the activities of the Oasis Forum and editorials that were critical of Chiluba's third-term ambitions.[90]

Fifth, it is important that the campaign against the unconstitutional extension of a presidential term is founded on issues with which people can readily identify. Thus, the increased poverty and high unemployment levels affecting them made the masses receptive to the message of the anti-third term campaign in Zambia.

A final assertion may be made. The factional turmoil that engulfed the MMD in the context of the third term issue undoubtedly played an important role in thwarting Chiluba's efforts to manipulate the republican constitution to enable him extend his stay beyond the constitutionally prescribed two terms. The MMD had initially been formed as a platform to spearhead the campaign for the ousting of UNIP and the reintroduction of a multiparty democracy. However, the disintegration, within a few years after assuming power, of the broad support for these aims by the various interest groups that had formed the MMD, made it easier for those within the party who were opposed to the third term to form, together with opposition parties and other actors, a significant counterweight to Chiluba's unconstitutional aspirations. It can therefore be contended that internal opposition within the political party of an incumbent seeking an unconstitutional extension to their tenure would appear to be a significant factor.

Notes

1. UNIP was founded in October 1959 as a successor to the Zambia African National Congress (ZANC) which had been banned in March that year. It was initially led by Mainza Chona since ZANC leader Kaunda had been imprisoned, but upon his release from prison in January 1960, Kaunda assumed the leadership of the party.
2. At the time, Angola, Mozambique, Rhodesia (now Zimbabwe), South Africa, and South West Africa (now Namibia), were all under colonial or white minority rule.
3. The Kaunda government supported the National Union for the Total Liberation of Angola (UNITA, in Angola), the Zimbabwe African People's Union (ZAPU, in Rhodesia), the African National Congress (ANC, in South Africa), and the South West Africa People's Organization (SWAPO, in South West Africa).
4. See, e.g., Hanania Lungu and Naison Ngoma, "The Zambian Military—Trials, Tribulations and Hope," in M. Rupiya (ed.), *Evolutions and Revolutions: A Contemporary History of Militaries in Southern Africa* (Pretoria: Institute for Security Studies, 2005), 321–322; Ann Seidman, *Apartheid Militarism and the US South East* (Trenton, NJ: Africa World Press, Inc., 1990), 49; William Minter, *Apartheid's Contras: An Inquiry Into the Roots of War in Angola and Mozambique* (Johannesburg: Witwatersrand University Press and London and New Jersey: Zed Books, 1994), 116–117; Melvin L. M. Mbao, "The Politics of Constitution-Making in Zambia: Where does the constituent power lie?" in Christina Murray and Charles Fombad (eds.), *Fostering Constitutionalism in Africa* (Pretoria: Pretoria University Law Press, 2010), 92–93; *Truth and Reconciliation Commission of South Africa Report*, vol. 2 (October 1998), 18, para. 72.
5. See Government Notice 374 of July 27, 1964. Other reasons given officially for the continuation of the state of emergency included tribal tensions within the country and economic problems.
6. See Government of Zambia, *Report of the Human Rights Commission of Inquiry (the Munyama Commission)* (Lusaka: Government Printer, 1995), app I.
7. See S. Mubako, "Zambia's Single-Party Constitution: A Search for Unity and Development" *Zambia Law Journal* 5 (1973): 2–3. In 1972, a total of 150 persons were detained without charge under the Preservation of Public Security Regulations, 1960.
8. Constitution of Zambia Act, No. 27 of 1973, which repealed the Zambia Independence Act 1964 and revoked the Zambia Independence Order 1964 and the Constitution contained in the schedule thereto. The Schedule to Act 27 contained the new Constitution. Article 4(1) of the new constitution proclaimed: "There shall be one and only one political party

or organization in Zambia, namely the United National Independence Party (in the Constitution referred to as the Party)." Clause 2 of article 4 provided that "[n]othing in the Constitution shall be construed as to entitle any person lawfully to form or attempt to form any political party or organization other than the Party or to belong to, assemble or associate with, express opinion or do any other thing in sympathy with, such political party or organization." Although this measure was justified by reference to the need to prevent ethnic conflict and promote national unity, critics have contended that the decision to introduce the one-party state was informed by, inter alia, "narrow partisan and survival" considerations. See Mbao, "The Politics of Constitution-Making in Zambia," 8; See also John M. Mwanakatwe, *End of Kaunda Era* (Lusaka: Multimedia Publications, 1994), 91–92; Muna Ndulo, "Constitution-making in Africa: Assessing Both the Process and the Content" *Public Administration and Development* 21, no. 2 (2001): 106.
9. Cephas Lumina, "Political Conditionality and its Implications for Human Rights: The Case of Zambia," Unpublished PhD dissertation (Griffith University, 1997), 130.
10. Douglas Williams, "Zambia" in Bard-Anders Andreassen and Theresa Swinehart (eds.), *Human Rights in Developing Countries 1991* (Oslo: Scandinavian University Press, 1991), 358.
11. The Commission was headed by the then Solicitor-General, Patrick Mvunga, hence the name "Mvunga Commission."
12. The Commission was appointed in terms of Statutory Instrument No. 135 of 1990.
13. The MMD was founded in July 1990 as a coalition of diverse interest groups aimed at campaigning for the reintroduction of a multiparty political system. It was launched as a political party on December 20 that year.
14. Of the twenty-two members of the Mvunga Commission, two represented the MMD. The two MMD members boycotted the commission in protest at the perceived UNIP control of the constitutional reform process. See https://www.princeton.edu/~pcwcr/reports/zambia1991.html, accessed April 20, 2017.
15. The Inquiries Act (Cap. 41 of the Laws of Zambia) under which constitutional review commissions are appointed, gives the government the power to accept or reject any or all recommendations from a constitutional review and to make any modifications.
16. Constitution of Zambia Act, 1 of 1991.
17. Constitution of Zambia (Amendment) Act, No. 20 of 1990, repealed article 4 of the Constitution which proscribed political parties other than the ruling UNIP.
18. Human Rights Watch, *Zambia: Elections and Human Rights in the Third Republic* 8, no. 4(A), 8, accessed April 20, 2017, http://hrw.org/

reports/1996/zambia.htm; See also The Carter Center, *Observing the 2001 Zambia Elections: Final Report* (Atlanta, GA: The Carter Center, October 2002), 17.
19. Boniface Madalitso Dulani, "Personal Rule and Presidential Term Limits in Africa," Unpublished PhD dissertation (Michigan State University, 2011).
20. Clearly, that did not cover the period served by Kaunda from 1964 to 1991. See Mbao, "The Politics of Constitution-Making in Zambia," 101.
21. Ibid., 97.
22. Mwanakatwe, *End of Kaunda Era*, 221; See also. Mbao, "The Politics of Constitution-Making in Zambia," 98.
23. Neo Simutanyi, *Zambia: Democracy and Political Participation*, Discussion Paper, A review by AfriMAP and the Open Society Initiative for Southern Africa (Open Society Foundations, March 2013), 6.
24. Simon Mwale, *Zambia's Constitutional Review: What Sort of Principles and Issues*, Policy Brief, Third Quarter 2005, Jesuit Centre for Theological Reflection, accessed April 20, 2017, http://www.jctr.org.zm/policy-briefs-doc/1018-3rdq-05-brief/file.
25. Constitution of Zambia (as amended by Act No. 18 of 1996), article 34(3)(b). Article 34(3) of the amended Constitution provided: "A person shall be qualified to be a candidate for election as President if – (a) he is a citizen of Zambia; (b) both his parents are Zambians by birth or descent; (c) he has attained the age of thirty-five years; (d) he is a member of, or is sponsored by, a political party; (e) he is qualified to be elected as a member of the National Assembly; and (f) he has been domiciled in Zambia for a period of at least twenty years."
26. Article 65(3) provided: "A Chief shall not be qualified for election as a member of the National Assembly." Clause (4) stated: "A Chief who intends to stand for election to the National Assembly shall abdicate his chieftaincy before lodging his nomination." See also article 129: "A Chief shall not, while remaining a Chief, join or participate in partisan politics." See further article 45(2) which required that the Vice-President be appointed by the President from among the members of the National Assembly. Since Kaunda's party deputy, Yeta, was disqualified from standing for election to the National Assembly, he, in effect, could not be appointed as the country's Vice-President.
27. It should be noted that earlier in the year, former president Kaunda, who had come out of his brief retirement from politics to take up again the presidency of UNIP, was preparing to challenge Chiluba for the republican presidency. See Jeremy Gould, "Postcolonial Liberalism and the Legal Complex in Zambia," in Terence C. Halliday et al. (eds.), *Fates of Political Liberalism in the British Post-Colony* (Cambridge: Cambridge University Press, 2012), 423.

28. Carter Center, *Observing the 2001 Zambia Elections*, 17; Claude Kambuya Kabemba, "Looking at the Management of the 2001 Zambian Tripartite Elections" *Journal of African Elections* 1, no. 2 (2002): 11.
29. It has been argued, however, that his subsequent attempt to remove term limits is indicative of the fact that his initial support for term limits was not a disapproval of personal rule but rather part of a strategy to create opportunities to ascend to power. See Paul Lewis, "Shifting Legitimacy: The Trials of Frederick Chiluba," in Ellen L. Lutz and Caitlin Reiger (eds.), *Prosecuting Heads of State* (Cambridge: Cambridge University Press, 2009), 209–210.
30. Lewis, "Shifting Legitimacy," 133. It has also been asserted that Chiluba's actions soon after he assumed office provide an indication of his autocratic style. In December 1991, for example, he unilaterally declared Zambia a Christian nation without consulting his Cabinet or Parliament. See Gero Erdmann and Neo Simutanyi, *Transition in Zambia: The Hybridization of the Third Republic*, Occasional Paper (Lilongwe: Konrad-Adenauer-Stiftung, 2003), 13.
31. Lewis, "Shifting Legitimacy," 133; Sarah Coleman, "Zambia: Third-Term Debate," accessed February 16, 2016, http://www.worldpress.org/Africa/1158.cfm.
32. *Sunday Mail* (Lusaka), January 11, 1998.
33. Lewis, "Shifting Legitimacy," 133.
34. Chomba Chella and Simon Kabanda, *Lessons in Effective Citizen Activism: The Anti-Third Term Campaign in Zambia*, SAIIA Occasional Papers 6 (Braamfontein: South African Institute of International Affairs, July 2008), 2.
35. *Times of Zambia*, December 2, 1991, 1, cited in Chella and Kabanda, *Lessons in Effective Citizen Activism*, 2.
36. Erdmann and Simutanyi, *Transition in Zambia*, 48.
37. Dulani, "Personal Rule and Presidential Term Limits in Africa," 26.
38. Simon Kabanda, *Citizens Forum Zambia*, Practitioner Reflection, Working Paper 8, July 2010, 6.
39. Gregory Mthembu-Salter, "Zambia: Recent History," in Katherine Murison (ed.), *Africa South of the Sahara 2004*, 33rd edition (London and New York: Europa Publications, 2003), 1200.
40. Ibid.
41. http://news.bbc.co.uk/2/hi/africa/1162462.stm.
42. See Erdmann and Simutanyi, *Transition in Zambia*, 17.
43. Bornwell C. Chikulo, "Corruption and Accumulation in Zambia," in Kempe Ronald Hope and Bornwell C. Chikulo (eds.), *Corruption and Development in Africa: Lessons from Country Case-Studies* (Houndmills: Macmillan Press Inc. and New York: St. Martin's Press, 2000), 171.

44. Chance Chagunda, *Presidential Terms and Good Governance,* Briefing Paper 87, Southern African Catholic Bishops' Conference, Parliamentary Liaison Office, December 2002, 3.
45. Mthembu-Salter, "Zambia: Recent History," (2003), 1201; See also Chagunda, *Presidential Terms and Good Governance,* 2.
46. "Nine MPs Suspended for Opposing Chiluba's Third Term Bid," accessed February 15, 2016, http://panapress.com/Nine-MPs-suspended-for-opposing-Chiluba-s-third-term-bid--13-446657-18-lang1-index.html.
47. Comment by Angel Mumba, *The Post,* April 25, 2001, 12, cited in Chella and Kabanda, *Lessons in Effective Citizen Activism,* 3.
48. http://panapress.com/Nine-MPs-suspended-for-opposing-Chiluba-s-third-term-bid--13-446657-18-lang1-index.html. See also Manoah Esipisu, "MPs in Court to Stop Chiluba's Third Term Bid," April 19, 2001, accessed February 15, 2016, http://www.iol.co.za/news/africa/mps-in-court-to-stop-chiluba-s-third-term-bid-64635.
49. IRIN, "Zambia: Ruling Party Convention Goes Ahead," April 27, 2001, accessed February 16, 201, http://allafrica.com/stories/200104260504.html, 6.
50. Gould, "Postcolonial Liberalism and the Legal Complex in Zambia," 442. See also paragraph 8 of the Affidavit of Christon Sifapi Tembo and paragraghs 4 to 6 of the Statement of Claim filed in the High Court on April 30, 2001, in the case of *Lieutenant-General Christon Sifapi Tembo and Brigadier-General Godfrey Miyanda (suing on their own behalf and on behalf of members of the Movement for Multi-Party Democracy opposed to the 3rd term) v National Secretary of the Movement for Multi-Party Democracy,* 2001/HP/0422, High Court of Zambia (unreported).
51. Gould, "Postcolonial Liberalism and the Legal Complex in Zambia," 442.
52. *Tembo and Miyanda v National Secretary of the Movement for Multi-Party Democracy,* 2001/HP/0422, Statement of Claim, para. 7.
53. Those expelled from the MMD included the country's Vice-President, General Christon Tembo, eight Cabinet ministers (namely, MMD vice-president and Minister of Education, Brigadier-General Godfrey Miyanda; Minister of Legal Affairs, Vincent Malambo; Minister of Labour, Edith Nawakwi; Minister of Natural Resources, Samuel Miyanda; Minister of Agriculture, Suresh Desai; Minister of Community Development, Dawson Lupunga; Minister of Trade and Industry, David Mpamba; and Minister of Mines, Syamukayumbu Syamujaye), three deputy ministers and eight Members of Parliament. See "Zambia's Ruling Party Expels Top Members," May 2, 2001, accessed February 15, 2016, http://www.iol.co.za/news/africa/zambias-ruling-party-expels-top-members-66144.
54. Mildred Mulenga, "Zambia: Chiluba Expels Nine Cabinet Ministers from Ruling Party," May 2, 2001, accessed February 15, 2016, https://allafrica.com/stories/200105030001.html.

55. *Tembo and Miyanda v National Secretary of the Movement for Multi-Party Democracy*, 2001/HP/0422, Ruling, May 23, 2001, 2.
56. Ibid.
57. *The Post*, May 4, 2001.
58. Lewis, "Shifting Legitimacy," 134.
59. Ibid., 133; See also Kabemba, "Looking at the Management of the 2001 Zambian Tripartite Elections," 12.
60. Chris McGreal, "Zambia's Neighbours Edgy at Leader's Bid to Stay in Power," *The Guardian*, May 4, 2001, accessed April 20, 2017, https://www.theguardian.com/world/2001/may/04/chrismcgreal.
61. Gould, "Postcolonial Liberalism and the Legal Complex in Zambia," 439.
62. Chapter 31 of the Laws of Zambia.
63. *The Post*, January 22, 2001, cited in Gould, "Postcolonial Liberalism and the Legal Complex in Zambia," 440.
64. Zambia Episcopal Conference, "The Third Term Bid by President Chiluba," Press Release, 25 January 2001, 1, para. 1.
65. Ibid., 2, para. 5.
66. Ibid., 2, para. 6.
67. IRIN, "Civic Groups Condemn a Third Term for Chiluba," February 22, 2001, accessed February 16, 2016, http://www.irinnews.org/report/18751/zambia-civic-groups-condemn-third-term-chiluba. The meeting was attended by more than 1200 people, including church leaders, parliamentarians, lawyers, traditional leaders, as well as representatives of civil society and community-based organizations. See Kabanda, *Citizen Forum Zambia*, 6.
68. The name of the declaration derives from the venue of the meeting, the Oasis Restaurant. See "Zambia: Oasis Declaration: Civil Society Rejects Third Term," www.allfrica.com, 23 March 2001.
69. Gould, "Postcolonial Liberalism and the Legal Complex in Zambia," 441; See also Jeremy Gould, "Subsidiary Sovereignty and the Constitution of Political Space in Zambia," in Jan-Bart Gewald, Marja Hinfelaar and Giacomo Macola (eds.), *One Zambia, Many Histories: Towards a History of Post-Colonial Zambia* (Leiden: Brill, 2008), 282.
70. Gould, "Postcolonial Liberalism and the Legal Complex in Zambia," 438.
71. *The Post*, March 28, 2001.
72. Gould, "Postcolonial Liberalism and the Legal Complex in Zambia," 442.
73. Anthony Mukwita, "President Chiluba's Third Term Bid Dashed," accessed February 15, 2016, http://www.ipsnews.net/2001/04/politics-zambia-president-chilubas-third-term-bid-dashed/.
74. Ibid.
75. See News24 Archives, "Impeachment Motion Filed Against Zambia's Chiluba," accessed July 14, 2016, http://www.news24.com/Archive/Impeachment-motion-filed-against-Zambias-Chiluba-20010504.

76. Esipisu, "Chiluba Drops Third Term Bid," http://www.news24.com/xArchive/Archive/Chiluba-drops-third-term-bid-20010505, accessed February 16, 2016.
77. Dulani, "Personal Rule and Presidential Term Limits in Africa," 5.
78. IRIN, "Decision on Chiluba Impeachment Delayed," May 30, 2001, accessed July 14, 2016, www.irinnews.org/report/21859/zambia-decision-chiluba-impeachment-debate-delayed.
79. Ibid.
80. Erdmann and Simutanyi, *Transition in Zambia*, 43.
81. Mthembu-Salter, "Zambia: Recent History" (2003), 1202; See also Erdmann and Simutanyi, *Transition in Zambia*, 70.
82. Denis Venter, "Democracy and Multiparty Politics in Africa: Recent Elections in Zambia, Zimbabwe and Lesotho," *Eastern Africa Social Science Research Review* XIV, no. 1 (2003): 10; McGreal, "Zambia's Neighbours Edgy at Leader's Bid to Stay in Power."
83. Ibid.
84. Gould, "Subsidiary Sovereignty and the Constitution of Political Space in Zambia," 283, note 15.
85. Lewis, "Shifting Legitimacy," 133.
86. Ibid., 134.
87. Gould, "Postcolonial Liberalism and the Legal Complex in Zambia," 438.
88. Chella and Kabanda, *Lessons in Effective Citizen Activism*, 10.
89. Ibid.
90. Lewis, "Shifting Legitimacy," 134.

Constitutionalism and the Future of Presidential Term Limits in Africa

Jack R. Mangala

In the aftermath of the end of the Cold War, the vast majority of African presidential regimes adopted the constitutional rule limiting the number of terms their chief executives could serve in office. Among other political and institutional reforms initiated at that time, this cardinal rule of democratic governance was intended to create constitutionally binding constraints on the presidents in order to move the countries past the era of "big men" that had defined Cold War politics, and anchor them on the path of democratic transition. Even though, in some instances, leaders embraced term limits more for cosmetic purpose intended for foreign consumption than as a genuine constraint on the power of incumbency, the adoption of term limits is nonetheless credited with contributing to an emerging political culture in which leaders could not simply impose themselves on their countries as had been the case decades earlier.

While it is possible to argue, *in abstracto*, that the lack of term limits is not, per se, undemocratic as long as elections are free and fair, any informed view on the inner working of presidential regimes and

J. R. Mangala (✉)
Grand Valley State University, Wyoming, MI, USA
e-mail: mangalaj@gvsu.edu

© The Author(s) 2020
J. R. Mangala (ed.), *The Politics of Challenging Presidential Term Limits in Africa*, https://doi.org/10.1007/978-3-030-40810-7_8

the power of incumbency would lead one to conclude that the lack of term limits is fundamentally undemocratic and term limits on the chief executive are different from all other institutions. They represent "an institutional demarcation line that separates democratic rulers, however powerful, from tyrants."[1] In presidential regimes, it has been established that presidents cannot be re-elected ad infinitum (or even more than once) without the whole state apparatus becoming uniquely and dangerously responsive to the executive branch and further contributing to personalizing power. Thus term limits are an important democratic safeguard, the respect of which is a key contributing factor to the process of democratic consolidation that stresses, at its core, the idea that institutions and norms are more important than individuals, no matter how capable or visionary they might be. No one is indispensable. This echoes the idea of equality that underlined the adoption of the principle of office alternation in ancient Greece. The sense of enthusiasm that was palpable when term limits were being adopted by African presidential regimes in the early part of the 1990s speaks to the importance of this cardinal rule for democratic consolidation.

While, on the one hand, it can be argued that term limits rules are impacting on the trajectory of African political leadership in important ways, we have also witnessed, on the other hand, a strong reversal movement in nearly a third of the countries where term limits had been adopted in the early 1990s, which seems to suggest that personal rule remains as much alive among the post-authoritarian generation of African leaders as before. These two contending currents are captured in the case studies included in this volume. While there is cause for concern that any leader would choose to subvert the constitution and stay in power longer than mandated, the fact that term elongation bids have been defeated, as discussed in the three cases included in the second part of the book, seems to lend credential to the argument that there is an undercurrent working in favor of democratic consolidation on the continent and that term limitation rules, even though still challenged by some, are however taking root in Africa's political landscape. To this optimistic view, some would respond that the relatively high number of successful challenges to term limits, as captured in the three cases included in the first part of the book, underscores the fragility of the democratic transition and the entrenched personal nature of power in African politics, bringing to focus the delicate lines of tension and complex interplay between the role of formal and informal institutions, with the latter offering, ultimately, a better window into the onset of the phenomenon of new Caesarism and the outcomes of third-term bids in Africa.

The qualitative narratives provided in the case studies have addressed these contending currents and shed much-needed light on why and how challenges to the term limits rules unfolded and were ultimately settled in specific national contexts. Case study narratives have provided a deeper understanding of the term limits debate as well as a wealth of scholarly insights on the motivations of leaders who have challenged the term limits rule, the lines of argument for and against *continuismo*—often delivered with colorful national nuances—put forward by clashing actors and various parties in the term limits debate, the strategies employed by each side to ensure victory, and the specific factors that have most impacted the outcomes. Case studies have dissected, with remarkable surgical precision, the stakes and significance of the challenges to the term limits rule in six African countries. A few cross-case and general observations will be offered in the ensuing sections.

1. Ever since their institutionalization in the early years of the post-Cold War era, term limits have acquired a great measure of public acceptance and legitimacy. There seems to be a strong support for term limits rules across the borders, both in countries that have them and those that do not because the president succeeded, through a parliamentary majority or other procedural maneuvering, in removing them. This is a positive development for the future of democracy in Africa. It contradicts the narrative about the "people's call" often presented as a rationale by leaders—and their coterie of clients—who wish to stay in office beyond constitutionally mandated terms. The people-driven third-term bid is often no more than a mythical excuse used by leaders throughout history that has never been supported by any empirical data. A leader decides to hang on to power first, then engineers the people's call as a convenient justification. It does not work the other way around. That is why term limits alteration via a parliamentary vote—where they can control the outcome through corruption, intimidation, and patronage—rather than a popular referendum is the preferred modus operandi for presidents seeking political immortality.
2. When considering the question of term limits at the individual level of analysis which deals with the leaders' personal motivations in clinging to power rather than at the level of institutional variables

that determine the outcomes of processes aimed at altering term limits rules, narratives from the case studies have confirmed the critical importance of rent-seeking and, in some instances, concerns over personal immunity, in the leaders' decision to subvert the constitution. The importance of rent-seeking and personal immunity as key drivers of *continuismo* at the personal level of the leader has significant policy implications. Making the presidency (and other state institutions) less attractive in terms of the spoils of office and increasing the cost of holding that office through constitutional subversion, while ensuring the availability of opportunities for income-generating activities for former presidents, would help in strengthening the institution of term limits. Incentivizing leaders not to think of the office they hold as their personal property represents a key challenge in transforming the presidency in Africa and, in the same token, the state itself. As long as many leaders will continue to approach the presidency as a golden opportunity for wealth accumulation, they will find ways to hold on to power whatever the ultimate cost to themselves and the state.

3. The examination of the determinants of the outcomes of term limits alteration processes in the case studies has highlighted a number of important factors. They include the extent of patronage and state penetration of the network of clients a leader commands; the relative unity among the political forces opposing term limits change; the existence of fractures along ethnic, regional, or ideological lines within the ruling coalition; the determination and mobilization creativity of civil society actors; and the vested interests of key international actors in the outcomes. For example, in the case of President Yoweri Museveni of Uganda, the United States had a vested interest in seeing him stay in power because of terrorism and growing militant Islam concerns in East Africa (Sudan, Somalia, and Kenya). Museveni was politically savvy enough to play that card and smartly positioned himself as a key US ally in the fight against terrorism, thus securing a tacit OK from the latter in his decision to alter term limits. The same is true, albeit for a different set of reasons (post-genocide guilt, stability, and economic recovery), for President Paul Kagame's 2017 successful term limits alteration in Rwanda.

Narratives from the case studies have also underscored the complex dynamics between various variables at play in defining the outcome in a particular situation. No outcome was explained by one single factor. In the aforementioned examples about Uganda, terrorism and militant Islam as high-stake issues for a key international actor (USA) along with other factors such as political violence and the division of the opposition contributed to successful term limits alteration in that country. In the case of Rwanda, post-genocide guilt on the part of key international actors (UN, USA, UK) coupled with the militarization of the regime and the relative stability and economic recovery since the genocide, all of which led to a successful subversion of term limits by Kagame and his allies.

4. An important contribution to the literature on presidentialism and term limits from the case studies included in this volume is their thorough examination of the tactical strategies deployed by opposing sides in the term limits debate to achieve their goals. Once a decision has been made to alter term limits (or oppose such constitutional alteration), victory in the political arena will depend, ultimately, on the strategies used by various camps, and on the means at their disposal to execute such strategies. With all the advantages and spoils of office, presidents seeking to alter term limits and their allies have often resorted to the use of money, violence, intimidation, control of state media, and ethnic manipulation to ensure a successful outcome. For forces committed to defending the integrity of the constitution, victory has often depended, among other things, on their capacity for building large coalitions, around a common platform, between political parties and actors from the civil society. Adequate framing and messaging of the issue at hand and the stakes at play seems to have impacted the outcomes of term limits debates analyzed in the case studies. While those supporting change to term limits rules have generally framed the debate in terms of stability, efficiency, popular will, and the leader's exceptional qualities, the opposition's ability to effectively counter this political narrative by mobilizing various constituencies around higher societal stakes centered on the dangers of personalism, and the imperative of democratic consolidation for national development has been essential in understanding the outcomes of the term limits debate.

Looking beyond the case studies discussed in this volume, and against the backdrop of the authoritarian reversals observed in Africa and elsewhere in the developing world, it is worth reaffirming two important points. First is the centrality of binding term limits for democratic consolidation. The latter, which occurs when democracy becomes the only game in town, calls for the establishment of strong institutions—geared toward the common good—that hold primacy over individuals regardless of the latter's personal qualities. Trying to subvert the constitution in order to extend one's term in office is antithetical to democratic consolidation. It perpetuates a culture of personal rule that has not served Africa and its people well. Second, the cardinal importance of constitutionalism in building a democratic culture cannot be overstated. Constitutionalism is the heartbeat of the republic, the unflinching belief in a government of laws, not of men. Constitutionalism postulates that all actors, above all the one actor holding the most power—the president—show total adherence to the law and spirit of the constitution. That remains the *sine qua non* of national development.

In the early 1990s, the wave of democratization that swept across Africa and the ensuing adoption of term limits rule was, to a greater extent, the result of a shifting international context resulting from the end of the Cold War. The emerging new international era, marked by what has been referred to as the "rise of the rest,"[2] has seen China "altered the strategic context in Africa"[3] through a sustained economic and political penetration over the past decade. The growing influence of China on the continent has led to a weakening of Western Countries' leverage and a slow realignment of their priorities: combatting terrorism and Islamic fundamentalism seems more important today than promoting democracy. China, on the other hand, has not only offered African countries some leverage in their dealings with the West, it has also presented itself as an alternative political and economic model. This is why the March 2018 Amendment to the Chinese Constitution abolishing term limits on the Presidency is of particular significance when discussing the future of presidential term limits in Africa.[4]

The above international context has, without any doubt, given more ammunition and political cover to those seeking to abolish term limits. The current picture of term limits in Africa seems mixed and shows a clear regional contrast. While the institution has survived alteration attempts in West Africa (Benin, Burkina Faso, Senegal, and Nigeria), it has however suffered important setbacks in Central Africa (Congo, Burundi, Rwanda, and Uganda). Current trends toward authoritarianism—the so-called rise of strong men—around the world and in some African countries like

Tanzania and Kenya, seem to suggest the institution of term limits will face more challenges in years to come.

"Why so many African presidents are ditching term limits?" asks *The Economist*. Rather giving into the usual exoticization of African politics and societies, the answer to this question underscores the fact that these leaders are rational actors and "they calculate that the costs of doing so are low."[5] Kagame in Rwanda and Sassou Nguesso in the Congo knew that, beyond diplomatic pronouncements and toothless political declarations, they would not face any serious backlash from the international community. Both leaders are considered "reliable partners" by international partners. The lowering of the costs of clinging to power is a function of the changing international order described above that seems to prioritize the fight against terrorism and stability over democracy and whose alternative leader (China) has invested neither in matters of democracy at home nor democracy promotion abroad.

Against this backdrop, and unless the people of Africa themselves—which is the true essence of democracy—take ownership of the norm of presidential term limits as a common good and fight for its preservation by imposing a higher cost (the international community is not willing to impose) on leaders who attempt to or deviate from it, a growing number of African presidents would try to subvert it, and they would succeed more than in past decades in extending their term in office.

Notes

1. Alexander Baturo, *Democracy, Dictatorship, and Term Limits* (Ann Arbor: The University of Michigan Press, 2014), 11.
2. Fareed Zakaria, *The Post-American World* (New York: W.W. Norton, 2008).
3. Anthony Lake and all, *More Than Humanitarianism: A Strategic U.S. Approach Toward Africa* (Washington, D.C.: Council on Foreign Relations, 2006).
4. See Anthony Kuhn, "Why Abolishing China's Presidential Term Limits is Such A Big Deal," *NPR*, March 14, 2018. Available online at https://www.npr.org/sections/parallels/2018/03/14/593155818/why-abolishing-chinas-presidential-term-limits-is-such-a-big-deal.
5. "Why So Many African Presidents are Ditching Term Limits," *The Economist*, August 4, 2017.

Index

A
Accountability, 13, 15, 46, 58, 59, 83, 110, 119, 120, 126, 151, 153, 172, 173
African Development Bank (ADB), 70, 89
African National Congress (ANC), 218, 220
African Union (AU), 26, 29
Amin, Idi, 105, 106, 108, 109, 112, 118
Argentina, 5, 16
Aristotle, 9
Arkansas, 12, 30
Autocratic regime, 120, 122, 133, 159

B
Besigye, kiiza, 116, 117, 121, 122, 126, 130, 132
Blair, Tony, 51, 116, 117
Bolivia, 5
Bongo
  Ali, 67, 83–88, 94–96
  Omar, 1, 2, 7, 39, 65–67, 69–86, 89–96, 99
  regime, 66, 67, 70, 71, 73, 75, 76, 78, 80, 81, 83–85, 87–95
  system, 1, 74, 79, 89, 96
Bush, George W., 25, 180

C
Caesarism, 18, 25, 229
Chiluba, Frederick, 2, 53, 207–219, 222–224
Civil, 10, 37, 38, 52, 53, 84, 106, 108, 132, 176
  disobedience, 142, 156
  society, 7, 22, 28, 40, 46, 47, 52, 54, 73, 78, 84, 93, 122, 126, 128, 129, 143, 144, 146, 147, 149, 150, 152, 153, 155, 156, 158–164, 166, 167, 177–179, 210, 213, 215, 216, 218, 219, 225, 230, 231
Clinton
  Bill, 51
  Hillary, 52, 63

© The Editor(s) (if applicable) and The Author(s), under exclusive license to Springer Nature Switzerland AG 2020
J. R. Mangala (ed.), *The Politics of Challenging Presidential Term Limits in Africa*, https://doi.org/10.1007/978-3-030-40810-7

Cold War, 1, 2, 6–8, 18, 29, 37, 227, 229, 232
Compaoré, Blaise, 96, 141–160, 162–169
Congrès pour la Démocratie et le Progrès (CDP), 142–144, 148, 150, 152–166
Constituent assembly (CA), 110–112, 173
Constitutional
   change, 20, 29, 45, 49, 51, 53, 54, 80, 116, 143, 145, 210
   council, 152, 214
   revision, 40, 45, 49, 54, 56
Continuismo, 29, 229, 230

D
de Gaulle, Charles, 68, 69, 98
Democratic
   consolidation, 10, 49, 191–193, 195, 228, 231, 232
   deficit, 38, 85
   experiment, 38, 74, 83, 95
   institution, 3, 6, 9, 14, 37, 38, 46, 49, 95, 96, 142, 145, 147–149, 153, 165, 166, 175, 191, 192, 228, 232
   norm, 2, 6, 7, 9, 37, 85, 175
   reform, 2, 7, 37, 38, 145, 147, 150, 227
   safeguard, 38, 228
   transition, 21, 50, 145, 165, 207, 227, 228
Democratic Green Party, 47, 48, 55
Democratic Republic of the Congo, 2, 6, 8, 27, 67
Democratization, 6, 7, 38, 73, 76–78, 85, 147, 153, 165, 175, 232
Development indicator, 43
Dictatorship, 6, 25, 38, 45, 65, 94, 208
Dominant party, 43, 49, 166

Dynastic succession, 67, 83

E
East Africa, 230
East African Community, 55, 111, 121
Election
   management, 122, 128, 129, 144
   process, 73, 76, 78, 85, 119, 123, 130, 132, 214
   results, 66, 86–88, 108, 125, 129, 130, 132, 160, 209
Electoral
   commission, 55, 56, 108, 122
   dominance, 148
   finances, 91, 125
   fraud, 66, 83, 85, 86, 91, 95
   performance, 145, 169
Equatorial Guinea, 7, 39, 119
European Union (EU), 50, 60, 62, 88, 130

F
Federal government, 177, 196
Fiscal federalism, 177
Front populaire, 146, 147

G
Gabon, 1, 2, 6–8, 29, 39, 65–74, 76–78, 80, 81, 83–86, 88–91, 93–96
Gates, Bill, 51
Gender equity, 42
Genocide, 38, 41–44, 46, 50, 51, 55, 57, 60, 61, 231
Governance, 38, 43, 44, 47, 51, 58, 110–112, 173, 174, 181, 193
   democratic, 7, 27, 113, 177, 227
   good, 7, 12, 13, 17, 111, 116, 117, 172

Gross domestic product (GDP), 42, 70, 91, 94, 186

H
Hamilton, Alexander, 13, 16, 17, 31

I
Imihigo, 43
Incumbency, 10, 12–14, 17, 38, 44, 120, 227, 228
Indispensability, 4, 25, 41, 185
Institutionalization, 6, 229
Insurrection populaire, 142, 146
International, 7, 26, 27, 41, 46, 50–52, 56, 90, 116, 129, 162, 178, 180, 181, 185, 194, 217, 218, 230–233
  Crisis Group, 57
  debt, 181

J
Jefferson, Thomas, 9, 11

K
Kabaka, 107
Kabila, Joseph, 27, 33, 49, 67
Kagame, Paul, 38, 40–51, 53–58, 61, 112, 230, 231, 233
Kampala, 45, 108, 127, 129–137
Kaunda, Kenneth, 205–208, 218, 220, 222
Kenya, 63, 121, 125, 230, 233
Kérékou, Mathieu, 72, 74, 95
Kigali, 49, 50, 52, 53
Kinyarwanda, 43

L
Leadership
  alternation, 10, 14–16, 38, 39, 42, 59, 106
  crisis, 106
  rotation, 9, 12, 13, 16, 17, 20
  succession, 106, 172
Liberation, 96, 116
  movement, 43, 205
  struggle, 205
Libya, 67
Lord's Resistance Army (LRA), 107, 118

M
Madison, James, 9
Mba, Léon, 68, 69, 98
Mexico, 15
Militant politics, 105
Militia force, 123
Mugabe, Robert, 39, 117, 119
Multiparty politics, 65, 66, 71, 84, 113, 122
Museveni, Yoweri, 2, 38, 39, 51, 53, 106–119, 121–128, 130–135, 230

N
Namibia, 2, 8, 53, 205, 220
National
  Conference, 65–67, 72–78, 89, 147, 158, 168
  Resistance Army, 106, 109, 129
  Resistance Movement, 106, 109, 112, 113, 118, 122–128, 131, 133
  Revolutionary Committee, 146, 147
Nigeria, 2, 29, 49, 53, 129, 172–175, 177–183, 185–189, 191–196, 198, 232
Nkurunziza, Pierre, 39, 49
Nyerere, Julius, 109

O
Obama, Barack, 26, 32, 49, 162, 170
Obasanjo, Olusegun, 2, 20, 53, 129, 172, 175–181, 185–188, 190, 191, 194, 197, 198
Obote, Milton, 105–109, 112, 116, 119, 133, 134
Odinga, Oraila, 50
One-party
  state, 206, 214
  system, 65, 70, 71, 75, 207
Ouagadougou, 141–143, 157–159, 161, 162, 165, 170

P
Paris agreements, 85
Participation, 9, 11, 12, 73, 86, 88, 89, 106, 111, 112, 120, 146, 147, 175, 193, 219
Patrimonial regime, 38, 150, 152
Patronage politics, 38, 66, 83, 89, 127
Personalistic
  politics, 38, 39
  regime, 38
Political
  compromise, 150, 208
  corruption, 66, 83, 85, 89–91, 93, 95
  culture, 4, 93, 127, 146, 164, 227
  governance, 7, 52, 58
  instability, 14, 15, 38
  miscalculation, 143
  mobilization, 146, 150, 153
  opponent, 10, 27, 69, 89, 90, 92, 95, 130, 142, 159, 186
  opportunism, 41, 172
  opposition, 47, 49, 72, 73, 84, 89, 93, 96, 106, 113, 122, 126, 127, 142–144, 147–151, 153, 155, 156, 158–164, 206, 208, 213, 218, 219, 231

pluralism, 207
Popular vote, 110, 125, 167
Poverty, 42, 59, 70, 91, 120, 172, 186, 219
Power
  alternation, 1–3, 10, 12, 27, 38, 66, 76, 85
  shift, 186, 189
  usurpation, 4, 11
Presidential
  leadership, 22, 58, 121, 152, 154, 160, 161, 173
  majority, 2, 6, 75, 76, 80, 86, 142, 144, 162, 227
  system, 6, 7, 74, 153, 154, 170, 171, 173–175
Putin, Vladimir, 15, 30, 118

R
Rectification, 147, 149
Referendum, 50, 55–57, 72, 79, 85, 134, 142, 147, 162, 167
  national, 47, 55
  popular, 55, 56, 115, 161, 163, 229
Régiment de sécurité présidentielle (RSP), 143, 144, 157
Rent-seeking, 26, 27, 211, 230
Ruling party, 10, 22, 44, 48, 74–76, 83, 85, 86, 106, 115, 120, 121, 123, 126–128, 164, 206, 215
Russia, 8, 15, 30, 118
Rwanda, 2, 6, 8, 29, 37, 38, 40–45, 47–60, 112, 230–233
Rwandan Patriotic Front (RFP), 37, 40, 47

S
Sankara, Thomas, 146, 147, 149, 150, 156, 164, 167–169
Senegal, 67, 165, 167, 232

Short-termism, 17
Social Democratic Party (PSD), 47, 48, 55, 75
Soros, George, 51
South Africa, 24, 205, 218, 220
Southern Africa, 205, 218, 222
State institution, 132, 165, 230
Status quo, 39, 121
Strong men, 37, 162, 232
Structural adjustment program (SAPs), 90, 109
Sub-Saharan Africa, 38, 42, 72

T
Tanzania, 24, 105, 109, 121, 125, 233
Term, 2–19, 21–29, 37–40, 42, 43, 45–51, 53–56, 58, 59, 67, 76, 78–81, 95, 106, 107, 111–119, 121, 131, 133, 141–146, 148–153, 155, 156, 158–166, 171, 172, 174, 176, 178–180, 185, 187, 188, 192, 195, 199, 207–216, 218, 219, 227–232
  elongation, 3, 8, 20, 24, 172, 188–193, 195, 228
  extension, 18, 115, 172, 178–181, 185–187, 189–195, 207, 210, 219
Transparency International, 52, 93
Tyranny, 9, 11

U
United States (US), 5, 7, 9, 16, 26, 29, 44, 49–52, 70, 90, 135, 162, 170, 180, 185, 186, 195, 230, 231
US Africa Summit, 162

V
Venezuela, 5, 8, 30
Voter participation, 12, 85, 88

W
Washington, George, 5, 23
West Africa, 146, 205, 220, 232
World Bank, 70, 90, 109, 112

Z
Zimbabwe, 39, 117, 119, 205, 220

Printed by Printforce, the Netherlands